ORIGINAL SERMONS,

BY MATTHEW MEAD, OF STEPNEY.

THE SERMONS
OF
MATTHEW MEAD

ORIGINAL SERMONS

ON THE JEWS;

AND ON

FALLING INTO THE HANDS OF THE LIVING GOD

BY MATTHEW MEAD,
OF STEPNEY
AUTHOR OF "THE ALMOST CHRISTIAN"

EDITED FROM MSS. PRESERVED
IN THE FAMILY OF
SIR THOMAS W. BLOMEFIELD, BART.

WITH A MEMOIR BY THE EDITOR, AND A BRIEF PREFACE
BY THE REV. E. BICKERSTETH
RECTOR OF WATTON, HERTS.

ALSO HIS
FAREWELL SERMON
AS AN EJECTED MINISTER

Soli Deo Gloria Publications
...for instruction in righteousness...

Soli Deo Gloria Publications
213 W. Vincent Street, Ligonier, PA. 15658
(412) 238-7741

∗

First printed in 1836 in London
by James Nisbet and Company

This Soli Deo Gloria Reprint is 1991.

∗

ISBN 1-877611-29-8

PREFACE.

Having been favoured with a sight of the Manuscript Sermons of MR. MEAD respecting the Jews, having advised their publication, and being informed that the profits will be given (after remunerating the publisher) to the Society for Promoting Christianity among the Jews, I cannot but comply with a request which has been made to me to prefix a few recommendatory words.

Mr. Mead's character, as a holy and practical writer, is however so well established, that his books need no recommendation from me. It is through the kindness of Sir Thomas William Blomefield, in whose family the Manuscripts have been preserved, that they are now sent to press. The Sermons have, indeed, sufficient internal evidence of their authenticity, and bear the stamp of the vigorous, enlarged, and devout mind of the Author. It is very gratifying to see that the attention of Christians was with so much judgment, and piety, directed to the case of the Jews above a century and a half since.

May it please God, our Heavenly Father, that these Sermons on the Jews may rouse all Christians to holy zeal in our blessed Master's service, and those published with them by the same Author, "On falling into the hands of the living God," may awaken many careless sinners from indifference, to a just concern for their everlasting welfare.

EDW. BICKERSTETH.

WOTTON RECTORY, HERTS,
Sept. 8, 1836.

CONTENTS.

BRIEF MEMOIR.*

THE Editor feels himself called upon, before he proceeds to detail the few particulars he has been enabled to collect respecting the life and character of the author of the Sermons, now for the first time given to the public, to state the circumstances under which they came into his possession.—In looking over some old books and papers which devolved to him upon the death of his relative the late Edward Wilmot, Esq. of Lansdown Grove, Bath, he discovered two volumes of M.S. sermons, bound; the one with the following M.S. title page, " Five Sermons; preached at Stepney by Mr. Matthew Mead, transcribed from short hand notes written after him. James Andrews scripsit, 1710." The other, " Twelve Sermons preached at Stepney by Matthew Mead, transcribed, &c. (as above) 1703." The name of Anthonina Hatfield,

* The Editor has consulted, among others, the following authorities:—Palmer's Non-conformist's Memorial, Edits. 1775 and 1802.—Granger's Biographical History of England.—Burnet's Works.—Neal's History of the Puritans.—Grey's Impartial Examination of Neal's, &c.—Peirce's Vindication of Dissenters —Walker's Numbers and Sufferings of the Clergy.—Encyclopædia Britannica.—Brook's Lives of the Puritans.—Rapin's History of England, &c.—Watts's Bibliotheca Britannica.—Biographical Dictionary.—Rees's Cyclopædia.

the mother of Mr. E. Wilmot, and the daughter of
M. Hatfield, Esq. of London, is written in the title
page of each volume; a connexion by marriage between
the families of Mead and Wilmot may perhaps account
for the manuscripts being in the possession of one of
the branches of the latter family; Sir Edward the
Grandfather of the present Sir Robert Wilmot, Bart.
of Chaddesden, Derbyshire, having married Sarah
Marsh, the eldest daughter of the celebrated Richard
Mead, M.D. who was the eleventh son of Mr. Matthew
Mead.—In addition to these circumstances, and the
internal evidence of style and matter, their authenticity further appears from the fact, that an extract from
one of the Sermons was incorporated by the Author in
his life time, into the sermon which he published on
" Ezekiel's Vision of the Wheels."

The Editor finding himself in possession of these
manuscripts, thus providentially committed to his
trust, and having been advised to publish them by
several friends, upon whose judgment he could rely,
among whom he would especially name the Rev. E.
Bickersteth, deems it a pleasing and sacred duty to
give them to the Church of Christ, trusting that the
preacher " being dead, will yet speak" by them to the
present generation. May the Lord vouchsafe to ac-
company the perusal of them with his Holy Spirit,
and use them as instruments, not only of awakening
in the hearts of his believing people, a more lively
sympathy with the Jewish nation, but of saving many
who are now in danger "of falling into the hands of the
living God," and thus making ready a people prepared
for him at his second and glorious appearing.

Matthew Mead, the well known author of that ex-

cellent work " The Almost Christian, or the false professor tried and cast," was born in the year 1629, and
is said to have descended from a considerable family
in Buckinghamshire, in which county he inherited a
handsome patrimony; but nothing is recorded respecting the place of his birth or education. The
first account we have of him is that he held the living
of Great Brickhill, Bucks, from which he was removed
by Oliver Cromwell on 22d January, 1658, to the cure
of the New Chapel, Shadwell.

We next find from the sermon which he published
in 1660, on " Spiritual Wisdom improved," and which
he dedicated " to the congregation at Stepney, who
were the auditors of it," that he was then engaged
as Assistant Minister to the Rev. Mr. Greenhill,
at that time the Incumbent of the parish church.
—The occasion of his publishing it was that a charge
of treason and rebellion had been brought against him,
in consequence of his having deprecated " a sinful
compliance with ceremonies against conscience." He
says in the dedication, " I had thought I might have
continued with you long enough to have outlived my
design upon this text, but the wise God, in whose
hand my times are, hath given me a " quietus est," not
only in reference to my place, but to my conscience also.
The greatest evil I shall wish to those that succeed me
shall be, that they may be as true to the interest of
your precious souls, as I did always desire, and to my
power endeavour to be. God is my record, that I
sought not yours but you; my care and prayer hath
always been, that you might receive heavenly treasure
out of a poor earthen vessel. I may say, that no part
of God's vineyard in the whole nation hath had more
choice and eminent labourers, (myself excepted) than

this of Stepney,* for several years together, and in this regard I had a hard province to write after such copies; but who looks for a man's head upon a child's shoulders? nor will God require the improvement of ten talents, where he gives but one." Notwithstanding his anticipated dismissal here alluded to, we may however collect from a passage in Mr. Howe's funeral sermon (from which a copious extract has been subsequently given) coupled with the Dedication to the first edition of " The Almost Christian," that he was engaged during the summer of 1661 in preaching to the same congregation.

In 1662, one of the most important events of his life, his ejection for non-conformity took place, but whether from Stepney or Shadwell, or as some say from Great Brickhill, is not distinctly known. The sermon which he preached upon that affecting occasion, was afterwards published under the title of " The Pastor's Valediction," and the Editor trusts he shall need to offer no apology for reprinting it at the close of the present volume.

On dispassionately reviewing the history of these troublous times, it is impossible not to condemn and deplore this violation of the promises made to the Presbyterians in the Declaration of Breda, especially when we consider how materially their services had contributed to the restoration of the King, and that nothing would have been more suitable to a season of national rejoicing, than the oblivion of past animosities. Two thousand ministers of the Established Church, a large number of whom were men of devoted piety, were thus sacrificed to political intrigue, and the

* " Mr. Burroughs, Mr. Whittaker, Mr. Bridge, and till now Mr. Greenhill."

secret design entertained by the Court, of favouring the Popish party. This act of national injustice was followed by persecutions, similar to those which characterized the days of Archbishop Laud and of the Commonwealth, concerning which, so far as he himself was concerned, Mr. Mead thus cheerfully expresses himself, in the preface to a Sermon which he afterwards published, and which was preached partly in anticipation of the General Thanksgiving day, for the deliverance of the nation by the Prince of Orange, and partly on that day—" A deliverance to him who is redeemed thereby from nine years incessant vexations, by suits, by fines, by illegal housebreakings, by plundering and spoil, by imprisonments, by prosecution for life, by wandering in a strange land, must be far sweeter than it can be to him who is delivered only from his fears and sad expectations of what is to come ; and if, in the wise providence of God, the waters of a fuller cup, have been wrung out to one than to another, it is no wonder though he catches more hastily at the cup of consolation, which is given to wash them down ; as he that is forced to take some bitter potion, readily accepts any thing of a pleasant relish to put the former taste out of his mouth."

The next we hear of our Author is, that in 1663, he resided at Worcester House, * in Stepney, where he

* It appears from the early records of this Nonconformist Church, to which through the Christian kindness of Dr. Fletcher, the Editor has had free access, that this house was their own property, and that after the Revolution, they generously settled it upon Mr. Mead, in fee, as some compensation for the losses which he had sustained in his private fortune as their Minister, and as an acknowledgment of the services which he had rendered them. In this house his eleventh son Richard, the distinguished Physi-

bestowed a liberal education on his large family of thirteen children, under a private tutor at home.

We learn from the first entry in the church books, that a little company of believers met at Stepney, as early as the year 1644, over whom Mr. Henry Burton, * an eminent sufferer in the days of Archbishop Laud presided, at which time the Rev. Mr. Greenhill, before alluded to, was Incumbent of the Parish. Of this church Mr. Greenhill after his ejection for non-conformity in 1662, became the Minister; in 1668, Mr. Mead was appointed Assistant minister, and upon Mr. Greenhill's death, he was chosen his successor, and ordained Dec. 14th, 1671, by Dr. Owen, Mr. Caryl, Mr. Griffiths, and Mr. Collings. Can we wonder at the singular blessing which accompanied this choice, when we are informed, by the following entries, of the spirit in which it was made?

cian, as well as the Patron of Literature and Science, was born; and here on his return to England, after having completed his studies at Utrecht, under the celebrated Grœvius, he first commenced his professional career.

* An interesting account of Burton is given in Brook's Lives of the Puritans, vol. iii. page 40. Previously to his being put into the Pillory, and having his ears cut off, he said among other things, " Little do you know, what fruit God is able to produce from this dry tree. Through these holes (meaning the Pillory,) God can bring light to his church; my conscience in the discharge of my ministerial duty, in admonishing my people to beware of the *creeping in of Popery*, and in exhorting them unto a dutiful obedience to God and the King, was that which first occasioned my sufferings." The Editor has reason to expect that a detailed History of the Church at Stepney, over which Mr. Mead presided, is likely to be given to the public, by the individual most competent to undertake it, which he has no doubt will contain much valuable and interesting information.

October 13, 1671. " A day of fasting and prayer was kept in the church, and in the close of it, they proceeded to a choice, and Mr. Matthew Mead was chosen pastor of the church, by the consent of the whole church ;" and again, " Dec. 28. We kept a day of thanksgiving for the great mercy of making up our breach, and settling the church."

Oh that there were such an heart in us now ! that all our measures and mercies were thus preceded by prayer, and followed by Thanksgiving for an anticipated blessing!

On the the 10th of May, 1674, the foundation of the spacious Meeting-house was laid, of which the Rev. Dr. Fletcher is now the much-esteemed pastor; and so rapidly was it erected, that Mr. Mead preached the first sermon in it on Sept. 13th, in the same year. He adds in the church book; " The Lord make it a place for the begetting many souls to Christ." Previously to this, but at what time is not ascertained, Mr. Mead had been compelled for the purpose of escaping persecution, to retire into Holland. Upon liberty being granted to the dissenters, he returned to England, having preached at Utrecht during his residence abroad, where he gained the entire respect and esteem of the Government, and upon the erection of the Meeting-house, the States General presented him with the four pillars which support the roof of the edifice, as a token of their regard. So little confidence was however placed in " the Indulgence " then granted by the King, that the building was erected with a view to its being easily converted into dwelling houses, should such a necessity occur.

Here Mr. Mead became the minister of a very large
congregation, and no one was more followed than
himself, when he preached in the City.

On the 1st of May, 1674, Mr. Mead commenced a
Lecture, of the origin of which he gives the following account in the preface to the Volume which
he afterwards published, on the "Good of Early
Obedience." "In April, 1674 a gentleman, who
was till then a stranger to me, came with an earnest
request that I would undertake the preaching of
a sermon yearly, on every May-day, to the younger
people. I desiring to know his reason, why to
them, rather than to others, and why on that day
rather than on any other? he told me it had often
been the grief of his soul, to behold the vicious and
debauched practices of youth, on that day of liberty,
and did hope that many might be induced, either by
their own inclinations, or by the counsels of their
parents or masters, rather to spend their time in hearing a sermon, than in drinking and gaming, &c., by
which means, many might be converted and saved.
The design being so honest, and the reason so cogent,
I was persuaded to comply with it, and began upon the
following May-day, and so it hath been continued ever
since; and I may say it, not in any boast, but to the
praise of the glory of the grace of God, with great
success."

This interesting volume was dedicated to the
Lady Diana Alington, whom he thus faithfully ad-
dresses :—" Wherefore, Madam, let " Holiness to the
Lord," be written upon all your honour, and all your
enjoyments; whatever is entrusted with you ought to

be devoted to him, or it never can be rightly enjoyed, nor duly improved. God hath honoured you to be the fruitful mother of hopeful children; but remember, Madam, that as they derive honour from your loins in regard of your station in this world, so they derive guilt and pollution on another account. And what is worldly honour stained with damning guilt, which makes them children of wrath, even as others! There is a Nobility that is divine, and of a heavenly original, which hath Religion for the root, and God for the top of the kin; in comparison of which, all other nobility is but an empty shadow, and all worldly grandeur but as those apples which grow upon the banks of the Dead Sea, which, under a tempting outside, contain nothing but dust. This honour derives not from the first birth, but the second, and is peculiar to them only, who are " born not of blood, nor of the will of the flesh, nor of the will of man, but of God." (John i. 13.) Would your Honour have those pleasant branches thus ennobled? I know it is the matter of your prayers, and let me beg you to join thereunto your utmost endeavours, by a strict and pious education; the common want of which has stained the present age with as debauched a Nobility and Gentry, as ever any time brought forth. And, Madam, if to all this, you shall add the winning motive of your own example, so walking in all the precepts of Christ, and in all the virtues of the Holy Spirit, that they may be won into the ways of God by the beauty of your feet, oh, what an honour and rejoicing would this be to you in the near approaching day of Christ Jesus! How many children have been brought into love with the ways of God by the holy example of godly parents! and many more have perished by the contrary, who are now cursing the parents that begat them, and the loins that brought them forth."

The lecture has been continued to the present time, and as the Editor is assured, has been rendered eminently useful during the ministrations of successive pastors, no year having passed away without some instance being known of spiritual good received.

We now come to a most trying period of Mr. Mead's life, when the enemy of God and man appears to have been permitted to put forth all his malice for the purpose of ruining his character, and accomplishing his destruction; but the Lord whom he served, did not leave him in his hand, He "brought forth his righteousness as the light, and his judgment as the noon day; for the Lord loveth judgment, and forsaketh not his Saints; they are preserved for ever, but the seed of the wicked shall be cut off." (Ps. xxxvii. 6, 28.)

It is well known that the secret policy of King Charles's reign had long been directed to the furtherance of the Popish cause; and we find from the following entries in the Church Records of Stepney, in the handwriting of Mr. Mead, the apprehensions then entertained of a still darker day, and the spirit in which they sought to avert the impending danger.

1679. Tuesday, March 9th, was kept a day of prayer in the church to prepare them for a solemn renewing of their covenant with God.

1679. Tuesday, March 16th. The church in a day of fasting and prayer, solemnly and unanimously renewed their Covenant with God, it being a time of very great darkness and danger, by reason of the

Popish plots and designs on foot; which Covenant
was renewed in these words :—

" Wee who are here present before the Lord as a
church of Jesus Christ, whom he hath been graciously
pleased by his special power and mercy, to call out
of the world unto the saving knowledge of himself in
Christ, and therein unto the faith and fellowship of
the Gospel, having seriously considered, and deeply
laid to heart our many and frequent backslidings from
God, and sad decays in grace, and manifold failings in
duty, both as to faith, love, and obedience ; in all
which we have greatly reproached our high and heavenly calling, to the great dishonour of Christ, the
grief of the Holy Spirit, the scandal of the blessed
Gospel, and the wounding of our own souls; by all
which we have highly provoked the anger and displeasure of God, not only against the nation, but
against the churches, and against this church in
particular ; so that he may justly remove his candlestick out of this place, and cause the glory to depart
from us. Therefore being deeply affected with the
dread of his present dispensations, and considering the
loud call of his Word, to remember from whence we are
fallen, and to repent and do our first works, we do
with shame, and self-abhorrency, desire to lie low
before the Lord, and humble ourselves with confusion of face for all our sins and abominations, and do
as in the sight of the Lord, renounce them with indignation and abhorrency ; and being fully convinced,
that, under such grievous backslidings, the duty is to
take words and to return to the Lord ; and setting
before us the holy example of the churches of God in

former ages, who upon sense of their backslidings and
revolts, have renewed their covenant with the Lord,
we do look upon it as a special duty incumbent upon
us as a church of Jesus Christ, to renew our covenant
with the Lord, which we have so often violated and
broken.

"Wherefore in humble confidence of the Lord's gracious acceptance of us in Jesus Christ, who hath promised upon our hearty return to take away all iniquity,
accept us graciously, and love us freely, we do return
unto him this day with our whole hearts, and do
humbly and solemnly resign up ourselves to him as our
God in Christ, and we call heaven and earth to record
this day, that we do faithfully engage our souls, that
for the time to come, we will constantly adhere to him
as our God, and that we will endeavour by the strength
of his grace, and assistance of his Holy Spirit to walk
more closely with him, and more humbly and fruitfully
before him, and that wee will with all diligence observe
and do the things which our Lord Jesus hath commanded us, as to all the dutys, ordinances, and institutions of his holy worship, and that we will walk in mu-
tual love among ourselves unto the glory of Christ, and
the edification and comfort of each other. And we do
each one in particular, male, and female, lift up our
hands to the Most High God, as a witness to this our
explicite consent hereunto, and to testify unto the
Lord, the sincerity of our hearts herein; and the great
God, for Christ's sake, accept it, and grant that this
holy covenant, which we do now solemnly renew on
earth, may for ever be ratified in Heaven."—*Matthew
Meade, Pastor, and thirty-four Members.*

Thus was this holy man preparing himself and his little flock, for the coming storm, and seeking as a true Patriot, to avert an anticipated National judgment by personal humiliation, repentance, and prayer. He was not permitted, however, to escape unmolested, but was accused in the year 1683, together with Dr. Owen, and Mr. Griffiths, of being privy to what was called the Rye-house Plot, for which the great Lord Russell suffered death. It is stated that on this occasion, Mr. Mead, though conscious of his innocence, again withdrew to Holland, leaving his Son Richard under the care of Mr. Singleton an able classical scholar, who had been ejected as a non-conformist from the office of Second Master of Eton School.* The truth of this account, however, appears to be very questionable, inasmuch as we learn from a List, which was afterwards published, that many who fled beyond seas were consequently outlawed; and it can scarcely be doubted that the Government would have proceeded against him with equal severity. If the statement be true, he at all events soon returned and obeyed the summons to attend the Privy Council, at which the King was present; and Mr. Mead on that occasion answered the interrogatories put to him in so satisfactory a manner, that His Majesty himself ordered him to be immediately discharged.

Notwithstanding this honourable acquittal, King James II. soon after his Accession to the throne, sanctioned and published an account of the plot,

* These particulars are taken from Rees's Cyclopædia; but in the Biographical Dictionary, it is affirmed, that Richard Mead was placed under the care of Mr. Singleton, in 1688, which was more probably the fact.

which had been drawn up by Dr. Thomas Spratt, Bishop of Rochester, in the lifetime of King Charles, and under his special direction, in which the same charges were renewed against Mr. Mead, and others.* The accusation principally rested upon the evidence of William Carstares, a witness who was subjected to the cruel torture of the Thummikins in Scotland, for an hour and a half, without making any confession.† On the following day he was brought forth to undergo the still more dreadful torture of the Boot, but his arms being swelled with the late torture, and being already in a fever, he was prevailed upon to make a confession on the 8th Sept. 1684, which, however, contained nothing respecting the Ministers in question. This confession was renewed on the 18th. Sept., and Carstares then added: " The deponent did communicate the design on foot to Dr. Owen, Mr. Griffiths, and Mr. Mead of Stepney, who all concurred in the promoting of it, and were desirous it should take effect." In reference to this confession, the Royal

* The Editor is grieved to add that this charge against Mr. Mead was reiterated by Dr. Nicholls in his " Defence of the Church of England," and by Dr. Grey, in his " Impartial exnation of Neal's History of the Puritans."

† Further particulars respecting this barbarous transaction, may be found in Burnet's History of his Own Times, 2d vol. 418, Oxford Edition, and Peirce's Vindication of Dissenters, part i. p. 258. Mr. Peirce there says of Mr. Mead, " This worthy man was my guardian, and therefore I think myself bound to pay so much respect to his memory, as to take this occasion of acquainting my reader, if he does not know it already, that he was a gentleman, and a scholar, and a most excellent preacher; and that his reputation was too well established among those who knew him, to be lessened by such reproaches as are here cast upon him."

account adds, " Which part of Carstares' oath is the more remarkable, because the king solemnly affirms, that the Duke of Monmouth, in his confession to his Majesty, and his Royal Highness, did particularly name those very three men, as conscious of the plot, and withal declared in these very words, "That all the considerable Non-conformist Ministers knew of the conspiracy." An instance that alone, if there were not many more such, were a sufficient instruction to all Separatists, of what tender consciences the men are, whom they choose for the principal guides of their consciences; since after all this, Mead deposed before his Majesty, "that he had never heard of any disturbance intended against the government, but that on the contrary, he himself had once advised Ferguson, upon discourse of some libel of his, then newly made public, that it was not their part to do such things." Nay, their great Oracle Dr. Owen, being examined upon oath before the Lord Chief Justice Jones, and being asked, " Whether he had not heard of a horrid plot against the life of the King," did not long before his death take God to witness, and subscribed to it with his dying hand, "that indeed he had heard of such a plot by the means of the King's proclamation, but no otherwise !' "*

Is it surprising that a Government which could thus attempt to defame the faithful ministers of Christ, with a view to the introduction of Popery, and the establishment of arbitrary power, should within the short period of four years cease to exist ! Surely the prayer of the Psalmist would then have received a

* True Acount and Declaration of the Horrid Conspiracy. p. 81.

signal answer, " Slay them not, lest my people forget,
scatter them by thy power, and bring them down, O
Lord our shield." (Psalm lix. 11.)

We may easily conceive with what devout thanksgiving Mr. Mead hailed the deliverance of the kingdom
from Popery and Slavery by the Prince of Orange,
whom (as he declares in the title page to the sermon
before alluded to,) "God raised up to be the instrument thereof." It is a discourse admirably adapted to
elucidate a most difficult portion of Scripture, " The
Vision of the Wheels," in the first and tenth chapters of
Ezekiel.

At this threatening period of our National history,
the Nonconformist ministers, though still smarting
under the rod of recent persecution, nobly forgot their
wrongs, and united with the Church of England in
their opposition to Papal domination. Happy would
it have been for the nation, and just towards themselves, had some plan of comprehension been then
carried into effect, for the purpose of relieving their
scruples, and re-admitting them within the bosom of
the National communion ; but notwithstanding all the
efforts of King William, their claims were disregarded,
and the rent, thus widened, was perpetuated in the land.

At that time, so far from desiring to disunite
religion from the State, Mr. Mead justly remarks :
" It is the great wisdom and goodness of God, that
our National rights and Religious concerns should be
so interwoven, the one with the other, as that they
cannot easily (if at all) be separated ; otherwise probably we might have done like wanton children, *lick off
the honey, and then throw away the bread ;* but being
happily thus twisted together, the contesting of one

proves the vindication of both, and so "the Earth helps the Woman." (Rev. xii. 16.)*   And at a later period, Mr. Neal, in his preface to the fourth volume of his "History of the Puritans," when arguing in favor of Liberty of conscience, justly remarks; "Upon these principles, it is evident, that freedom of religion, in subordination to the civil power, is for the benefit of society, and no ways inconsistent with a Public Establishment."

It is indeed contended in the perilous times in which we live, that nationally we have no concern with God, nor He with us, and that as a nation we are not bound to establish his Worship, nor to provide for the ministry of his Word, and the observance of his Sabbaths.

It cannot be denied, that the Holy Scriptures reveal God to our notice from the earliest ages, as dealing with nations no less than with cities, families, and individuals;—with man in the aggregate as his creature, the inhabitant of his earth, and with every division and subdivision of the great human family which he has ordained; for "He divided to the nations their inheritance and separated the sons of Adam." (Deut. xxxii. 8.)   It is true that as the "King of nations," (Jer. x. 7.) he was pleased to select the Jews to be a peculiar people in covenant with himself, to whom the custody of his oracles should be specially committed, yet in them we find numerous prophecies relating to Canaan, Egypt, Assyria, Babylon, and the other nations of the earth, and records of the different visitations by which God, as the "God of nations," was pleased from time to time to lay bare his arm,

* Sermon on the Vision of the Wheels, p. 103.

"that he might be sanctified in their sight." (Ezek. xxxix. 27.)

But further, he appears to have constituted the Jewish nation, the great medium of communication through which he would promulgate to the different kingdoms of the world, his will concerning them, and to have invested the Jewish prophets with a commission which sometimes extended to the remotest corners of the earth. We have a remarkable instance of this in the case of Jeremiah—The Lord had said to him, " See, I have set thee over the nations, and over the kingdoms, to root out, and to pull down, and to destroy, and to throw down, to build and to plant." (Jer. i. 10.) In pursuance of this authority, the prophet is commanded. (chap. xxv.) to take the wine cup of the fury of the Lord, and to cause " all the kingdoms of the world which are upon the face of the earth to drink of it." Again, in (chap. xxvii.) he is directed to send bonds and yokes, by certain messengers, to the kings of the several nations there enumerated, with a command to them from the God of Israel, to submit themselves to the king of Babylon, accompanied by a promise and threat, severally annexed to their obedience or disobedience to his revealed will. In like manner Ezekiel is commanded to prophesy against the Ammonites, and to say unto them, " Hear the word of the Lord" (Ezek. xxv. 2, 3.); and in (chap. xxix.) he is directed to set his face against Pharaoh King of Egypt, and prophesy against him, and against all Egypt, and to speak and say, " Thus saith the Lord God, I am against thee, Pharaoh, King of Egypt".—Jonah was also sent in person to Nineveh, that great and wicked city, to cry against it. Is it not reasonable to conclude that these, and similar messages from the Lord of Hosts, reached their appointed destination, that his Word did not return unto him void, but that in spite of their idolatries, the nations were thus taught to reverence " the God of truth, the living God, the everlasting King." (Jer. x. 10.)*

And can it be supposed that Christianity was intended to dissolve this relation which previously subsisted between God and the nations of the earth, and that individuals and families are now his only concern? If Egypt refused to listen to the Word of the Lord by the ministry of Moses, and was overwhelmed by judgment; while wiser Nineveh repented at the preaching of Jonah, and was spared,—shall not the nations of the earth be held responsible *as nations* for the reception which they give to the Revelation of Him, who is at once set before them as " the Lamb of God which taketh away the sin of the world," and as " the Prince of the kings of the earth?"

Shall Tyre, " the crowning city, the mart of nations, whose merchants were princes, whose traffickers were the honourable of the earth," (Is. xxiii. 8.) the particulars of whose national prosperity, the Lord has so minutely registered in the prophecy of Ezekiel, (chap. xxvii.) be visited with desolating ruin, because she sinned against her measure of light and knowledge, and therefore was without excuse ; shall Capernaum, a

* It has been suggested to the Editor, as worthy of remark, that in the verse which follows this, (ver. 11.) the prophet breaks out in the Chaldee Language, as if prompted by the Spirit of God, in addressing the nations, to overleap the barriers of his National Dialect.

city exalted to heaven, and blessed with Spiritual privileges which had never been vouchsafed to Tyre and Sidon, be thrust down to Hell, because she beheld the mighty miracles of her Messiah, and yet believed not; and shall England hope to escape a far heavier doom, if she forget the God who has exalted her among the nations, and crowned her with unparalleled mercies both in Providence and Grace; if " wiser than Daniel," she renounce at length her National responsibilities and "lift up her heart as God?" (Ezek. xxviii. 6.) It is true that the Gospel of the grace of God is intended to penetrate the heart of the individual sinner, and "to take out of the Gentiles a people for his name" (Acts xv. 14.), a purpose which neither the wickedness of man, nor the gates of hell can defeat; but it is no less the will and purpose of God, that as "the Gospel of the kingdom it should be preached in all the world, as a witness unto *all nations*, and that then should the end come." (Matt. xxiv. 14.)

Oh that, if it be possible, we as a nation to whom this witness has come, and who have professed to receive it, may know, even we, at least in this our day, the things which belong unto our peace ! the repentance of Nineveh, even if sincere, would not avail us now: more has been given to us, and more is required at our hands. It is to the sceptre of Jesus Christ our Incarnate GOD that we are required to bow, and in the spirit of national humiliation, to confess and forsake those iniquities, which are a reproach to us now, and will otherwise eventually prove our ruin. Oh, that our National Zion may be purified, its pillars strengthened, and its efficiency increased, till it commend itself to every man's conscience in the sight of God, as adapted to the Spiritual necessities of our entire population.

The only subsequent notices of Mr. MEAD handed down to us, are his publishing a few occasional Sermons, (which, on account of their intrinsic excellence, it is the desire of the Editor to reprint, should it please God to give his blessing to the present publication,) and having thus faithfully served his generation by the will of GOD, he fell asleep on the 16th of October, 1699, and was gathered to that Blessed company, who have finished their testimony and entered into rest.

His funeral sermon was preached at Stepney, by the Rev. JOHN HOWE, from (1 Tim. iv. 16.) " Thou shalt both save thyself and them that hear thee"—from which the following Extract is taken :—

" The loss is great and grievous beyond all expression, above all our lamentation, when such are taken away, as have made it their business to save themselves and those that heard them. In their endeavour to save themselves they have been great examples; in their endeavour to save others, they may have been great instruments of much saving good to many a soul. How few are they that drive such designs ! How fast doth their number decrease ! How fitly may we take up that of the Psalmist when " the godly man ceases, and the faithful fail from among the children of men", and what could be said with greater pathos? " Help, Lord," as in a common ruin, " Help, help, for God's sake; help, Lord, help !" My friends, are you not sensible you have lost such an one, even while you are not yet saved, while you yet need to be working out your salvation ? The effectually called it is true, are saved, (2 Tim. i. 9.) " Who hath saved us, and called us with an holy calling;" and (which in substance is the same thing) the regenerate are saved; " Not by works of righteousness which we have done, but of his mercy he saved us, by the washing of regeneration and the renewing of the Holy Ghost." (Tit. iii. 5.) But if this were the case of you all, how much yet remains to be done, in order to your full and consummate salvation? You have yet mighty difficulties to overcome, a body of death which you are not yet delivered from; for are not these some of your groans in reference to it, " O, who shall deliver us!" a world full of troubles and snares; your adversary the devil that goes about seeking whom he may devour; all the principalities and powers of the kingdom of darkness, that you are to contend with, and with whom you are to dispute every step of your way to heaven. And do you not need such a leader in that way? And if any are fallen into drowsy slumbers, do you not need his awakening ministry? If dead, how often hath the blessed Spirit breathed life into you by his quickening ministry? How often hath God used him to enlighten you when you have been in the dark, to clear up the great doctrines of the Gospel, when you have not distinctly understood them; to establish you in the faith when you have wavered; to resolve you in matters of practice when you have been in doubt; to encourage you in your fears and faintings, to comfort you in your sadness and sorrows! I wonder not that there are many weeping eyes, and should much wonder if there be not many aching trembling hearts among you, for what you have lost, and from an apprehension how hard and almost hopeless it is, your loss should be soon or equally supplied.

" He was long in forming and preparing to be what

he was when you lost him. His station among you
in this neighbourhood, when first he undertook the
pastoral charge of this Church, over which the Holy
Ghost made him Overseer, required a man of as much
wisdom and grace as any such station could well be
supposed to do; considering how numerous, how intelligent, and well instructed a people he was to take
the care of. I well remember, that about three or four
and forty years ago, being desired to give some help on
a Lord's Day to that eminent servant of Christ, Mr.
Greenhill, whose praise is still in all the Churches, I
then first heard him preach; and (if my memory fail
not) he had about that time in hand some part of that
excellent discourse of the "Almost Christian." I had
then the opportunity of beginning an acquaintance
with him. His excellent good natural parts, his inge-
nuous education, his industry, his early labours in
preaching the Gospel of Christ in his native county,
in the city, and in this place; his conjunction and
society for some years with that excellent servant of
God before named; above all, the gracious assistances
he had from Heaven, gave him great advantages to be
a minister of Christ, approved unto God, a workman
that needeth not to be ashamed, rightly dividing the
word of truth. And his multiplied years unto the
seventieth, with the continual addition thereby to the
rich treasury of his experiences, still improved him
more and more: so that there being no decay of his
natural endowments, and a continual increase of his
supernatural, you had the best of him at last; whereby
indeed your loss was the greater, but your obligation
was also the greater, that God continued to you the
enjoyment of him so long, and that in a serviceable

state.   But when he could be no longer serviceable in
his stated delightful work, it was by the decay not of
the inward but the outward man; so that when he
could preach to you and converse with you no longer,
he could earnestly and fervently pray for you to the
end, and God did not afflict you by leaving long among
you the shadow, the outside of the man, and of such
a man!

    " He took little pleasure in embroiling himself or his
hearers in needless and fruitless controversies.   The
great substantial doctrines of the Gospel were his
principal study and delight, such as lay nearest the
vitals and the very heart of religion and godliness,
and most directly tending to the saving them that
heard him.   The subjects which he chose to insist
upon from time to time in the course of his ministry,
shewed, as to this, his spirit and design.   Having
formed from the Holy Scriptures that scheme of
thoughts which satisfied him, and gave him a clear
ground whereupon to preach the Gospel with an
unrecoiling heart, he loved not to discompose it.   His
judgment in things that had that reference, being
constantly moderate, and unexceptionably sound;
remote from rigorous and indefensible extremities on
the one hand and the other.   Hereupon he drove at
his mark without diversion, not so much aiming to
proselyte souls to a party as to Christ, and to engage
men, as much as in him lay, to be sound and thorough
Christians.   Hitherto tended his sermons from year
to year.   The great subject he had in hand, and
which he left unfinished, when God took him off from
his public work, was manifestly pointed this way,
viz. of the Covenant of God in Christ: and his annual

course of preaching a sermon on May-day to young
men, had the same manifest scope and aim, God so
ordering it, that his last sermon was this year on that
day.

" His judgment in reference to matters of church
order, was for union and communion of all visible
Christians, viz. of such as did visibly hold the Head, as
to the principal *credenda* and *agenda* of Christianity, the
great things belonging to the faith and practice of a
Christian, so as nothing be made necessary to Christian
communion, but what Christ hath made necessary, or
what is indeed necessary to one's being a Christian.
What he publicly essayed to this purpose the world
knows, and many more private endeavours and
strugglings of his for such a union, I have not been
unacquainted with; the unsuccessfulness of which
endeavours, he said not long before his last confinement, " *he thought would break his heart,*" he
having openly, among divers persons, and with
great earnestness some time before expressed his
consent to some proposals, which, if the parties
concerned had agreed in the desire of the thing itself,
must unavoidably have inferred such a union, without
prejudice to their principles, and on such terms as
must have extended it much farther, else it had
signified little. But this must be effected, as is too
apparent, not by mere human endeavour, but by an
Almighty spirit, poured forth, which, after we have
suffered awhile, shall καταρτισαι "*put us into joint,*"
and make every joint know its place in the body,
(1 Pet. v. 10.) shall conquer private interests and
inclinations, and overawe men's hearts by the authority
of the Divine law, which now, how express soever it

c

is, little availeth against such prepossessions. Till
then, Christianity will be among us, a languishing,
withering thing. When the season comes of such an
effusion of the Spirit from on high, there will be no
parties ; and amidst the wilderness desolation which
cannot but be till that season comes, it matters little,
and signifies to me scarce one straw, which party of
us is uppermost; the most righteous, as they may be
vogued, will be but as briars and scratching thorns ;
and it is better to suffer by such than to be of them.
In the mean time, it is a mark of God's heavy displeasure, when persons of so healing spirits are taken
away; and if it awaken any of us, that will tend to
prepare us for the effects of it, which preparation
seems a thing more to be hoped for than prevention.

" But this worthy servant of Christ, sees not the
woful day, whatever of it he might foresee. He was
long languishing and even dying daily; but amidst
surrounding death, as a relation told me, there was no
appearance of any the least cloud upon his spirit, that
obscured the evidences of his title to a blessed Eternity.
Being asked how he did, he said " *Going home, as every
honest man ought, when his work is done.*" He was
much in admiring God's mercies under his afflicting
hand, saying, " *Every thing on this side hell is mercy ;
that the mercies he received were greater than his burdens,
though in themselves grievous ; that he rested upon that
promise, that his Father would lay no more upon him
than he was able to bear ; that he expected to be saved
only by the righteousness of Christ imputed to him,*"
though he well understood, as I had sufficient reason
to know, that Christ's righteousness is never imputed
to any, but where, if the subject be capable, there is

an inherent righteousness also, that is no cause of our salvation, but the character of the saved. And having before precautioned some as were about him, not to be surprised " *if he went away suddenly*," he repeated the ejaculation, " *Come Lord Jesus, come quickly*," and renewing the former caution, by saying, " *Remember what I said before*," as he sat in his chair, with all possible composure, he bowed his head, and without sigh or motion expired in a moment. The sighing part he left to others that stay behind, and I do even feel the sorrows of his most afflicted family, his mournful widow, his sorrowing sons and daughters, his destitute church, with all others that got good, or might have done, by his quickening, spiritful, piercing ministry, or had the advantage and satisfaction of his acquaintance and converse.

" Your grief cannot but be measured by your love, and your love by his in the several kinds and objects of it: his conjugal, paternal, pastoral, friendly love, as he was an affectionate husband, a tender father, a vigilant pastor, and a pleasant friend. But withal let your consolations be measured by the proper grounds thereof. It is a most improper, irrational, unchristian way of being comforted in such a case, only to let time wear away your sorrows: it is but a negative, a heathenish, yea, a worse than heathenish method of receiving comfort: for I have observed it to be animadverted upon, as an intolerable absurdity by some among the Heathens, that time should work that cure of grief and sorrow, which reason and prudence work not. And thus it is plain, we shall be relieved, not by holy thoughts, but by not thinking. So it may in time be forgotten, that ever such a man as Mr. Mead was minister in Stepney! and what is this to Christian consolation ?

" But we need not wander from the text, for a positive and a solid ground of comfort. Remember, it was his business to save himself, and those that heard him. As you have no doubt of his salvation, which I believe none of you have, make sure of your own. Put on with the breast-plate of faith and love, that helmet, the hope of salvation. You are of the day; watch and be sober as those that are " not appointed to wrath, but to obtain salvation by Jesus Christ" (1 Thess. v. 7, 8, 9.) and then consider, (as I doubt not many a soul will bless God for him for ever) how glorious a sight it will be to see him one day appear in the head of a numerous company of saved ones, and say as a subordinate Parent in the Apostle's sense, (1 Cor. iv. 15.) " Lord, here am I, and the children thou hast given me."

Such was the testimony of this very eminent servant of Christ, respecting Mr. Mead, himself so well qualified to discern and appreciate the excellencies of his ministerial character.

He was interred near the south-west door of Stepney church, his tomb being still kept in repair by the members of the church to which he belonged, and upon it is the following inscription :—

H. S. E.

Quicquid mortale fuit

MATTHÆI MEAD, V. D. M.

Honestâ inter Cattieuchlanos familiâ orti,

A pietate, Doctrinâ, Facundiâ præclari,

Qui

Assiduis et insignibus Laboribus

Pro Patriâ, Religione, Libertate,

Invicto animo defunctus,

Vitæ tandem et laudis satur

Ad Cœlitum Domum, quam diu optaverat,

Lassus et anhelus placidissimé ascendit,

Ann. Ætat. suæ 70. 17 Kal. Novembr. CIƆIƆCXCIX

Et

Boni Civis,

Amantissimi Conjugis,

Optimi Patris,

Theologi veré Christiani,

Clarum reliquit posteris Exemplum.

Of which the following is a Translation :—

Here lie interred

The Mortal Remains

of MATTHEW MEAD, Minister of the Gospel.

Descended from an honourable Family in Buckinghamshire,

Eminent for Piety, Learning, and Eloquence,

Who having completed his unremitting and distinguished Labours

For his Country, for Religion, for Liberty,

With an invincible Zeal,

Full of Days and Honour,

Weary and panting for repose, but with unclouded spirit,

Ascended to the long-wished for abode of the Blessed,

In the 70th Year of his age, on the 16th Oct. 1699,

Leaving to Posterity the bright example

Of a Good Subject, a most affectionate Husband,

An excellent Father, and a truly Christian Divine.

It may be well to remark the peculiar providence which has postponed the publication of these sermons, till the subjects upon which they treat, the Restoration of the Jews, the future destinies of the Church of Christ as closely connected with that event, and the Second coming of our Lord, have acquired such deep and increasing interest in every thinking mind: nor is it to be regretted that the Protest against Popery which they contain should be given to the world at a time, when the dangers which threatened the over-throw of the Protestant church at the Æra of the Revolution, have again assumed a magnitude and im-portance, which has belonged to them at no intervening period of our National history.   Mr. Mead remarks, " So that things were come to a great extremity with the Protestant interest; though it was not like Lazarus, dead and buried, yet it was like Isaac laid upon the altar, and bound, with the knife at the throat, but God "remembered us in our low estate, for his mercy endureth for ever." (Ps. cxxxvi. 23.)* The following monitory reflections of Bishop Burnet, in reference to the same times, though some of his ex-pressions may sound harsh and uncharitable to those who are unable to distinguish between Love for the individual, and hatred against the false system of Re-ligion by which he is spiritually enslaved, are also well worthy of being laid to heart by the present generation.

" But while we let our thoughts out to wonder at the wisdom and goodness of God, let the admiration of these produce somewhat like them in ourselves: we ought to grow wise, for our experience has cost us

* Sermon on the " Vision of the Wheels."

dear, and had almost proved a very dreadful School to us. We now see the folly of trusting to that religion, and of imagining that any weight was to be laid on all the promises that could be made us by them. It is not to be doubted, that many were so little acquainted with the depths of Satan, that are in that black society, as to believe that it was possible for them to maintain truth, honour, and good nature, *notwithstanding the points of speculation that are in their Schools;* we resolved to make the experiment, and they have taken such pains to let us see our mistake, that it is to be hoped we shall never at any time hereafter, relapse into the like error. The goodness of God, that appears now in such endearing characters to us, ought likewise to form the like temper in us. Our minds have been too much embittered on all hands, by reason of some inconsiderable differences, which our enemies have always managed with so much address, as to engage us to weaken our common force, by dividing ourselves into parties, and by a fatal series of woful accidents, these sparks have been blown up into such a flame, that they had almost quite consumed us. But it is to be hoped, that we shall study to be all of one mind; or if we cannot arrive at so great a blessing, that at least we shall love one another, and remember that we are Brethren, fellow Christians and fellow Protestants, that must have been destroyed together, and therefore must now support and bear with one another.

" But as I doubt not but the happy disposition of all people's minds will now produce a desired temper in those matters, so we must not bind our charity within so narrow a compass. No, we are Christians and therefore we must not only love our brethren, but even our enemies and our persecutors, and so overcome their evil with good. For how hard thoughts soever we may justly have of the spirit and counsels that govern that Church, yet many among them in the simplicity of their heart, and according to the implicitness of their principles, follow those opinions that have been dropped into them from their childhood; they have not strength of thought to look narrowly into them, nor do their rules allow them in so bold a thing, as to examine whether they are in the right or not; and though it is hard to imagine how any should go over to them, yet it is easy to imagine how those who are among them should be shut up blindfold, and muffled up with the awful bonds of Authority and Infallibility."*

It is true, that the Popery of the present day no longer dares to assume the attitude of accredited persecution, but adopts the language and attempts to mask itself under the disguise of that modern Liberalism, upon which in the decrepitude of its old age, it is compelled to lean for support. That its principles are nevertheless unchangeable, and its thirst for power unabated, the present state of Ireland abundantly proves;† while through the supine indifference

---

* Sermon preached before the Prince of Orange, 23rd Dec 1688.

† After comparing the recent deliverance of the nation with that of the Israelites out of the power of Pharaoh, Bishop Burnet says,

" This is that Egypt out of which we are delivered,—I wish I could say delivered,—Alas ! Ireland is not, but is still in bondage with her children, and like to be a long scene of blood and misery ; nor can *our deliverance be complete*, till that is perof modern Protestants, it has obtained an ascendancy in the Legislature, and an establishment in the land, which are sufficient to arouse all who value the blessings of the Reformation to a sense of their increasing danger.

> ————sidelong he works his way,
> As when a ship, by skilful steersman wrought,
> Nigh river's mouth or foreland, where the wind
> Veers oft, as oft so steers, and shifts her sail;
> So varied he————

Such was the character of its first approaches, so long as caution was necessary, till at length, however remote may be the danger of our Protestant *light* being extinguished in the land, our *National* recognition of Protestant *principle* has almost ceased to exist.

It may be said indeed, that Infidelity rather than Popery, is the master spirit of the age in which we live; but it must never be forgotten, that popery and infidelity, however apparently opposed to one another, are in fact but diversified forms of Government, by which the Prince of this world maintains and exercises his dominion in Apostate Christendom : we need not wonder then that they should exist together, and play into one another's hands. " May God remember us now in our low estate, for his mercy endureth for ever."

The Editor will only add, how great a privilege he deems it, as a warmly attached member of the Church of England, to be permitted to testify by this publica-

fected; and though we here are not at present in their power, yet it is but too evident, that many wish we were." (Exhortation to peace and union, a Sermon preached at St. Lawrence Jewry, 26th November, 1689). Prophetic words ! It is from the shores of Ireland that the Tide of Popery is now rolling back upon ourselves, in just judgment for our past indifference and neglect.

tion, the love and honour which he bears to one, who though compelled by conscientious scruples to relinquish his preferment, and to fulfil his ministry out of the visible communion of the church, of which he had been ordained a minister, was nevertheless, a bright and shining light and witness for Christ, in his day and generation. Upon this subject, he would again refer to the sentiments of Bishop Burnet, and desire to be enabled cordially to adopt them as his own. " While St. Paul was a prisoner for the gospel, some thinking to add affliction to his bonds, preached Christ not sincerely, but out of malice and envy ; yet so triumphant was the spirit of universal love, and of zeal for the honour of his blessed Master in him, that he rejoiced in this, that Christ was preached. And then do we become his followers, when by a degree of the same spirit, we can so far raise our minds above all the narrownesses of a party, that *though we were assured that those men who differ from us, were in the wrong, and had ill designs against us,* yet we would conquer them in the spirit of the Gospel, and so overcome their evil with good."* Weapons like these were taken from the armoury of heaven, and are worthy of a Christian Bishop

It is indeed delightful to contemplate the character of such men, the holy Peacemakers of the age in which they lived ; preserved themselves by divine Grace, from imbibing the spirit of the times, and enabled, as ministers of the Everlasting Gospel to take heed to their ministry that they fulfilled it, and to keep themselves unspotted from the world. And

* Exhortation to Peace and Union.

may we not consider them as still addressing us from Heaven in the language of warning and encouragement by their writings and example?

Is this a nation so fearing God and working righteousness, that there would be little danger, nationally or individually, of our "falling into the hands of the living God," were he now to come to Judgment? Might not the faithful minister of Christ justly reply to the confident assertion, "I have kept the commandment of the Lord," with Samuel of old, — "What meaneth then this bleating of the sheep in mine ears, and the lowing of the oxen which I hear?" (1 Sam. xv. 14.) What, our luxury? our maxims of temporizing expediency? our idolatry of wealth on the one hand, and of intellect on the other? Our neglect of relative duties? our contempt of God and of his ordinances? our profanation of his Sabbaths? our treasury replenished by the consumption of ardent spirits, and the consequent drunkenness, uncleanness, and swearing, for which "the land mourneth." (Jer. xxiii. 10.) The Apostle testifies of heathen Thessalonica, that among them drunkenness was a sin which shunned the light of day? He says, "They that are drunken, are drunken in the night." (1 Thess. v. 7.) Could this be truly affirmed of Christian England? Let the public resorts of the drunkard on the morning of every Sabbath, answer the question.

Again, do we live in days, in which the character of "the Almost Christian" is so entirely unknown, that there is no need to try our profession of religion, where any is made? Are our lamps so well trimmed, and our vessels so replenished with oil, that the midnight cry, "Behold the bridegroom cometh," would take none of us by surprise, and awaken in every bosom no other feeling than that of holy joy ?   Great, blessed be God, is the spread and preaching of his word among us, but how very few believe the record which it contains ! Have *we* received the truth in the love of it ? and is it our chief concern to adorn the doctrine we profess to have received, by a holy and consistent life?   And if it be, is not the Prayer of the Psalmist still most suitable to our condition, " Search me, O Lord, and know my heart, try me and know my thoughts, and see if there be any wicked way in me, and lead me in the way everlasting." (Psa. cxxxix. 23, 24.)

We are living, it is true, in an age of such pretended liberality and compassion for all, that the Jew, rejected himself for his rejection of Christ, shall nevertheless be deemed a fit Legislator for a Christian community : but is there an equal pity felt for the benighted condition of his soul ? a no less ardent desire that the veil of Spiritual blindness may be removed from his heart, and that he may become a Citizen of that only free and great city, the new and heavenly Jerusalem? These are solemn and deeply interesting inquiries ! They are suggested to the Reader of the following pages, with an earnest entreaty that he will institute them for himself, as if addressed to himself alone, and ask with uplifted heart, " Lord is it I ?"

It is proper here to remark that a few words wanting in the manuscripts, have been supplied by the Editor. They are printed in italics between brackets, in order that the Reader may either adopt them, or select for himself any preferable expressions. The Manuscripts have been deposited for the convenience of public inspection, in the British Museum.

The following is a list of the Works already published

by the same Author.

———

1. Spiritual Wisdom improved, a Sermon on Ephes. v. 15, 16. 1660 4to, London, 1678, 12mo. 4th edition.
2. The Pastor's Valediction, a Farewell Sermon on 1 Cor. i. 3. 1662, 4to. and 12mo.
3. The Almost Christian Discovered, or the False Professor tried and cast. 1661, 8vo. 1666, 8vo. London, 1684, 12mo. 8th. edition. Glasgow, 1755, 12mo. Glasgow, 1825, 12mo., with an Introductory Essay by the Rev. D. Young, Perth. London, 1832, 12mo. London, 1834, 12mo.
4. The Good of Early Obedience, on Lam. iii. 27. 1683, 8vo.
5. The Life and Death of Nathaniel Mather, 1689, 8vo.
6. The Vision of the Wheels, a Sermon on Ezekiel x. 13. 1689, 4to.
7. Funeral of Thomas Rosewell, on Job. xxxiii. 23, 24. 1691, 4to.
8. Two Sticks made One, or the Excellence of Unity. A Sermon preached by appointment of the Ministers of the Congregational, and Presbyterian Persuasion at their Union. 6th April. London, 1691, 4to.
9. Sermon, London, 1692, 4to.
10. Sermon, London, 1697, 4to.
11. Funeral Sermon on the Rev. Timothy Cruso, from Romans viii. 11. 1698, 4to.

ORIGINAL SERMONS, &c.

SERMON I.

_____

"*And he said unto me, Son of Man, can these bones
live?   And I answered, O Lord God, thou knowest.*"
—Ezek. xxxvii. 3.

THERE are two great prophecies in this chapter, one
concerning the dry bones, the other is concerning two
sticks made one.   The latter of these I have upon occasion spoken to elsewhere.   This of the dry bones I
would now speak to; and because I shall have re-
course to many things in the prophecy, it will not be
amiss to read the whole prophecy. (Ezek. xxxvii.) "The
hand of the Lord was upon me, and carried me out in
the Spirit of the Lord, and set me down in the midst
of the valley which was full of bones, and caused," &c.

In this prophecy, (now read) you have a description
of the sad and deplorable condition of the Jews in their
present captivity in Babylon, and a prophecy of their
wonderful and unexpected deliverance out of that
thraldom.   Both these are couched under the type of
dry bones, from the first verse to the eleventh, and
there he explains the meaning of the bones,—these
bones are the whole House of Israel, that is, these
bones are the emblem or hieroglyphic of the House of
Israel; so that these dry bones are not to be looked

upon as a thing real, but only visional; not true in the history of the thing, but true in the signification of the emblem; for this you have intimated in the 1st verse, " The hand of the Lord was upon me, and carried me out in the Spirit, and set me down in the midst of the valley that was full of bones." He was carried out in the Spirit, not corporally, but visionally, as he saith, chapter viii. 3, " The Spirit lifted me up by a lock of my head between the earth and the heavens, and brought me in the visions of God to Jerusalem." He was then in Babylon, and it is not likely that the Spirit of God carried him by the hair of the head to Jerusalem. No! It was a vision. He brought me in the visions of God to Jerusalem; and he saw what was done in the temple, not by speculation, but by visional representation, which he was as fully assured of the truth of, as if he had seen it with bodily eyes. So here the prophet is in a valley of dry bones, walks round about them, communes with God about them, prophecies over them; sees the bones come together, and sinews and flesh come upon them, and life and breath come into them; but he tells you in the 1st verse, all this was in the Spirit. It is vain to inquire what or whose bones these were, seeing they are represented only in a vision, and designed of God only to set out Israel's sad case, and the condition they were now in. In this representation, or emblematical description of Israel's condition by the bones, you have four parts :—

The circumstances of these bones. (In ver. 2.)

The dialogue between God and the Prophet about them. (ver. 3.)

His prophecy over them, (verse 4, 5, 6, 7.)

The effects or consequences of this prophecy, from 7th to 10th verses.

1. The circumstances of these bones. As to number, nature, and place. As to number, they were many, very many. As to nature, dry, very dry. As to place, in the valley, in the open valley.

As to number, very many, (ver. 2.) So the 1st verse saith the valley was full of bones; they were so many that when the breath came into them, that they stood on their feet, they became an exceeding great army. (ver. 10.)

As to the nature and quality of them, they were very dry. No sinews, no flesh, no marrow, nor moisture, and so nothing in them that could cause the least hope of life. Dry bones do import an hopeless condition; therefore, say they in the 11th verse, "Our bones are dried, and our hope is lost."

These bones were in the open valley, and this is a further expression of their misery; for valleys, being low bottoms, are often put to express a low and afflicted state. And they are not only said to be in the valley, but in the open valley, exposed to all violence and injury of wind and weather. Such was their state in Babylon. How sad was their condition; they were very many, and what they felt lay very heavy, till they were past hope, the bones were very many, very dry, and in the open valley.

2. You have the conference or dialogue between God and the prophet, concerning these dry bones. When God had brought the prophet into the valley, and shewed him these dry bones, he asks him his opinion about them; "Son of man, can these dry bones live?" He doth not only say, Can bones live? but,

can these bones, can these that are dry, very dry, that lie in the open valley, can these bones live? The question may have a three-fold reference; either to the certainty of life, or the likelihood of life, or the possibility of life.

It may refer to the *certainty* of the thing. Is it sure these bones shall live? Dost thou believe it as a thing that shall really come to pass?

It may refer to the *probability* of the thing. Is it likely that bones thus dry, and scattered and exposed, should ever be made to live? And in this God condescends a step lower to try the prophet's faith; as if he should say, If thou canst not believe the certainty that these bones shall live, yet canst thou believe the probability that they may live? Or,

The question may refer to the *possibility* of the thing. Is it possible that such a thing can be? And here God condescends a step lower than before, to see what faith the prophet had in this matter, or whether he had any faith in it at all.

Now to this question the prophet gives his answer to God in the next words. " O Lord thou knowest." In which answer there are three things included.

1. An exclusion of all natural power of living. As if the prophet should say, It is manifest that these bones, so dried and scattered, so exposed, cannot live again by any power in themselves to live, or by any act or power in any creature to quicken them.

2. It implies the hesitancy of his own thoughts about the event of the thing in question, whether they should live again or not. O Lord thou knowest, but as for me, I know not; as I see no hope, so I do not know what to think.

3. The answer is such as refers all to God; who is infinite in power, wonderful in council, and excellent in working. " O Lord thou knowest ;" as if he should say, Thou art omniscient, and knowest what thou wilt do ; and omnipotent, and canst do whatever thou hast a mind to do. Though I do not know what will become of this thy poor people that are dead and past hope, and cannot say whether ever thou wilt restore and relieve them again, yet, O Lord, thou knowest. And from the words thus opened, you may take this observation,

That the Church and people of God may be so low brought by long and sore suffering and bondage, that their deliverance and redemption may pose and non-plus the faith and hope of the best of the saints of God.

I shall speak to it as briefly as the thing will bear, under three heads:

I. That the church and people of God are many times under very great and long bondage and sufferings.

II. That these sufferings may bring them very low.

III. The lowness of their condition may be such as to nonplus their faith and hope of any redemption.

I. The church and people of God may be, and sometimes are, under very great and long bondage and suffering. Consider two things to make this out.

1. That the Scripture hath set no bounds either to the quality or continuance of the church's trial and suffering.

(1.) Not to the quality of it. What or how great it shall be—sometimes it is very great. The prophet speaks of great bitterness, (Isa. xxxviii. 17.) Of great and sore troubles, (Psa. lxxi. 20.) And you read of great wrath from the Lord of Hosts, (Zech. vii. 12.) And the apostle speaks of a great death, (2 Cor. i. 10, &c.) Their sufferings in this world may be as great as those of the wicked, and greater too, for the greatness of their sufferings is reserved for another world.

(2.) Nor doth the Scripture determine the continuance of their sufferings. It saith how long they shall not be, they shall not be for ever, Christ hath freed them from eternal sufferings by suffering for them; but it may be for a long time. This we know, that all the church's sufferings are timed by God; and the malice and rage of wicked men cannot stretch them beyond God's appointed time: but when that time shall be, when it shall end, is a secret hid in the breast of God. But this we find, that it is sometimes very long. "For thy sake we are killed all the day long." (Romans viii. 36.) "We which live are alway delivered to death for Jesus sake." (2 Cor. iv. 11.) Indeed, the sufferings of God's people are sometimes said to be short, for a little time, for an hour, (Rev. iii. 10.) Afflictions for a moment, (2 Cor. iv. 17.) But this is to be understood with respect to eternity; for as time itself is very short, if compared to eternity, so are sufferings too. And therefore the Holy Ghost calls them the sufferings of this present time. So that they sometimes last as long as a man's life; his whole life may be exposed to sufferings. Israel's abode in Egypt was a long time; and seventy years Judah lay in captivity in Babylon. A long time! and therefore the Holy Ghost doth here compare their case to the dry bones scattered in the valley.

2. The carriage and behaviour of the church under her sufferings is such as speaks them to be very great and long. When God, by the continued pressure she

is under, puts her to her " how long !" it argues her
sufferings to be very long. " How long wilt thou be
angry, O Lord ! for ever ? How long shall the wicked
triumph ?" So under the fifth Seal, you read that the
souls of them that were slain for the word of God,
cried with a loud voice, " How long, O Lord, holy
and true, dost thou not judge and avenge our blood
on them that dwell on the earth !" This " how long"
doth imply that their sufferings were great and of long
continuance. When the hope of God's people fails by
reason of sufferings, then it is a sign they are great
and long. (Lam. iii. 18.)—" I said, my strength and
hope is perished from the Lord." (Isa. xl. 27.)
" My way is hid from the Lord, and my judgment is
passed over from my God." As if he should say, He
neglects to plead my cause, and give judgment against
my enemies ; he hath left us in their hands, and our
case is past hope : and therefore their case is compared to these dry bones.

II. These great and long sufferings do sometimes
bring the church of God very low. (2 Chron. xxviii.
19.) " The Lord brought Judah low." (Psa. lxxix. 8.)
" Let thy tender mercies speedily prevent us, for we
are brought very low;" past the hope of all human
help. He speaks as if their case was utterly desperate,
without the help of an Omnipotent arm. Now here I
shall show you two things,—

1. In what sense the people of God may be said to
be in a low condition.

2. Why God deals thus with them.

1. In what sense they may be said to be in a low
condition. I do not speak of that lowness, which is a
disposition of heart opposed to high-mindedness and

spiritual pride, but of such a lowness as is provi-
dential, and is occasioned by the severe dealings of
God.   And in this sense they may be said to be low,

(1.) In respect of privileges and present enjoyments.
In Scripture it is reckoned a very great honour, to partake of and enjoy the Gospel and ordinances of God.
As it gives them advantages above other people, (Rom.
iii. 1, 2.) so it advances them in honour. It is a greater
honour to be born under the Gospel and the privileges
that come by it, than to be descended from the loins of
Princes. Of Israel it is said, " What nation is there so
great ?" What made them so great? was it their number,
their large borders, their vast dominions ? No ! for the
Lord tells them, (Deut. vii. 7.) " He did not set his love
upon them because they were more in number than
others, for they were the fewest of all people ;" but
that which made them great was the ordinances of God
among them.   " What nation is there so great that
hath God so nigh to them ?" (Deut. iv. 7.) Two things
make a people great, a special presence and righteous ordinances, and both these this people had, and,
therefore, are said to be great.

(2.) A people may be said to be low with respect to
strength and power. Their strength may be wasted
and their power gone. (Deut. xxxii. 36.)   "The Lord
will repent himself for his servants when he sees that
their power is gone," and therefore they are called, "Dry
bones."   Bones that are in a living body, and clothed
with sinews and flesh, are strong ; but bones, that are
dead and dry, have no strength in them ; that question
of the prophet is like this in the text—" By whom shall
Jacob arise, seeing he is very small ?" (Amos. vii. 2.)

(3.) They may be said to be low with respect to

honour and reputation. These set a people on high. (Deut. xxviii. 1.) " If thou keep his commandments the Lord will set thee on high." (Psa. cvii. 41.) He pours contempt upon princes, and sets the poor on high. And when a people are made vile and dishonourable, then they are said to be laid low.

(4.) They may be said to be low, as to faith and expectation. Their sufferings may be so great and so long, that they may be bereft of all hope of deliverance. So was Israel in Egypt; they hearkened not to Moses when he said, God sent him to deliver them; and, therefore, the case of Israel in Babylon, is compared to dry bones, because they were past hope of life. In the 11th verse, " These bones are the whole house of Israel, behold they say, Our bones are dried, and our hope is lost; we are cut off for our parts." Then are a people low indeed. But why doth God suffer his people to be brought thus low? First, negatively, it is not because God takes pleasure in it; no, it is far from Him. Judgment is his strange work. If he hath no pleasure in the sinner's death, surely it can be no pleasure to him to see his people in deaths oft, killed all the day long; and their bones scattered at the grave's mouth, the stones of the sanctuary poured out on the top of every street; nay, it is so far from his pleasure, that it is his affliction. " In all their afflictions he was afflicted." (Isaiah lxiii. 9.) Nor is it for want of love to his people; for "as a father pitieth his children, so the Lord pitieth them that fear him." God hath very great ends in doing this. Ends that have far greater good in them than there can be evil in all their sufferings. As for instance,

(1.) God hath a design hereby to glorify his attributes.

His *wisdom* is greatly honoured by his people's afflictions.

1. In timing their afflictions, when it is most seasonable, when there is most need.

2. In his wise ordering of them—how, what sort, and how long. What sort of sufferings we shall feel; this is under the guidance of God. There be many kinds of death endured for Christ; one dies in his name, another in his enjoyments, another in his relations, &c. How much we shall undergo is directed by his wisdom: he doth not lay the same burden upon all, but suits the burden to the back, or the back to the burden. "He stays his rough wind in the day of his east wind." How long they shall suffer, is also directed by his wisdom. "After two days he will revive us, and we shall live in his sight." God knows how to order all our crosses and put an end to them; when we are at our wits end, and know not what to do, God is never at the end of his wisdom, but hath a thousand ways to relieve us.

He hath a design to glorify his *power*, and therefore he lets matters run to great extremity, that his power may be made manifest. He let Jairus's daughter die, and Lazarus lie in the grave, that his power might appear in raising them up again. Therefore he lets his people lie in Babylon till they become dry bones, that he may glorify his power in making them live.

He doth it for the glory of his *justice*, and this greatly shines forth in dealing so severely with his own people for their sin; he lets the world see that God is no respecter of persons. If his own people provoke him, they are brought low for their iniquity. (Psa. cvi. 43.) "He

gives his strength into captivity, and his glory into the
enemies hands;" he makes "judgment begin at the
house of God." (1 Pet. iv. 17.) He sends his people into
Babylon, there lets them lie till they become dry bones
in the valley. God is a just God, and answers his
people by terrible things in righteousness, and though
he forgives their sins, yet he takes vengeance on their
invertions.

His *faithfulness* is hereby greatly glorified. God
hath made promises to his people, that reach out hope
and relief to them in every condition; and that is
to be the prop and stay of their faith, that whatever
their case is, yet they may have a sure hold of God,
and encouragement to trust in Him. And there is no
prop like a promise. God many times suffers his
people to be very low brought, that his faithfulness to
his promise may be glorified.

This also gives great occasion to the glorifying his
sovereignty. No work magnifies God so much as that
which none can do but He. Many can set broken
bones, but none can put life into dry and dead bones
but He. Therefore he brings his people into great
deaths, that he may be known to be the Lord of Life.
" You shall know that I am the Lord when I have
opened your graves." He seals up the hand of every
man, that all men may know that it is his work; and,
therefore it is, that God usually lets things run to extremity. " In the mount of the Lord it shall be seen."
When the bricks were doubled, when the knife is at
Isaac's throat, then He stops the hand, and provides a
ram. Jairus's daughter is not fit to be cured, till dead;
nor Lazarus to be raised, till he stinks in the grave.
If you look for a clear day in the mysteries of God's

providence, you must stay till evening , for at "eventide
it shall be light :" and this is one reason why God lets
his people be in a low condition in this world, it is for
his own glory.

(2.) With respect to the enemies of his interest and
people.

To discover what is in their hearts. There is
the same end of the sufferings of the saints, as of
heresies in the church; it is that they that are of the
truth may be made manifest, and that the lusts and
corruptions of wicked men may be discovered. The
Evangelist speaking of the indignity and sufferings which
the Lord Christ should undergo in the world saith, it
is that the thoughts of many hearts may be revealed.
The times of Christ's personal sufferings, were times
of great discovery, and so are the times of his mystical
sufferings in his body the church; they discover the
thoughts of many hearts. The witnesses must die, and
their dead bodies lie in the street of the great city, and
by this will the hearts of many be revealed that will
not afford them a grave. It hath always been the
spirit of the enemies of God's people, to insult over
them and tread them down in their low condition.
Times of great suffering are times of great discovery.
Profession doth not so well reveal a man as persecution; then it is seen what the hearts of men are, for
Christ, for the truths of Christ, for the ministers of
Christ, and for the kingdom of Christ. Then we may
see who are for him and who not; who follow him for
love and who for the loaves. This is the fire that tries
every man's work of what sort it is.

It is *that the salvation of his people may appear
to be the work of God*, so as to put their enemies to

everlasting shame and silence, as when Israel came
out of Egypt, God did deliver them in that manner
that not a dog moved his tongue, so it shall be when
God puts forth his power to save his people; it is said,
all iniquity shall stop her mouth—it is the abstract for
the concrete, iniquity for men of iniquity. Wicked
men shall stop their mouths, and this is when he sets
the poor on high from afflictions. Great salvation
opens the mouths of the saints, but it stops the mouths
of the wicked, and that three ways;

1. By conviction. Full conviction stops the mouth.
Therefore, when Christ saith to the man without the
wedding garment, " How camest thou in hither?" it
stops his mouth, and he is speechless, so shall the enemies of God be. When God's people are in great
sufferings, then the mouths of wicked men are open to
reproach and judge and condemn them; but when God
appears in their behalf to deliver them, it shall be in
such a manner as shall convince the world that this is
the seed that God will bless.

2. Their mouths shall be stopped with shame. (Isa.
xxvi. 11.) " They shall see and be ashamed for their
envy at thy people." (Micah vii. 15.) " According
to the days of thy coming out of the land of Egypt,
so will I shew unto thee marvellous things;" and
what follows? " the nations shall see it and be confounded, they shall lay their hands upon their mouths."
(Isa. lxvi. 5.) " Hear the word of the Lord, you that
tremble at his word! your brethren that hated you,
that cast you out for my name's sake, said, " Let the
Lord be glorified;" but he shall appear to your joy,
and they shall be ashamed."

3. Their mouths shall be stopped with terror and

amazement at the work God shall do for the dry bones. When the spirit of life from God enters into the witnesses that they stand upon their feet, it is said great fear fell upon them that saw them. (Rev. xi.)

(3.) God brings his people very low to be as dry bones in the valley with respect to his people themselves.

In judgment for sin. God will not let his own children go altogether unpunished. Judgment begins at the house of God, and sin is the procuring cause of it, wherever it comes. (Jer. ii. 17.) "Thou hast procured this to thyself."

It is for trial. God loves to try the sincerity of his people, and the truth and strength of their grace, of what kind it is, and of what degree. Sometimes he tries what we can do for him, and what we can endure. Jairus comes to Christ for healing for his daughter; see how Christ tries him—he put her in the hands of Christ to save her life, and she dies in his hand; why doth Christ let her die but to try her father's faith? the father could believe for her when she was living, but Christ will go further, and know whether he will trust him for a dead child. So here in the text, " Can these dry bones live ?"

God doth it that he may by his carriage herein give such a witness and *experience of his power, and grace, and faithfulness to his people*, as may be an encouragement to faith for the future, whatever difficulties they meet with. The way that a Christian is to walk in, is full of difficulty from one end to another, like Israel's way out of Egypt. When they are got out of Egypt, there is a Red Sea to pass over; when they are got out of that, they have a wilderness to

wander forty years in. Now the way of God is to
make his deliverance an experience to us, that we may
hope in God in all future troubles. (Psa. lxxiv. 14.)
" Thou breakest the head of Leviathan and gavest
him to be meat to thy people, inhabiting the wilderness ;" that is, food for their faith when they were in
wilderness straits. Now remember (as if he said)
the Red Sea, how I delivered you from Pharaoh and
his host, and destroyed them in the sea. God hath
two ends in every salvation he works for his people, a
present succour, and after support, and the greater
the present deliverance is, the more encouraging it is
as to experience. And I tell you, whatever salvation
God works for his people at any time, you never make
a right improvement of it if you only believe it and
reap the present benefit of it ; but God designs it to be
food for your faith in after times of trouble : therefore,
when you hear of wars and rumours of wars and inva-
sions, if you that were delivered a while ago so wonderfully, if you cannot trust and rely upon God now, you do
not improve your former deliverance. It is a blessed
thing when we can trust God for the vindicating of his
name and power against all his enemies. God lets
things run to a low ebb before the tide turns and mercy comes in, for this very reason, that we may trust in
God for time to come. When there is none shut up
or left, when there is but an handful of meal in the barrel, when the bones are dry, then is God's time ; if
you can but trust him till then, God will deliver his
people in such a manner as shall make abiding impressions upon them. (John xi. 45.) When Christ
raised Lazarus from the grave, then many seeing the
things Jesus did, believed on him. (Ezek. xxxvii. 13.)

"You shall know that I am the Lord when I have opened your graves and brought you out." Though your captivity be as death, and your confinement be as the grave, yet I will bring you out, and ye shall know that I am the Lord. They shall have more experience of the love and faithfulness of God than ever they had before, and shall be brought to trust in God more than ever before.

III. The lowness of the condition of the church may be so great as may nonplus their faith, and put their hope to a stand about their redemption. To see a company of dry bones lay scattered up and down in a valley, who would believe that ever they should come together, bone to his bone. The poor Jews in Babylon had no faith nor hope about it; but they despaired of any such thing. "Behold our bones are dried, we are cut off for our part:" their faith was nonplust. Thus it was with Israel at the Red Sea. When the sea was before them, and the enemy behind them, and the mountains on each side, their faith was nonplust. Thus it was with Job in his particular case. "God hath destroyed me on every side and I am gone, my hope is removed like a tree." Language full of despair. There are three things by which he bespeaks his case desperate in his own opinion.

1. "He hath destroyed me on every side," my estate, children, person and peace, on every side is destroyed. It was once the envious complaint of the devil, that God had made an hedge about him on every side; but now it is the unbelieving complaint of Job, that God had destroyed him on every side.

2. "He hath destroyed me and I am gone;" he

speaks like one that is dying. As we say, such a one is going, and when dead, he is gone.

3. " He hath removed me as a tree" that is cut up and dry, that is, past hope. Thus Job's faith was nonplust.

Thus it was with David ; though God had promised him a kingdom, yet he cries out in the greatness of his persecution, " All men are liars ;" and, " I shall one day perish by the hand of Saul."

And so it will be when the Lord comes to save his people, to deliver them out of the hands of them that hate them, it will be when their faith is nonplust.

To apply this a little in a few inferences :—

1. Here we see the sad fruit of sin ; how low it brings a people. They provoked him with their inventions, and were brought low by their inventions. It brings them not only to death, but lays them under great degrees of death, till their flesh be consumed, and their bones dried and scattered in the valley.

2. I infer, hence, the case of God's people may be such as to be past all hope, as to sense.

3. How hopeless so ever their case may be, God can easily alter and better it. He can exalt the low tree, and make the dry tree to flourish. He made Aaron's dry rod to bud and blossom, and Sarah's dead womb to conceive. If God undertake any work it is easy. The God that quickens the dead, and calls things that are not as though they were, can easily do it. If he can by his word call things that have no being into being, and restore things that cease to be to their first being, then how easily can he better the case of his church, when they are past hope.

4. In the method of God's providence, when things are most desperate in our sense, then they are nearest redress. When the church is most under the power of death, then life is nearest. When the bones are dead and dry, then life comes. When the burdens of Israel were doubled, and the severity of their task-masters great, then deliverance is near. When the decree to destroy all the Jews was sealed with the king's seal and sent abroad, when the decree came near to be put in execution, then God turned it to the contrary. When Lazarus was sick they send for Christ to come and heal him, but Christ's hour was not yet come ; he grows worse and worse, and then dies, but still it is too soon; then he is buried and lays in his grave, but still it is too soon for Christ to raise him, till he stinks, and then it is a fit time for Christ to show himself to be God indeed. God loves to own his people when they are forsaken of their own hopes. Mercy never tarries too long, nor comes too late ; it is always given in the fittest season, which God knows better than we ; therefore let us trust him to the last. When John wept because there was none worthy to open the book, then Christ is discovered for the work. (Rev. v. 4, 5.)

5. I infer that mercy doth not always tarry for the fitness of his people to receive it, and it is well for us it doth not, we could never hope to be delivered. What fitness or disposition in dry bones, scattered in the valley, to live and stand upon their feet? God loves to show the freeness of his mercy, and it is then most free when he bestows it when there is no meet-ness for it, nor preparation to receive it. "I do not this for your sakes, O House of Israel, but for my

Name's sake:" this dew from the Lord tarries not for man, nor waits for the sons of men. I tell you, though God will not cut off his enemies till they are fit to be destroyed, yet he many times delivers his people before they are fit to be delivered. What fitness had Israel for deliverance when it came? Never a people more unprepared for deliverance than they were; nay, they were so far from being prepared for it, that they would not believe it, when God sent them word of it. What fitness had the church of God in Babylon for deliverance when it came? a company of dead dry bones scattered here and there! never a work so unfit to be brought about; but if God breathe on them, the dry bones shall live.

Again, by way of counsel. May the church of God be so low brought, that their deliverance may nonplus the faith of the best of God's people? then take heed of a desponding spirit in a time of difficulty and danger. However it may go with the Church of God, look to it that you be not discouraged; when faith is at a stand as to second causes, then refer all to the First Cause: do as the prophet doth here in the text, refer all to God, leave things in his hand. " Son of man, can these bones live? O Lord thou knowest." The words are very full of sense. First, they imply the creature's ignorance of the course of Providence. Secondly, they imply God's omniscience, and refer it to his power. Thou that knowest all things, knowest if they shall live; thou knowest thou canst do all things possible to be done; therefore, O Lord, thou knowest. Thou madest them dry bones, and therefore thou canst clothe them again. Thou knowest they can live, they have in them an obediential capacity to be whatever thou wouldest have them; thou knowest bones as dead and dry as these have lived. How dead was Israel in Egypt! how long in death! how deep the grave! and yet thou breathedst upon them and revivedst them. Lord, thou knowest! thou knowest how to make them live; thou canst command deliverance for Jacob. Thou canst tell how to raise up dry bones at the last, and therefore why not in a mystical sense before that day? thou knowest how to remove all obstructions that lie in the way of this. If it be sin, thou canst take it away; if it be unbelief and despair, thou canst remove it. All this is implied in the prophet's answer, " O Lord, thou knowest."

And, indeed, there are many questions that may arise from the word of God, and the works of God, to which no answer can be given but this of the prophet, " O Lord, thou knowest." Whence comes the wind and whither goeth it,—whether the word preached shall convert this soul or that, Lord, thou knowest! when the witnesses shall be slain and rise again, when the vials shall empty themselves on the proper objects, when Babylon shall fall and the woman shall be delivered, when the earth and the works of it shall be burnt up, and the new heavens and earth commence, who can tell! therefore, O Lord, thou knowest. Therefore let us not despond about things we do not understand; that which is out of your reach to remedy, refer to the power and wisdom of God to redress; but of all things, take heed that faith be not nonplust and at a stand, at the lowness of the cause of Christ. Shall faith wither because the bones be dry? God forbid. Consider,

1. It is one of the saddest things in the world to see

a believer without faith. A child of light walking in darkness, as to practice, and a believer lying in unbelief, as to God's providence, are very sad things: yet how common is it? A man may act faith in eternal recompence, and yet be in unbelief as to present providence. He may have a faith in the blood of Christ, and yet want a suitable faith in the work of Christ.

2. No death, no sufferings, can do you such mischief as the fainting of your faith in an evil day.

(1.) It gives Christ a loose from the promise. It doth quit and discharge him, and is not that a great thing? As long as you believe Christ stands engaged, but if faith fails, you have no hold of him, you let him go. God cannot do what he would in a way of judgment, when faith holds his hand; nor can he do what he would in a way of deliverance, when unbelief stands in the way.

(2.) This unbelief weakens his working hand. Christ could do no mighty works there because of their unbelief. Nothing is difficult to Christ that is feasible to faith. How much is this the spirit of the day we are in. Among professors the cause and interest of Christ is a sinking thing, a decaying thing. There is a death upon his cause and church, and therefore many forsake it; "trouble not the Master."

(3.) This makes your case worse, whatever it be. As the woman in her bloody issue, whatever means she used, yet still she grew worse, and the reason was because she used the wrong means. If the case of the church be bad, unbelief always makes it worse. Let there be never so many deaths upon it, yet this of unbelief is the sorest. This is the stone upon the grave's mouth. Therefore, as Christ said when he was to

raise Lazarus, take away the stone. So, believe and
it shall be done. What would God do for his church
and people, at this day, when there be so great things
upon the wheel, if his people could but follow him
with faith !

Labour then for a strong faith, a faith that no
temptation can conquer ; that no sufferings can nonplus, that no death can kill. Would you honour God,
would you advance his name and cause and interest ?
would you do worthily for God in your day ? Labour
for a strong faith ; a faith suited to the trial of the day.
Such a faith as Abraham had. The Holy Ghost com-
mends it for four rare properties—

1. He believed in hope against hope. Against
hope of sense—he believed in hope of the promise. O
that it was thus with us ! We can believe when sense
and hope go together. When faith acts by sense, that
is weak faith ; but when it acts without the evidence
of sense, then it is strong indeed. O that we could
get such a faith, and that we would beg it of God. Is
there none shut up nor left ? Yet, believe. Is the
knife at the throat of Isaac, in this day ? Yet believe.
Is Lazarus in the grave ? Yet believe. Is there a
sentence of death upon the cause of Christ in the
nation ? Yet believe. God will make you see his
glory.

2. Another property of Abraham's faith was this :
—He considered not his own body, now dead, nor the
deadness of Sarah's womb ; both dead as to a genera-
tive power. Now this he considered not, that is, so
as to have his confidence in God weakened. Here is
death upon death, a dead body and a dead womb, yet
a living faith overlooked both. O where is this faith

to be found now among you that are called believers among the seed of Abraham? If God make a promise and there be a living womb to make it fruitful, then we will believe. Can God furnish a table in the wilderness? Here a dead body is considered to the prejudice of faith in God. So, that of the disciples. " We trusted that it was he that should have redeemed Israel; and besides this is the third day."

3. Abraham staggered not at the promise through unbelief. A man may be said to stagger at the promise in three cases.

(1.) When he disputes either the truth of them, or the power of God to perform them.

(2.) When he despairs of the performance of them.

(3.) When he wavers and is off and on, double-minded. Jam. i. 6—8. Now of one mind—now of another. Sometimes hoping, sometimes desponding, as ready to leave God as to seek to him. Now such was Abraham's faith, that he staggered not at the promise through unbelief. He did not dispute nor despond about it. How often do we stagger at the very promise itself! If Providence cross it, if there be a dead body and a barren womb in the way, how do we stagger at the promise of God through unbelief?

4. Abraham was fully persuaded that what God had promised, he was also able to perform. He sets God's faithfulness and power against all deadness and weakness in the creature. What though my body be dead, yet God lives! Though not able to beget a son, yet I know God is able to get me one. This is another rare property of faith, that we should labour for some portion of it in a day of trouble; that we may be able to set God's faithfulness and omnipotency against

every discouragement we meet with in the world. O for such a faith as this in this day among dry bones! Bring a dying faith to a living promise, and that will make faith live till the dry bones live, and if there be any of you that have attained to such a faith as this, then let me, III. put you upon the exercise of it in some important duties that concern the present case.

1. Be much in prayer for the dry bones. The Papists make it a duty to pray for the dead: a foolish thing! but in this sense, it is a duty of all saints to pray for the dead, for the dead and dry bones. "Wilt not Thou revive us again, that thy people may rejoice in Thee?" or as he in Hab. iii. 2. "O Lord, revive thy work in the midst of the years; in wrath remember mercy." Is the cause of Christ dead? then put it into Christ's hands, he is the Lord of life. Are the people of God dead in their hope, in their spirits, in their frames? put all into the hands of Christ, and then it is in safe hands. Nothing can miscarry there. It may come under a sentence of death, but can never die utterly. The ruler's daughter was dead really, though not utterly. The widow's son was dead and carried out upon the bier, he died really but not utterly. So Lazarus died and was buried, really but not utterly, for he was raised again. O that we could by faith and prayer put all our difficult cases into Christ's hands, and try what he can do! your dead bones would live again. It is the greatest honour you can do him to put him upon difficult work: as it is an honour to a believer to believe great things, so there is nothing honours Christ more than putting him upon doing great things.

(1.) He is pleased when you put him upon great things.

(2.) He is angry when you distrust him. To look upon any work so as to think it out of the reach of God's power, is greatly to his disparagement. You cannot dishonour Christ more than to measure his arm by the length of yours.

(3.) If any thing provoke him to leave the dead, it is because the living will not trust him. Therefore he cures Martha's unbelief before he raises Lazarus. Because the interest of Christ's kingdom is low, and its enemies are high, therefore we think his kingdom will never be set up. Lord, help our unbelief!

(4.) A thing is never so fit for Christ's undertaking, as when it is beyond the reach of human power. When the lunatic man was brought to the disciples, and they could not cure him; then, saith Christ, " Bring him hither to me." When the woman had spent all upon the physicians, and she grew worse and worse, then virtue goes out of Christ to heal her. Therefore let us go to Christ and not let him alone. This will do it—" will not God avenge his own elect, which cry to him day and night?" when the spirit of prayer is up, then the enemies of God must down.

2. Be not drawn aside by any discouragements from this duty. Remember the woman of Canaan, what a faith she shewed in her coming to Christ, and nothing could put her off. So Jairus, when others laughed Christ to scorn, believed, and his child lived. They that laughed at the raising the dead were shut out, and they that believed were admitted in, and saw the work of Christ. They that have no faith shall not see his power.

3. Believe that your prayer shall have a remembrance, for the vision is for an appointed time, and in

the end it shall speak, and will not tarry. Believe
for a blessed issue to the saddest providences to the
church of God. "When I sit in darkness the Lord
shall be a light to me." (Mic. vii. 8.)   Therefore whether you live to see the interest of Christ uppermost
or no, yet live and die in the faith of it.   Let your
faith be like that of Joseph when he was dying;
though in Egpyt, yet by faith he made mention of
the departing of the children of Israel out of Egypt;
and therefore gave a charge to carry his bones with
them.

4. Let not the lowness of your condition, nor
delay of redemption make you weary of waiting nor
stagger in your faith; cry, "how long, Holy, and true!"
as the language of importunity, but not of unbelief.

(1.) Because our time is not always God's time.

(2.) Our sufferings have not attained the end upon
us for which they were sent, and until then they must
be endured.

(3.) The more your prayers and repentings are,
that come between your sufferings and your succours
—your death and redemption—the sweeter will your
redemption be when it comes.   In that day it shall
be said, "this is the Lord, we have waited for him,
and he will save us?"

The last use is a word of comfort; though the
bones are dry, though the state of the church is very
low, yet hear what the Holy Ghost saith, (Joel ii. 21.)
" Fear not, O Land, be glad and rejoice, for the Lord
hath done great things."   In the former verse, it is
said, " the enemy had done great things," great waste,
and spoil, and brought great death upon God's people,
but here is their comfort, God will do great things for

them, as the enemies had done great things against them before.

Therefore here is ground of encouragement to his people in their greatest troubles; for if Christ hath an interest that must live in the greatest difficulties and deaths, that do or can befall it, let who will lose in the shaking providences of God upon the world, to be sure Christ will lose nothing. He is always on the gaining hand. (Haggai ii. 7.) You read of a great shaking, but it is to bring Christ into the world. " I will shake all nations, and then the desire of all nations shall come." (Ezek. xxxvii. 7.) You read of another shaking; when God would bring his church out of Babylon there was a great shaking and God brought the bones together. Every shaking goes on Christ's side. (Heb. xii. 26, 27.) You read of another shaking, which is to shake all corrupt worship out of the world, and establish pure worship; "yet once more shake not only the earth but heaven;"—that is the church, and the end is to shake down all false worship." (Rev. xvi. 18.) You read of another shaking, the last that shall ever be in the world. " There were voices and thunderings and lightnings, and a great earthquake, such as never was since men were upon earth;" and mark the effect of it, " Babylon came in remembrance before God to give her the cup of the fierceness of his wrath;" and I am persuaded, that God is risen out of his habitation, and that this shaking of the nations, is to shake Popery out of the world, and to establish his own kingdom.

Again; here is comfort from the promise of God, Dry bones must live because God hath promised it: the witnesses may be slain and lie dead in the streets but the spirit of life shall enter into them, and they shall arise again, and ascend to heaven; for God will make them live, and make good his promise.

As Christ can do it, so nothing can discourage him in it. Cannot the deadness of the cause hinder him? no, he raised Lazarus when he was dead, and stank! Cannot dryness of the bones discourage him? no, I will cause flesh to come upon you, and breath to enter into you, and you shall live. But cannot the unfitness and unworthiness of his people hinder him? Indeed it is a great hindrance to the faith of his people to see what sins are found among them, and these call aloud for mourning and repentance; yet I tell you this, that all the unworthiness of his people cannot discourage or hinder Christ from delivering them. What fitness had these dry bones for life? What fitness had Israel for deliverance? Their deliverance is the fruit of covenant mercy, which is sure mercy. (Obadiah, verse 17.) "Upon Mount Sion there shall be deliverance and holiness." He doth not say, there shall be holiness, but deliverance and holiness. The mercy shall bring a fitness in it for those that receive it; though in making promises spiritual mercy goes before temporal; yet in deliverances there is temporal mercy, and then spiritual; deliverance first, and then holiness. And so it is here in the text: first there is a breathing upon the bones, and they live—there is temporal mercy; and then there is the promise of God's putting his Spirit in them. The time for all this is not afar off; God will not chide continually. The hiding of his face is but for a little while, and your darkness shall be turned into the morning, for mark the twelfth verse of this chapter, " Behold, O my people, I will open your graves, and cause you to come up out of your graves, &c." Therefore he that shall come will come, and will not tarry. Therefore lift up the hands that hang down, for the Lord will turn again the captivity of his people.

SERMON II.

" Thus, saith the Lord God, Behold, O my people I will open your graves, and cause you to come up out of your graves ; and bring you into the land of Israel ; and ye shall know that I am the Lord." Ezek. xxxvii. 12.

In the former part of this chapter, there is a description of the sad and deplorable estate of the people of God in their Babylonish bondage. In the text you have a comfortable prophecy and promise of their wonderful deliverance out of their captivity, under the notion of opening their graves, and raising them out of their graves.

The promise is brought in, first, by a note of attention. Behold! which, like a hand in the margin, always points to something very remarkable. God never, in Scripture, calls us to behold, but it is always something worth beholding.

2. It is brought in by a pathetical appellation. " O my people," a language filled with sympathizing bowels to his people, in their sad and spiritless condition. In the promise itself, you have three things :—

I. The depth of their misery intimated under the metaphor of graves, the burying place of all their comforts.

II. The way of their deliverance foretold, by opening their graves, and bringing them out.

III. Here is the Author of this deliverance, and that is God.

I. The opening this metaphor of the graves, wi_ give you the sense of the whole text.

Though God alone can open the graves, so as to give life, yet, I may open these words, so as to give light. The expression is metaphorical and allusive, and so not to be taken literally; it is used by the Holy Ghost, to express the depth and extremity of misery: the Jews (you must know) were now carried away captive to Babylon, stript of all their comforts and enjoyments, and not only so, but loaded with distresses and grief, and filled with reproach and misery without pity, and burdens without ease, and sorrow without comfort. Many enemies to vex and grieve her, but among all her lovers none found to comfort her. Thus we are to understand the grave in the text. And if you consult the lamentation that was made over this grave, you will find there were nine hands that digged it.

1. Their own sin. " Jerusalem hath grievously sinned, therefore she is removed, her filthiness is in her skirts, therefore she came down wonderfully." (Lam. i. 8. 9.)

2. The anger and wrathful displeasure of God for sin; and this, though it work at second-hand, yet hath a great hand in making this grave. " The Lord hath covered the daughter of Sion with a cloud in his anger, and cast down the beauty of Israel." (Lam. ii. 1.) Surely against me hath he turned and compassed me with darkness.

3. The strength and power of the Babylonians. This is another hand, and this was guided by the former, for God made Judah weak, and Babylon strong; and so gave one up into the hand of the other. "The Lord hath delivered me into the hand of those against whom I was not able to rise up; he hath cut off in his anger all the house of Israel." (Lam. i. 14.)

4. The greatness of the rage of their adversaries. The power and strength of the Babylonians was very great in itself; greater in Judah's weakness; but greatened more by their own rage and malice.

5. The treachery and deceitfulness of her friends. So long as she kept close to God, many nations sought her favours, and made leagues with her ; but they were now so far from helping her in her distress, that they helped her enemies, and dealt treacherously with her.

6. The derision and scorn of their enemies. "Thou hast made us the offscouring and refuse in the midst of the people."

7. The want of spiritual enjoyment. " He hath violently taken away his tabernacle, he hath destroyed his places of the assembly, &c." (Lam. ii. 6.) " The Law is no more, the Prophets also find no vision from the Lord." (ver. 9.) This is another hand that made her grave deep.

8. The loss of God's presence. (Lam. i. 16.) " The comforter that should relieve my soul is far from me" (Lam. iii. 44.) " Thou hast covered thyself with a cloud, that our prayers should not pass through."

9. Her despair of any redemption or deliverance out of these miseries. " My strength and hope is perished from the Lord." (Lam. iii. 18.)

These are the hands that digged the grave of this people. This was their state and case which made their captivity very great and heavy, and called here a grave; and indeed the comparison is very apt and congruous.

For 1. Their present state with respect to their former condition, was no better than a grave. Canaan was so pleasant and dear to them, that it was as death to them to be deprived of it; and their being carried out of this land into Babylon was as a remove from life to death: and their being continued there, was just like their being buried in the grave.

2. Their state is compared to a buried state, in pursuance of the metaphor of killing and death; to which the sufferings of the church are compared in Scripture. The sufferings of the church when they are great and heavy are frequently called death and killing. "For thy sake we are killed all the day long." (Ps. xliv. 22.) "In deaths oft." (2 Cor. xi. 23.)

3. There is a very great resemblance between a grave, and the condition of the Church of God in Babylon, especially in these six things.

(1.) The grave is a place of darkness, so Job calls it. (Job x. 21.) "I go whence I shall not return, even to the land of darkness;" that is the grave. It is a place of darkness! there is neither light within to see with, nor light without to see by; there the sun shines not, and there the eye beholds not, and therefore it is fitly called darkness. Now the state of suffering is a grave in this sense, it is a state of darkness. So was this of the church in Babylon, therefore she complains, "He hath brought me into darkness, but not into light, he hath set me in dark places, as they that be dead of old." She had no pity from man, no comfort from God, no hope in herself; her state was a state of darkness.

(2.) The grave is a place of silence. " The dead praise thee not, neither any that go down into silence," (Psa. cxv. 17.) that is the grave. (Isa. xxxviii. 18.) " The grave cannot praise thee." Why? It is a place of silence. Now their Babylonish bondage was like a grave in this sense—It was a place of silence. They were so oppressed and broken and grieved and discouraged under their sad bondage, that their mouths were stopped. Therefore the Church in Babylon is said to hang her harp upon the willows. (Psa. cxxxvii. 2.) The harp was appointed for the praising of God and rejoicing; but now such was their case that all their joy ceased; no voice of harpers to be heard in her. Therefore when their enemies in way of scoff called to them, " Sing us one of the songs of Sion," they answer, " How shall we sing the Lord's song in a strange land." It was a place of silence. Like that in Jer. viii. 14. " Let us enter into our fenced cities and be silent there, for the Lord hath put us to silence."

(3.) The grave is a place of consuming and wasting; all rots in the dust, it wastes both features and flesh; their beauty shall consume in the grave. Now this Babylonian bondage was to the people of God a grave in this sense. It was a wasting and consuming judgment. In Scripture great judgments are called consumptions. (Isa. x. 22.) " The consumption decreed shall overflow in righteousness."

(4.) The grave is a place of stinking and noisomeness; as the flesh consumes there it sends forth an ill savour.

Now great sufferings are a grave in this sense,
they send forth ill savours.   Persecutions are always
attended with reproaches and revilings; men are
seldom so wicked as to persecute out of a professed
enmity to Godliness, therefore they reproach their
principles or their professions, and then the persecution of Jerusalem is, because it is a rebellious and
bad city.   (Ezra iv. 12.)   Christ himself in his
suffering state, had his name made to stink, he was
called "an enemy to Cæsar, a friend of Publicans and
sinners," and a blasphemer.   So Paul is charged as a
mover of sedition, a pestilent fellow, and a ring-leader
of sectaries.   " We are made made as the filth of the
world and the offscouring of all things to this day."
Our Lord foretold it should be so, and pronounces
them blessed that should be so reproached.

(5.) The grave is a place of forgetfulness.   So
Heman calls it. (Psa. lxxxviii. 12.)   " Shall thy tender
mercies be known in the dark, thy faithfulness in the
land of forgetfulness ? " that is the grave.   The dead
are soon forgotten.   In the grave we forget others—
and others forget us.   Now the Babylonish bondage
was a grave in this sense : it was a land of forgetfulness.   They forgat all that, the remembrance whereof
might have been their comfort and support.   God
made very comfortable promises concerning their
return out of Babylon after seventy years.   But they
buried all the promises of God in the grave of despair.   " My hope and my strength is perished from the
Lord;" and in the 11th ver. " We are cut off for our
our parts."   All the promises were forgotten, all past
experiences were out of mind.

(6.) The grave is insatiable, nothing can satisfy it.

Feed it with the bodies of thousands of men, and it is as unsatisfied as ever. The word for grave in the Hebrew, signifies "to crave or desire;" and why? because it is always craving. Though it hath been eating flesh from Adam's day to this day, yet it is still hungry. Therefore in Scripture the grave is reckoned among the four things that are never satisfied; nor will it be so as long as there is a son of Adam living on earth. Now sufferings are fitly called a grave in this sense; for Babylon's wrath, was cruel wrath, unsatisfied wrath. Literal Babylon was so, and mystical Babylon is much more. Her rage and malice against the people of God is never satisfied. She hath been drinking the blood of saints and martyrs for 1200 years, and yet she is not satisfied.

Thus you see what the graves are, and how aptly great sufferings, as this of the captivity, are set out thereby.

What is meant here by opening their graves, and causing them to come out of their graves? I answer, as the graves are metaphorical and allusive, so is the opening and bringing them out. Now this may be explained particularly with respect to the Jews, or more generally with respect to the whole church of God.

As it respects the Jews—so the opening of their graves is the destroying the power of their enemies. For what was this grave but the power and wrath of the enemy; this brought them down, this kept them under: therefore, when God breaks the power of Babylon and recompences this wrath upon them, then he is said to open the graves of his people and cause them to come out. And this was done literally by

Cyrus's proclamation. (2 Chron. xxxvi. 23.) " All the
kingdoms of the earth hath the Lord God of heaven
given me, and hath charged me to build him an house
in Jerusalem: who is there among you of all his
people ? the Lord his God be with him, and let him
go up."

As it respects the Church of God,—(as doubtless
it doth) both Jews and Gentiles. So God may be
said to open their graves in two cases especially.

1. When he doth deliver them out of their sufferings, by removing insuperable difficulties which cannot
otherwise be removed. Who can open graves and
make men rise out of their graves? It is a wonderful work of great power. There are always such
difficulties in the church's case, as do utterly pose all
created power. Now when God removes these difficulties and makes way for their deliverance, then is
God said to open the graves and bring his people out.
There are many great difficulties in a grave state, especially two.

(1.) In the grave the prisoner lay bound, besides
being shut up and locked in. Now God removes both.
The prisoner is bound hand and foot in the grave.
And this was Israel's case in their graves in Babylon;
they were bound hand and foot, and those bands were
the Babylonish laws and power which they lay under
during the 70 years captivity. Now when the Lord
destroys Babylon's power, makes void their laws, and
releases his people from them, and puts an end to their
oppression, this is opening their graves.

(2.) He that is buried is shut up and kept in. Thus
it was with these people in their captivity, they were
not only in their graves, but kept in by a heavy grave-

stone; that is, great unbelief and despair. This appears in their heartless complaints. " Our hope is lost, and our bones are dried, and we are cut off for our part." Now when God removes this unbelieving despondency in the heart of his people, and doth encourage them to trust in his power, then he rolls away the grave-stone.

2. When God vindicates the names of his people from the reproach and ignominy that is cast upon them —for great sufferings are attended with great reproaches. Therefore when God gives his people into the hands of his enemies, he is said to give them to be a hissing and reproach among the people. Now when God vindicates their name, and cause, and rolls away the reproach in which their names lay buried; this is opening their graves and bringing them out. In short, as all afflictions are death, and great and long continuance therein is a being buried; so when God delivers them from these, he is said to open their graves, and cause them to come out.

And this also must not be omitted, that when God doth this, he calls upon his people to take notice of it, to behold it as a very wonderful thing. " Behold, O my people, I will open your graves, and cause you to come out." Doct. " When the Lord comes to deliver his people it shall be in a very wonderful way; it shall be a work full of wonder." This is a truth that is supported by two pillars in the text.

1. By the note of attention, " Behold," which always points us to something remarkable and wonderful.

2. By the promise of deliverance, under such a metaphor as opening the graves. He doth not only say, " I will deliver you or bring you out of Babylon,

there is seven times more in it than that: it is to show
that it shall not only be done, but by a wonderful power
and in a wonderful manner. To raise the dead, hath
always past as a work of wonder of the first nature and
kind. " Wilt thou show wonders to the dead !" (Psa.
xxxviii. 10.) that is, wilt thou raise them to life? intimating that to raise the dead is a wonderful work; and
the delivering his people is raising the dead. Therefore whenever God doth deliver his people out of the
hands of their enemies, it will be wonderful. Now I
shall shew you that it hath been so from the beginning,
and it was so in the instance in the text, and it shall
be so to the end of the world. And the last deliverances that God shall work for his people shall be the
greatest; they shall be more wonderful than God ever
wrought before.

I shall give you two instances :—

I. In God's redeeming his old people the Jews, and
raising them out of their graves where they have lain
these sixteen hundred years; this people will God
raise again from their graves.

II. I shall instance in his redeeming his present
church of the Gentiles out of the power of Antichrist,
under which they have lain for near twelve hundred years.

God will redeem the Jews again, and he will redeem
his Gentile Churches that have been oppressed so long
a time. I say, this hath been the way of God from the
beginning, to deliver his people in a way of wonders.
Look but upon that deliverance of the church of God
out of Egypt, it was a wonderful deliverance. And I
shall the rather speak to this, because the Holy Ghost
hath made the deliverance of the church of God out of
Egypt, to be the way and manner of his delivering his

church from their enemies, until Christ come again.
This was a deliverance that took every step in wonders, and because this deliverance was designed of
God as a type and pattern, which he would work by
in the redeeming his church to the end of the world,
there is much in it : for there God spake with us,"
" They went through the floods on foot, there did we
rejoice," &c. (Psa. lxvi. 6.) Now four things evince the
wonderfulness of Israel's deliverance out of Egypt :—

1. For God to deliver his people when they were
altogether unworthy and unfit for deliverance, is wonderful. Thus did God deliver Israel out of Egypt.
Pray, what fitness had they for deliverance? You read
of no repenting for sin, no humbling under the hand
of God, no faith in him; never any people more unfit
and unworthy to be delivered than Israel was in
Egypt. For,

(1.) When God had wonderfully spirited Moses to
slay the Egyptian that was striving with an Israelite,
which was done purposely to encourage their faith of
a deliverance by Moses's hand ; he thought that his
brethren would have understood that God by his hand
would deliver his people from Egypt, but they understood not, but thrust him away, saying, " Who made
thee a ruler over us ?" Now this was a slighting the
wisdom and love of God. Nay, when God was afterwards by Moses working their deliverance, yet then
they murmur and quarrel with him and Aaron. What
an unworthy people were these !

(2.) When God reminds them of his covenant,
and renews his promise to deliver them, and sends
Moses on purpose to tell them, one would think
that this should have made a blessed change among

them. Moses comes on purpose to them, and tells them, God remembers his covenant, and therefore said unto the children of Israel, " I will bring you out of Egypt, and redeem you out of bondage, and will take you to be my people, and I will be your God." Was not this a blessed message as ever was sent ! Now, how do they entertain it ? They hearkened not to Moses for anguish of spirit and cruel bondage. They are so far from believing God, and Moses that came from him with this promise, that they despaired of it as a thing impossible.

(3.) What wonderful judgments by flies, and lice, and hail, and locusts, and death of the first born, did God bring upon this land of Egypt ! and why was all this but to be a witness for God against Pharaoh and against Egypt, and to raise and encourage the faith and hope of his people in their approaching redemption ? And yet for all this they could hardly believe.

(4.) When deliverance was in the very birth, then their faith was giving up the ghost. How do they murmur at the Red Sea against Moses, (Exod.xiv.11.) " Because there were no graves in Egypt, hast thou taken us away to die in the wilderness ?" How provoking was this unbelief ! Well might David say, (Psa. cvi. 7.) " They provoked him at the Sea, even at the Red Sea." Well, then, was there ever a people more unfit for deliverance than Israel was ? and yet notwithstanding all this, God overlooks their sin and unbelief and unworthiness, and all their murmuring ; this makes it a wonderful deliverance.

2. To be delivered under the greatest improbabilities and unlikeliness of deliverance makes it great and wonderful. This was Israel's case in Egypt. They

were delivered when it was most unlikely, for this deliverance was by the ordination of God to be by the hand of Moses. And, indeed, while Moses was at Court, there were great hopes by him. But when he had slain the Egyptian, he was forced to fly. Will God deliver by this Moses, when fled and gone and fixed in a strange land, he takes a wife and begets children, and engages himself in a new calling? Forty years run out, and not a word of his return to Egypt. And when God appeared to Moses, and tells him he will send him to Egypt again, he refuses it four times before he would go. (Exod. iii. 11.)—"Who am I that that I should go to Pharaoh and bring Israel out of Egypt?" (Exod. iv. 1.)—"They will not believe me nor hearken to my voice, they will say the Lord hath not sent me." Again, (ver. 10.) "O Lord, I am not eloquent; I am not fit, thou hast not made me fit for this work." And in 13th verse, when God again bids him go; he doth in a manner positively deny it. "Nay, O my Lord, if thou wilt send, send by the hand of him whom thou wilt send." As if Moses should say, Lord do not lay the burden of this redemption upon me, it is fitter for God, for the Messiah that is to come. Now, the root of all this was, his carnal fear. This runs in his head, I have formerly killed an Egyptian, and now if I go again they will call me to an account and kill me: and though he was ashamed to say it, yet God saw it and fences against it, "For," saith God, "go and return to Egypt for all they are dead that sought thy life." How unlikely was this people to be delivered when he must be the man to do it!

When he did undertake it, with how bad success was his undertaking; for Moses no sooner spake for them to Pharaoh, but Pharaoh was more set against them ; and, because he speaks for their liberty, therefore the tyrant doubles their burden. How unlikely was this people to be delivered !

Nay, after all this, when they were upon their march how soon were they stopt, how sadly disappointed, and sorely entangled and greatly discouraged ! On each hand they had difficulties, and must go either forward or backward. If they go forward there is the sea, if they go backward there was the enemy. And yet God delivered them notwithstanding all these difficulties, and therefore it was a wonderful deliverance.

3. To bring about the deliverance by weak and unlikely means makes it a wonderful thing. Such was the deliverance of Israel out of Egypt. The sea must make way for them, or there is no way for escape, but the sea went back for the Israelites and overwhelmed the Egyptians.

4. I might add, the more complete a deliverance is, the more wonderful. When a deliverance is not only outward, but inward; not only political, but spiritual; from false worship and idolatry, as well as from bondage and slavery; this is a complete deliverance. Now such was the deliverance of the church of God out of Egypt.

It was, (1.) political. At first, Pharaoh would not let the men go ; then he would let the men go, but not the rest ; then he will let the women and children go, but not their flocks and herds, but that would not do ; it mnst be male and female, young and old, flocks and herds, not a hoof must be left behind.

(2.) It was not only political as they were a people, but ecclesiastical and spiritual as they were a church, a deliverance from the false worship which they had learned in Egypt; and the great strife between God and the King was chiefly about the matter of his worship. God will have his people serve him his own way, and according to his own direction. "Let my people go, that they may serve me in the wilderness." "No," saith Pharaoh, "go and sacrifice to your God in the land;" here is the king's law set against God's, and he thinks he hath as good a right to command as God had. "Who is the Lord that I should obey him?" The controversy is about worship, who shall give laws to conscience, and govern in matters of religion, God or the King? Whenever this is, God interposes, for he is in nothing so jealous as the matters of religion. Therefore, whoever opposeth himself to God in this matter, is sure to fall before him. So did Pharaoh, he fell in the quarrel of religion, he would not let God be worshipped in his own way, and where this is, God is concerned to vindicate his name.

You have seen somewhat of this in England. God would have Protestantism set up.—No, we must have Popery; but God enters the controversy, and you know what became of him that opposed God. So that Israel's deliverance out of Egypt was wonderful.

By way of use then. The doctrine hath been proved, that whenever God works deliverance for his people, it is in a wonderful way. It is proved plainly from the instance of the Church of old.

But, you will say, what doth this concern the church of God in this day? Much every way. For look, in what way and manner God saved his church when in Egypt, so he will save it to the end of the world (Micah vii. 15.) When the prophet prays for the church in Babylonish bondage, that God would deliver them, " Feed thy people in Bashan and Gilead, in their own land ;" what doth God answer ? " According- ing to the days of thy coming out of Egypt, will I shew unto him marvellous things." So consequently the deliverance of the church from mystical Babylon shall be after the manner of Egypt.

1. From hence, then, you may learn how dear the church is to God. If once God takes a people to be his people, he will be true to them and true to his co- venant, and his covenant is to save them. (Isa. lxiii. 8.) " He said, Surely they are my people ; so he was their Saviour." It seems to refer to their deliverance from Egypt. God values no nation nor people in the world when they stand in competition with the Church's safety. The Babylonians, a warlike nation, shall be bread to the sword of Cyrus, to make way for the re- demption of captive Israel.—Saith God to his own people, " I have loved thee, therefore will I give men for thee, and people for thy life." (Isaiah xliii. 4.)

2. We may learn how vain all the attempts of the church's enemies are against it. " Why do the heathen rage, and the people imagine a vain thing ?" (Psa. ii. 1.) It may be a fair warning to all the powers in the world, to take heed how they carry it to the church of God, or how they oppose it. Pharaoh is set up for an ex- ample to all generations, to warn the great ones of the earth not to oppose them whom God hath engaged to preserve. Though they are weak in their persons, yet they are strong in their confederacy, for the Lord of hosts is their Redeemer and he is strong ; the Lord of hosts is his name.

3. Hence, we learn that the church may be very low

brought, but never so low as to be past help.   She
may be persecuted, but not forsaken ; cast down, but
not destroyed ; "God is in the midst of her, she shall not
be moved :" therefore we ought not to be discouraged
at the greatest distresses of the church.   Never any
distress greater than of the people at the Red sea, nor
ever a people prouder than the Egyptians, who said
" We will pursue, we will overtake," &c. ; but God
blew with his wind, the sea covered them, they sank
as lead in the mighty waters.   If God be for us, who
can be against us ?   Many may be against us, malici-
ously and designedly and actively, but if God be for
us, none can be against us successfully.   Get but into
covenant with God by faith, and make sure an interest
in God ; and make conscience of close walking with
God in sincerity and uprightness of heart, as a covenant people should, and you shall find that one God
is more than all your enemies, as the prophet said to
his servant, " Be not afraid of the Syrians for there be
more with us than with them.   With them, is an arm
of flesh ; but with us, Almighty God." Again, God is
more in power, "for who hath an arm like God." You
have heard much of the potent and mighty, but did
you ever hear of any that were omnipotent and almighty, but God alone ?   And the consideration of
this is not rightly improved, unless it be extended
and applied to our outward as well as our spiritual
enemies.

How secure is the justification of a soul whom God
will pardon ! there is none can hinder it ; " It is God
that justifieth, who is he that condemneth ?" (Rom. viii.)
How sure is the believer's weak grace to gain and increase ! for he that hath begun a good work will per-

fect it, and all the lusts of the heart, and all the devils in hell, shall not hinder it. Again, how sure is the believer's perseverance in the ways of God, for he is kept by the power of God through faith unto salvation. How secure is the believer's everlasting inheritance! "for whom he justifies them he also glorifies."

4. What an encouragement doth this truth afford to faith and trust! which is one of the great duties of the day we are in. "The just shall live by faith." (Hab. ii. 4.) When was this duty enjoined? "Now the just," &c. viz. when the Jews were in Babylon. God tells the prophet they shall be certainly delivered after the seventy years; therefore the great duty of their state and condition was to live by faith. It is not meant of living by faith for a personal salvation, but a living by faith for the church's redemption. And what more the duty of the people of God than this, in the time we are in? I tell you, the church of God is now in Babylon in a great measure, and there is a time for redemption. It is written in the book twelve hundred and sixty days. And though it tarry, yet it will come and will not tarry. Therefore the just shall now live by faith. The time is not out, though I believe it is nearer than we are aware of. If ever it was a duty for the church of God to live by faith, it is now; and what greater encouragement can we have than the remembrance of this deliverance out of Egypt; "for this was written for the generation to come." (Psalm cii. 18.) Mercy to the church of God in one age should be an encouragement to faith of God's people in all after ages. O for faith in God at such a time as this! when Egypt's deliverance is to be acted over again. "The Lord hath said, I will bring again from Bashan, I will bring my

people again from the depths of the sea;" (Psa. lxviii. 22.) that is, I will give my people such a deliverance out of the Babylonish power, and from the oppressing enemies of the church in the latter day, as I did of old when I saved them out of Egypt and Bashan. (Isaiah xi. 11.) "In that day he will set his hand a second time," and when that blessed time is come, he will set his hand a second time to recover the remnant of his people from Egypt. O what a blessed day will that be! therefore, *believe it* that God is coming to work as glorious a redemption for the New Testament Church in the latter day as ever he did in former days.

5. Here is encouragement to a patient waiting until the fit season comes : for as all the church's enemies are numbered, and their wrath limited, so their ruin and the church's redemption are exactly timed. God hath set a time and he will keep the time to a day. "It came to pass, that at the end of the four hundred and thirty years, even the self-same day, that all the host of Israel went out of the land of Egypt. (Exod. xii. 41.) The vision of Babylon's destruction and Israel's redemption is for an appointed time ; therefore, saith the Holy Ghost, "though it tarry, yet wait for it." It is said of the beast, (Rev. xiii. 5.) "Power was given him to continue 42 months ;" and then in the 10th ver. it is added, "Here is the patience and faith of the saints ! their patience in suffering and their faith in expectation of redemption." Let us wait patiently. God is an exact observer of times and prophecies. He never missed a day; he never gathers his fruit until it be ripe, nor lets it hang until it is rotten. He never gives mercy too soon or too late. He is a God of judgment, therefore let us wait for him. There is

great encouragement to exercise the grace of waiting;
for it concerns God more to hasten deliverance in
point of glory, than it doth us in point of security. We
many times get more good by waiting for, than enjoying a mercy. Such a posture keeps the soul humble.

6. Let us learn to take heed of avoiding suffering
by sinful means. This was the spirit of Israel in Egypt,
rather to comply with the Egyptians, than bear the
smart of a Providence. " It is better for us to serve the
Egyptians than to die in the wilderness." This is a
very great evil and never answers the end; but many
times brings us into the very mischief we would avoid.
It is like sinking the ship, to avoid the storm. Let
them that want a God to relieve them, use sinful and
unworthy shifts in a day of straits; and yet it hath
been the practice of too many, but it is an un-
doing policy. Stand still when you can go no farther,
and see the salvation of God. If the case be such
that you cannot go forward in the practice of duty,
yet never go backward by apostacy, but trust God in
the most difficult condition, and you shall never fail to
see a most glorious deliverance.

7. What encouragement this is to prayer. It was
this that moved the bowels of God to pity his people
in Egypt; " For," saith God, " I have heard their cry,
and am come to deliver them." God is always at the
call of prayer. This is a standing rule between God
and his people. " Call upon me in the day of trouble
and I will deliver thee, and thou shalt glorify me."
And let me tell you, of all prayer, prayer for the church
of God shall never fail of being heard. It is according
to God's own heart, and suitable to his interest; nay,
it is that which God will give himself no rest until it

be done, until the prayers of faith be answered with respect to his Jerusalem. And when he is resolved to have no rest, we cannot please him better than to give him no rest. Therefore, it is observable when the church of God was in trouble, this was their standing remedy; and when the church was in distress, still in their crying to God, they fetched their arguments from Israel's deliverance out of Egypt. And for your encouragement in this duty, know this, that all the persons in ELOHIM, all the persons in the Godhead are actually engaged in the design to deliver the church. There will be no rest in heaven until this be done. The Spirit of God will not be at rest until then; for He hath undertook this great work upon earth, to bring about the design of the redemption of his people. (Zech. vi. 8.) You read of quieting God's Spirit. See what it was that quieted his Spirit. You read of black horses to go forth into the north country, that is, into Babylon, where his people were in captivity, and they destroy the enemies of his church; and then come the white horses, and they denote the deliverance of his people; and then, in the 8th verse, " He cried to me, These that go towards the north country have quieted my Spirit." When Babylon is destroyed, and God's people redeemed, then his Spirit is quiet. The Lord Christ will have no rest in heaven until this be done; for what ! do you think that Christ hath no business in heaven? Doth he not live there for his church, and appear for his people and against his enemies? and he is " heard in all he asks." Nay, let me add, God the Father will not rest, until this be; for he hath declared it, " until the church be delivered, I will have no rest, until the righteousness thereof go forth as brightness,

and the salvation thereof as a lamp that burneth."
Now, what greater encouragement can we possibly
have for prayer? If the Spirit of God will give him
no rest—if Christ, as Intercessor, will give him no
rest—if God will give himself no rest, till his church
be redeemed, and their enemies destroyed, then it is
our duty to stir up faith in prayer, and give God no
rest until he establish Jerusalem and make her a praise
in the whole earth. And in this we shall fall in
with the design of God, and if we fall in with God in
the way of obedience, God will not fail of deliverance,
for thus saith the Lord of Hosts, "Behold, O my people, I will open your graves and cause you to come
out of your graves, and ye shall know that I am the
Lord."

SERMON III.

———

*" Therefore prophesy and say unto them, Thus saith
the Lord God, Behold, O my people, I will open your
graves, and cause you to come up out of your graves, and
ye shall know that I am the Lord.*—Ezek. xxxvii. 12."

THE doctrine I am at present upon is this—That
when the Lord comes to deliver his people it will be
in a very wonderful way; therefore he puts an " Ecce,"
upon it, " Behold;" which always points at some great
thing, and therefore is put before it to quicken our
animadversions. " Behold, the man is become as one
of us." (Genesis iii. 22.) It denotes a wonderful
apostacy. " Behold, I establish my covenant with
you." (Gen. ix. 9.) Wonderful condescending mercy.
" behold the bush burned with fire, and the bush was
not consumed." (Exodus iii. 2.) A wonderful deliverance. " Behold, a virgin shall conceive and bear
a son;" these are works of great wonder, and therefore
this note is put before them; and such is the use of it
in the text, it points us to the opening of graves, and
bringing the church of God out of their graves, which
is a wonderful thing; and therefore this expression of
opening graves is repeated four times in two verses.

See the 12th and 13th verses. I propounded three mediums to make out the truth of this doctrine, that the deliverances God works for his people in great distresses, are always in a wonderful way; thus he wrought in the beginning for Israel in Egypt, as I have shown you—thus he wrought for the church in Babylon, the instance in the text—thus he will work in the end, in the day of redemption of the church at last, of spiritual Zion out of mystical Babylon. I have done with the first instance, to wit, the deliverance of the church of old out of Egypt. I come now to the second instance, to wit, the deliverance of the church out of Babylon—to prove it was a wonderful deliverance. As she was wonderfully brought down, (Lamentations i. 9.) so she was wonderfully raised up. As the day of her captivity was called the great day, because of the greatness of the judgment, (Jer. xxx. 7.) " Alas ! for that day is great, so that there is none like it." It is not a natural day that is here meant, but a day made up of many days; as the year is made up of many days, so the day in the text is made up of many years; it is the day of their bondage in Babylon, which is a day of seventy years long; and this day is said to be great, not only from the length of it, but from the greatness of the judgment inflicted in it ; the day when God brings great sore judgments upon his people for sin, is called a great day. (Zeph. i. 14.) " The great day of the Lord is near, it is near and hasteneth greatly, even the voice of the day of the Lord." What day that is, he tells you in the 15th verse. That day is a day of wrath—a day of trouble—a day of wasting and desolation—a day of darkness and gloominess—a day of clouds and thick darkness; that is the great day Jeremiah speaks of, great for judgments inflicted, so there is a day mentioned which is great for the greatness of the deliverance wrought; great "shall be the day of Jezreel:" it is great mercy, great redemption, that makes this a great day; then shall the children of Judah and the children of Israel be gathered together, and appoint themselves one head and they shall come up out of the land, for great shall be the day of Jezreel. When God shows the greatness of his power in working great deliverance and in destroying great enemies, this makes a great day, a great day of mercy, a great day of thanksgiving and wonder; " and ye shall praise the name of the Lord your God that hath dealt wonderfully with you." (Joel. ii. 26.) He that views but the emblem, that this redemption is set out by, cannot but see it is full of wonder. For bones, dry bones in an open valley, for these to live is a wonder; and that appears by the question God puts to the prophet, " Can these bones live?" which plainly shows that they could not live but by a mighty power working wonderfully in them; they could live by no power but God's, and the manner of their life is wonderful. It is by prophecy and by the power of this, the bones should come together, bone to his bone, and this must needs be a wonderful work; and that which augments the wonder is, that it is by a shaking, " behold a shaking, and the bones came together, bone to his bone." (ver. 7.) The Babylonian empire is shaking to pieces, to make way for the coming of these bones together. But more particularly that which makes the deliverance of this people out of Babylon to be more wonderful is, that it is after the manner of Egypt; the promise was that it should be so, and it was so. (Psalm lxviii. 22, and Isaiah x. 24, and in several other places.) And that it is so, will appear evidently, if we compare the one with the other in the things wherein the wonderfulness of that deliverance out of Egypt consisted. I did instance in some things last time, that which makes the deliverance very wonderful; I must reflect upon it again to make the truth of the thing more evident.

I. God delivered Israel out of Egypt, notwithstanding all their unworthiness and unfitness, which was very great; they were no ways fit for deliverance, as I showed you at large, when God delivered them; the Holy Ghost sets forth this most appropriately in comparing their case, when God brought them out of Egypt, to that of a new-born infant.—"And as for their nativity, in the day that thou wast born (that is, brought out of Egypt) thy navel was not cut, neither wast thou washed in water to supple thee; thou wast not salted at all, nor swaddled at all. None eye pitied thee, to do any of these unto thee, to have compassion upon thee; but thou wast cast out in the open field, to the loathing of thy person, in the day that thou wast born." (Ezek. xvi. 4, 5.) All these allusive expressions are to show what the state of Israel was when God came to deliver them out of bondage, a most wretched state, as polluted as a new born infant, as unpleasant and loathsome to behold as an unwashed infant in its natural filth; and he goes on, (verse 6.) " when I saw thee polluted in thy blood, in thine own blood, I said unto thee when thou wast in thy blood, Live; yea I said unto thee when thou wast in thy blood, Live." Here are three things to be taken notice of,

1. Her great unfitness and unworthiness of deli-

verance. She was polluted in her own blood; great and horrid sins are in Scripture set out by blood, and to show the greatness of her sins, blood is three times mentioned in this verse.

2. This unfitness and unworthiness was not unknown by God, nor unobserved by him. And he takes a particular notice of all her unworthiness and unfitness; " I saw thee polluted in thy blood, in thine own blood."

3. Here is a deliverance wrought in the midst of all unfitness, seen and discovered; "I said unto thee when thou wast in thy blood, Live; yea, I said unto thee when thou wast in thy blood, Live; it was twice repeated to a two-fold end.

(1.) To bring them to an humble sense of their own unworthiness.

(2.) To show the freeness of grace in delivering of them.

In the midst of all unworthiness there was nothing to deserve it; love and pity was the moving cause of it, and therefore he adds, (ver. 8.) " When I passed by thee, and looked upon thee, behold, thy time was a time of love;" what time this was is certain; it was not a time of washing and making clean, a time of repenting and turning; no, it was the time aforenamed, called the day she was born in; (ver. 4, 5.) not washed, not salted, not suppled, not swaddled, nor pitied, then was the time of love. What admirable mercy is this! a time of blood to be a time of love! a time of misery to be a time of pity! a time of filthiness to be a time of deliverance! here is mercy, but no manner of fitness for mercy; redemption, but no manner of fitness for redemption; and this makes it wonderful. Now, such was the deliverance of the Jews out of Babylon; their case was like that of Israel in Egypt, a people altogether unworthy of deliverance and unfit for it, when God brought it about; inquire into their case and you will find it so.

(1.) Fitness for deliverance supposes repentance for sin, especially for those sins that procured the judgment: a people that are under judgment for sin, and do not repent of sin, but continue in it notwithstanding the judgment, are in no fitness for deliverance; and thus it was with this people, sin pulled down the judgment, but there was no repentance to remove it; sin had digged their graves and buried them, but there was no repentance to roll away the stone and bring them out. God calls them to repent before the judgment is come, to prevent it; " I will judge you, O house of Israel, every one according to his own way, saith the Lord God. Repent, and turn yourselves from all your transgressions; so iniquity shall not be your ruin." (Ezek. xviii. 30.) " Therefore also now, saith the Lord, turn ye even to me with all your heart, and with fasting, and with weeping, and with mourning : and rend your hearts, and not your garments, and turn unto the Lord your God : for he is gracious and merciful, slow to anger, and of great kindness, and repenteth him of the evil." (Joel ii. 12, 13.) They are called to repent before judgment comes, that they might prevent it, but they repented not ; and then he calls upon them, when the judgment is come, to repent, that he might remove it. " If thou shalt return unto the Lord thy God, and shalt obey his voice according to all that I command thee this day, thou and thy children, with all thine heart, and with all thy soul :

that then the Lord thy God will turn thy captivity, and have compassion upon thee, and will return and gather thee from all nations, whither the Lord thy God hath scattered thee." (Deut. xxx. 2, 3.)   But yet they repented not; God repented of the judgment, but they had not repented of the sin that caused it. "If ye will still abide in this land, then will I build you, and not pull you down, and I will plant you, and not pluck you up: for I repent me of the evil that I have done unto you." (Jer. xlii. 10.)   It was the mercy of their deliverance that melted down their hard hearts into a mournful and penitent frame.   "Then shall you remember that I had pity, for mine holy name which the house of Israel had profaned among the heathen, whither they went;" (Ezek. xxxvi. 21.) what doth this then point at? the 24th verse tells you; "For I will take you from among the heathen, and gather you out of all countries, and I will bring you into your own land."   So Jer. xxiv. 6, 7, "For I will set mine eyes upon them for good, and I will bring them again to this land: and I will build them, and not pull them down; and I will plant them, and not pluck them up. And I will give them an heart to know me, that I am the Lord: and they shall be my people, and I will be their God: for they shall return unto me with their whole heart."   Deliverance and repentance came together, and they were so far from repenting of sin in their captivity, that they continued in their wickedness to the great reproach of God among the heathen. "And when they entered unto the heathen, whither they went, they profaned my holy name, when they said to them, These are the people of the Lord, and are gone forth out of his land." (Exek. xxxvi. 20.)

God takes notice of it, and charges them with it five times together in four verses, and that those that continue in sin under judgment, are very unfit for deliverance.

(2.) A fitness for deliverance supposes some faith and hope in the expectation of it. Unbelief can never be a qualification for any mercy, it weakens the working hand. As faith holds the hands of vengeance and so keeps off judgment, so unbelief holds the hands of mercy that would remove judgment. " He could not do many mighty works there, save that he laid his hands upon a few sick folk, and healed them;" (Mark vi. 5.) not from any defect of power, but the exercise of divine power is always regulated by wisdom, and he foresaw his miracles would be without any saving effect, and therefore he would not expend his power among them by working miracles. Their infidelity was a great provocation to him, and therefore he could not show his power among them. Nothing can obstruct mercy like unbelief, and this was the great sin of this people. Though God had promised to visit them after seventy years, and bring them out of Babylon, yet they had no faith in the promise, but despaired of any deliverance; "Behold, they say, Our bones are dried, our hope is lost: and we are cut off for our parts." (Ezek. xxxvii. 11.) They had no expectation of deliverance, and where there is no faith there can be no fitness for it; and therefore when God doth deliver them, he tells them it was not for their sakes; as if he had said, I do it not because of your worthiness for it, but for the glory of my own name. " I do not this for your sakes, O house of Israel, but for my holy name's sake. (Ezek. xxxvi. 22.) And again, (ver. 32.) " Not

for your sakes do I this, saith the Lord God, be it
known unto you : be ashamed and confounded for your
own ways, O house of Israel." As if he had said, It
is mercy that is the spring and cause of what I do for
you, and nothing that you have done to deserve it,
and this makes their deliverance wonderful, and magnifies grace exceedingly. Grace to an unworthy, to
an unmeet unbethinking people, is great grace indeed !
Deliverance without repentance, without faith, and
hope, this makes deliverance wonderful ! thereby it
was a deliverance after the manner of Egypt.

II. To deliver a people when they are at the greatest extremity, at the lowest ebb, and seem forsaken of
their own hope   this makes deliverance wonderful.
Such was the deliverance of the church out of Egypt ;
and such was it out of Babylon ; it is the usual method
of God to let things run to extremity before help
comes; there never was any eminent deliverance of
the church, but it was ushered in by some amazing
distress. "For the Lord shall judge his people, and
repent himself for his servants, when he seeth that
their power is gone, and there is none shut up, or left."
(Deut. xxxii. 36.) God loves to take such opportunity
wherein his power and wisdom may be most conspi-
cuous ; when Israel was at the brink of the sea, and
beset with difficulties and dangers round about, then
God awakes to deliver them ; God's time to deliver the
three children is not until they are in the fiery furnace ;
when Lazarus was dead and buried, then was Christ's
time to raise him ; God loves to let a sentence of death
pass upon his mercies, that so he may be known to be
the Lord that raises the dead ; thus it was with the
churcn s deliverance here. She and her hope must be

buried together in the grave, and then, " Behold, O my people, I will open your graves, and cause you to come up out of your graves," this makes the deliverance wonderful.

III. To deliver a people that can do nothing towards their own deliverance, makes the deliverance wonderful. What could dry bones do to relieve themselves? what could Israel in Egypt do to deliver themselves out of Pharoah's power? They had no arms either offensive or defensive, a poor naked multitude, many for number, but destitute of power; and therefore God takes the work into his own hand. " I am the Lord, and I will bring you out from under the burdens of the Egyptians, and I will rid you from out of their bondage, and I will redeem you with a stretched out arm, and with great judgments." (Exod. vi. 6.) And, accordingly Moses, when they were in their greatest hazard, in the very mouth of dangers, encourages their fainting spirits and dying hope, by faith in the power of God. " And Moses said unto the people, Fear not, stand still, and see the salvation of the Lord, which he will shew to you this day : for the Egyptians whom ye have seen to day, ye shall see them again no more for ever. The Lord shall fight for you, and ye shall hold your peace." (Exod. xiv. 13, 14.) They did nothing to deliver themselves; God did all : and so it was in Babylon, it was a deliverance wrought by the mighty power of God's Spirit. " Not by might, nor by power, but by my Spirit, saith the Lord of Hosts." (Zech. iv. 6.) Therefore you read of the black horses going forth into the north country, and of the white horses going after them to quiet the spirit. (Zech. vi. 8.) The north

country, that is, Babylon, which lays north of Judea ;
the black horses are certain ministers of God's vengeance, that are sent to execute his wrath upon Babylon ; the white horses are ministers of God's mercy and
compassion to his people, whose work is to preserve
them, and deliver them out of Babylon. Now here
are four things very remarkable, and to our purpose,
concerning these black and white horses.

1. There is the place from whence they come, and
that is from between the mountains of brass. " Behold there came four chariots out from between two
mountains, and the mountains were mountains of
brass." (ver. 1.) These mountains set forth the righteous decrees of God ; " thy righteousness is like the
great mountains." (Psa. xxxvi. 6.) And these are said
to be mountains of brass, to show the firmness and immutability of God's decree and counsel, to save and
deliver his people ; and the coming out of these chariots
and horses from between the brazen mountains, teach-
eth us that the whole work, whether of vengeance upon
Babylon, or deliverance to Zion, is to execute the
purpose and decree of God.

2. Here is their commission for their work, and
that is from God ; and therefore they are said to
" go forth from standing before the Lord of all the
earth." (ver. 5.) Their standing before the Lord in
a waiting posture, shows their readiness to do his will ;
their going forth from before the Lord, shows that
what they do, either in a way of judgment or mercy, is
in obedience to a command of God.

3. Here is their order in working ;—the white
horses follow the black : this is the usual method of
God with his church, as it was in Abraham's vision.

" Behold a smoking furnace and a burning lamp :" (Gen. xv. 17.) the smoking furnace sets forth their future bondage in Egypt; the burning lamp their deliverance out of Egypt. Sufferings and trouble go before, light and comfort follow after; as it was with Elijah, first a great wind, then an earthquake ; first a fire, then a still voice and God in it. (1 Kings xix. 11, 12.) And so it was in the vision of the prophet, black horses first, and then the white. (ver. 6.) The black horses go forth into the north country, and the white horses go forth after them, to show us that the enemies must be destroyed, before his church can be completely delivered.

4. Here is the great end of their working, and that is to quiet the Spirit, (ver. 8.) " these are they that have quieted my spirit in the north country." Pray consider this expression a little. Who is this that calls the spirit here, my Spirit ? it is the angel, as you may see, verses, 4, 5 ; and who this angel is, you may see, chap. i. 8, 9. The angel in the 9th verse is the same with the man among the myrtle trees, in the 8th verse, and that is the Lord Christ ; so that is the Spirit of Christ that is here said to be quieted. Now, for the understanding of this, you must know that the whole government of the world and the church is given by the Father into the hands of Christ. " The Father judgeth no man, but hath committed all judgment to the Son." (John v. 22.) It was prophesied so of him of old. " The government shall be upon his shoulder." (Isa. ix. 6.) And the Spirit acts in this government, as a " Pro Rex ; " as He acts under the Father, the Spirit acts in the mediatory kingdom under

Christ, which is set out to the life in the vision of the
wheels, and the living creatures, and the Spirit, which
Ezekiel saw.   The wheels are the affairs of the world,
and the living creatures are the angels of God; now in
the vision, you read that the wheels moved, and the
living creatures act in the wheels, (Ezek. i. 19.) and
the Spirit acts in the living creatures; (ver. 20.) and
the Lord Christ acts in all.   In the 26th verse you
read of a throne above all, and a man upon the throne,
to show that Christ rules all, so that the Spirit acts in
the mediatory kingdom under Christ, and will never
rest till all things in that kingdom be consummated;
and, to confirm this farther, see that in Rev. v. 6, where
it is said, "there stood a Lamb as it had been slain,
having seven horns and seven eyes which are the
seven spirits of God sent forth into all the earth;"
what are these seven spirits? It is the Spirit of Christ
which is thus described by seven, a great number of per-
fections to set out the number and variety of his gracious operations; these seven spirits are said, in Rev.
i. 4, to be "before the throne of Christ," to show their
readiness to fulfill all the purposes and designs of
Christ, both in the church and in the world; and here
these seven spirits are said to be "sent forth into all the
world," and that with a peculiar respect to the church,
as in the 2 Chron. xvi. 9, " The eyes of the Lord run
to and fro throughout the whole earth, to show himself strong in behalf of them whose heart is perfect towards him."   These eyes of the Lord are the spirits,
called in Rev. v. 6, the " eyes of the Lamb."   He is
both the seven horns and the seven eyes of the Lamb,
perfect in wisdom, for he hath seven eyes; and perfect

in power, for he hath seven horns : so that he knows
how to deliver his church, and he is able to deliver
them, and he will deliver them, for he is sent forth
into all the earth ; and this being sent forth, denotes
a great trust reposed in him, and a great work committed to him by Christ with respect to his people in
the world; and in pursuance of this trust it is, that
he influences all the affairs of the world, and manages
matters with this design, to wit, to destroy all his
enemies, and to redeem all his people, and he will
never be fully at rest until this be done ; and therefore
it is that he here sends forth the black horses to Babylon for their destruction, and the white horses after
them for the church's deliverance and redemption;
and when Babylon is destroyed, and the church delivered, then the Spirit is said to be quieted ; as Pharoah was drowned and all his hosts to make way for
Israel out of Egypt, so all the Chaldean's power was
destroyed to make way for the Jews out of Babylon ;
so that the deliverance and redemption of the church
out of Babylon, was the sole work of the Spirit of God;
when the "enemies of God shall come in like a flood,
the Spirit of the Lord shall lift up a standard against
him." (Isaiah lix. 19.) And this is a wonderful deliverance.

4. I as wonderful, in that it was not only a
political, but a spiritual deliverance. Some think this
deliverance was only political, and the life that these
dry bones were raised to was only a political life, but
to me it seems plain that it was a spiritual deliverance
as well as political. This prophecy doth indeed respect
their civil state, but not solely nor chiefly ; but it hath
respect to their spiritual and religious state also. And

this will be evident, if you consider these seven particulars.

1. That the deliverance out of Egypt was the great pattern of this out of Babylon, and therefore they must answer and correspond one with another. Now when Israel was delivered out of Egypt, it was not only a political, but a spiritual deliverance; there was not only a civil, but a spiritual life conferred upon them; and this is intimated in Ezek. xvi. 6, "And when I passed by thee and saw thee polluted in thine own blood, I said unto thee, when thou wast in thy blood, Live; yea, I said unto thee when thou wast in thy blood, Live." Here is a twofold state of blood mentioned, and accordingly a twofold state of life conferred. Here is a bloody state of bondage, by reason of their sufferings which were great, especially when Pharoah made that bloody edict that all their males should be destroyed; and then there is a bloody condition by reason of their sins and idolatries. Now, answerable to this twofold state of blood, there is a twofold state of life; the one, political life out of their sufferings, the other, a spiritual life from a state of sin; "I said unto thee when thou wast in thy blood, Live." There is a political life, a life from sufferings: and then it follows again, "I said unto thee in thy blood, Live:" there is a spiritual life, a deliverance from a state of sin; now, the deliverance from Babylon must answer to this or else it is not as God promised it should be, namely, after the manner of Egypt. To be brought in bondage for sin, and not delivered from sin when delivered, is to make the deliverance a judgment as well as the bondage; to be delivered and not pardoned is no deliverance. Therefore, this was not only a de-

liverance from bondage and sufferings; but from sin
and guilt. " I will punish the King of Babylon and
his land, as I punished the King of Assyria, and
I will bring Israel again to his habitation." (Jer. l. 18,
19.) Here is a political deliverance; but that is not
all, for mark the 20th verse, " In those days and in
that time, saith the Lord, the iniquity of Israel shall
be sought for and there shall be none, and the sins of
Judah and they shall not be found, for I will pardon
them whom I reserve." Here is a spiritual deliverance
with the political, and thus it answered to the deliverance from Egypt.

2. It appears further, if you consider what was the
procuring cause of their captivity.—It was sin. " Jerusalem hath grievously sinned, therefore she is removed." (Lam. i. 8.) Their captivity was to punish
their sin, especially that abominable sin which God so
hated and they so much loved; and that was idolatry.
They were guilty of many great sins, but the greatest
were blood and idols. " Son of man, when the house
of Israel dwelt in their own land they defiled it by their
own ways and by their doings, their ways were before
me as the uncleanness, wherefore I poured my fury
upon them for the blood that they had shed upon the
land, and for their idols wherewith they had polluted
it." (Ezek. xxxvi. 17, 18.) And if the design of God
in their captivity was to punish their idolatries, then the
end of it was to purge them from their idolatries.
And so it is still after the manner of Egypt. For one
great end of God in delivering Israel, was to purge
them from the idolatries of Egypt; that they might
serve and worship their own God in his own way.
That is the great message Moses is sent from God to

Pharoah upon. " Let my people go that they may serve me ;" (Exod. iv. 23, and chap. v. 3,) " Let us go that we may sacrifice to the Lord." Moses never comes to Pharoah but this is his message, " let my people go that they may serve me ;" so that it is a controversy about the worship of God. And their redemption was to purge them from the idols of the land, that they might worship God in his own way. And so it was in this case, as is evident from Ezek. xxxvii. 23, " they shall not defile themselves any more with their idols, nor with their detestable things, nor with any of their transgressions, for I will save them out of all their dwelling places wherein they have sinned, and they shall be my people and I will be their God ;" and, (Ezek. xxxvi. 25,) " Then will I sprinkle clean water upon you and ye shall be clean, from all your filthiness and from all your idols will I cleanse you," (viz. when I take you from among the heathen, as in the former verse, " then will I sprinkle," &c.) And it was so ; for after their deliverance from the Babylonish captivity, we do not find that ever they turned to idolatry again. And so that word was fulfilled, " I will take away the names of Baalim from out of her mouth, and they shall no more be remembered by their names ;" (Hosea ii. 17.) and hence it was evident that the deliverance was not only political but spiritual.

3. God, in this deliverance, mingles spiritual promises with temporal mercies ; now, that deliverance in which God makes good spiritual as well as temporal promises, is a spiritual as well a political deliverance ; when Israel was delivered out of Egypt there were spiritual mercies mingled with temporal. " I will bring you out from under the burdens of the Egyp-

tians, and I will rid you out of their bondage, and I will redeem you with a stretched out arm and with great judgments." (Exod. vi. 6.) Here is a political deliverance; and then it follows, " I will take you to me to be a people, and I will be to you a God;" there is a spiritual deliverance joined with it, and this is that which he alludes to in Ezek. xvi. 8, " When I passed by thee and looked upon thee, behold thy time was a time of love; and I spread my skirt over thee and covered thy nakedness, yea I sware unto thee, and entered into a covenant with thee, saith the Lord God, and thou becamest mine." And so it was in their redemption from Babylon, " Behold, I will gather them out of all countries whither I have driven them in my anger, and in my fury, and in my wrath; and I will bring them again to this place, and I will cause them to dwell safely;" (Jer. xxxii. 37, 38.) there is their temporal deliverance: and then it follows, " they shall be my people and I will be their God;" there it was a spiritual deliverance, and so in this chapter, Ezek. xxxvii. 26, 27; " I will make a covenant of peace with them, it shall be an everlasting covenant with them, and I will place them and multiply them, and I will set my sanctuary in the midst of them for evermore, my tabernacle also shall be with them; yea, I will be their God and they shall be my people."

4. If their rising from their graves was as the dead body of Christ, then it must be a spiritual resurrection. But so it was. " Thy dead men shall live, together with my dead body shall they arise, awake and sing, ye that dwell in the dust, for thy dew is as the dew of herbs, and the earth shall cast out the dead." (Isaiah

xxvi. 19.) It is Christ that speaks ("thy dead men,"
&c.) to the captived Jews, that in the text are represented as in graves, and therefore in this verse said
to dwell in the dust; now Christ here promises, not
only that they shall arise, but arise, as his dead body,
that is, as in union to Christ the head, which is explained by that of the Apostle, in Rom. vi. 4, "as Christ
was raised up from the dead by the glory of the Father,
even we also should walk in newness of life;" and
therefore it must be a spiritual resurrection that is here
intended, as well as a political. How else, do they rise
as Christ's dead body?

5. The truth of this may further appear in the
manner, and by the means, through which their resurrection was brought about, and that was by prophecy,
(ver. 4, 7.) now the prophecies were not only for their
civil restoration, but to awaken and call them to repentance, that so there might be deliverance and holiness. It had been a poor deliverance without this, for
to be outwardly redeemed and inwardly enslaved by
their old lusts is but a preservation, not a redemption;
and therefore there is a twofold prophecy here mentioned, one in the 7th verse, and that was for their
civil deliverance, and then in the 10th verse there is a
prophesying again; the first prophecy brought in a political life, in the virtue of which the bones came together, bone to his bone. But this was a life without
breath; that is a political life without spiritual breath,
and therefore he must prophecy again to bring breath
into them. (ver. 9. 10,) "Come, O breath, and breathe
upon these slain that they may live. So I prophesied,
as he commanded me, and the breath came unto them

and they lived and stood upon their feet, an exceeding great army;" here is a spiritual life, and accordingly God himself interprets the prophecy, when he applies it to the Jews. He plainly points at a double deliverance, one in the 12th verse, " O my people, I will open your graves, and cause you to come up out of your graves, and bring you into the land of Israel;" there is the political deliverance : and then in the 13th verse, " and ye shall know that I am the Lord when I opened your graves, O ! my people, and brought you up out of your graves, (ver. 14.) and shall put my spirit in you, and ye shall live, and I shall place you in your own land." There the breath comes in, and that there is a spiritual deliverance, two things in the words plainly evince.

(1.) It is such a work as by which they shall know the Lord, (ver. 13.) Now to know the Lord by a work of opening graves, is so to know as to acknowledge and believe, and fear, and love, and serve him ; acknowledge his power, believe his promises, fear him for his goodness, and love and serve him with thankfulness, according to the known rule, words of knowledge imply affection.

(2.) It is such a deliverance as is completed with the pouring out of the spirit, (ver. 14.) " I will put my Spirit in you, and ye shall live, and I shall place you in your own land; then shall you know that I the Lord have spoken it, and performed it, saith the Lord;" so that to make this a political deliverance only, (as some do) and not spiritual, is to strip these bones of that flesh and sinews that God hath clothed them with; or rather, to leave them as a lump of flesh and bones, without spirit and life. I might add,

6. As their captivity was spiritual as well as political, so must their deliverance be; or else, how are their graves opened? The resurrection would no ways answer the death, nor the opening their graves and bringing them out, correspond to the burying and shutting them in. The deliverance would be far short of the bondage.

7. The deliverance had not answered the promise of God to them, had it not been spiritual as well as political; for the promise, as I hinted, held forth spiritual mercies to them as well as temporal, to cleanse them as well as to redeem them, (ver. 23,) to make a covenant of peace with them, to set his sanctuary in the midst of them, to be a God to them, as well as to deliver them; most plainly, therefore, it appears that their redemption out of Babylon was not only political but spiritual. Thus you have the doctrine further confirmed by an instance taken from the old Church in Babylon, that when God comes to deliver his church and people, it will be in a wonderful way.

Now these things are of great use to the church of God in the present day, and therefore his showing mercy and favour to Zion, and building her up when the set time is come, (which is at the end of the seventy years) is appointed to be written for the generations to come. (Psalm cii. 18.) The salvation and deliverance which God works for his church in one age, are to be made use of for the instruction and comfort of all after ages. And therefore from this wonderful deliverance of the church out of Babylon, we may be instructed and encouraged in these six truths.

1. That no enemy is so high, so great and potent, as to be out of the reach of God's arm; what a mighty

enemy were the Babylonians! what a city, what a
King, what a people were they! Their city is called
the golden city. "Thou shalt take up this proverb
against the king of Babylon, and say, How hath the
oppressor ceased, the golden city ceased?" (Isaiah
xiv. 4.) It is called the destroying mountain, the
glory of kingdoms, the hammer of the whole earth.
Historians tell us, that the city was sixty miles about,
her walls two hundred feet high, so thick that two
chariots might go a breast on the top of them, they
had a hundred great gates, many of them of brass.
Her prince was styled, "King of kings, of mighty
strength and glory." (Daniel ii. 37.) He is called,
"Lucifer the son of the morning," (Isaiah xiv. 12.)
So great that in the pride of his heart he deals blas-
phemously, rivals the power of God. "I will ascend
to heaven, I will exalt my throne above the stars of
God, I will sit also upon the mount of the congregation in the sides of the north, I will ascend above the
heights of the clouds, I will be like the most High."
(Isa. xiv. 13, 14.) And if you look upon their inhabitants
they are called "the mighty men of Babylon." (Jer. li.
30.) And yet how easily, how suddenly doth God destroy the Babylonish power, break in pieces the gates
of brass, and cut asunder the bars of iron.

2. The church can never be so low as to be past
help. She may be like a ship tossed in a storm, and
like to sink, but Christ is in the ship, who can turn
the storm into a calm, and make the winds and the
seas to obey him. Never were any people in a more
desperate and deplorable case than the Church was
in Babylon, therefore set out here by bones, dead
bones, dry bones, scattered bones in the open valley:

E

no life, nor hope of life in them, and yet these bones are brought bone to his bone, and made to live again. Oh the power of God ! "though ye have lien among the pots yet shall ye be as the wings of a dove, covered with silver and her feathers with yellow gold." (Psalm lxviii. 13.)

3. How weak and foolish is the wisdom of man to set itself against the Church of Christ, which is the only interest that God hath engaged to preserve; and against which the gates of hell shall never prevail. It is throwing the gauntlet to the Almighty, and wrestling with omnipotent providence, just as if a worm should design to dig down a mountain, or a poor fly to stop the motion of a millstone. O how foolish is this ! It is very sinful, very unsuccessful, and utterly destructive, and therefore the height of folly.

(1.) It is sinful, for whatever is done against the church is done against God. And, therefore, the church's enemies are called God's enemies, and they that combine against her, are said to combine against God. "Thine enemies make a tumult, and they that hate thee have lifted up the head." (Psalm lxxxiii. 2.) And see how this is interpreted, " They are confederate against thee." If the Church be God's dwelling place, as she is, then to violence her is to make a forcible entry upon God's right : and he will certainly bring his eject-ment against all that have a hand in it. And therefore

(2.) It will certainly be unsuccessful; "for who hath hardened himself against God and prospered?" (Job ix. 4,) see that, (Isaiah viii. 9, 10.) " Associate yourselves, O ye people, and ye shall be broken in pieces, and give ear all ye of far countries, gird yourselves, and ye shall be broken in pieces, take counsel together and it shall come to nought, speak the word and it shall not stand, for God is with us."

(3.) It is a very destructive enterprise. God will not bear always. He may, upon great provocation, give his people into the enemies hand for a time; who may deal cruelly with them, but it will cost them dear, for God will reckon it to them in vengeance. So it was here—God gave the Church into the power of Babylon, and she was unmerciful and cruel to her. "I was wroth, says God, with my people, (Isa. xlvii. 6.) I have polluted mine inheritance, and given them into thine hand; thou didst show them no mercy, upon the ancient hast thou very heavily laid thy yoke;" and see how God retaliates it, (ver. 11.) "therefore shall evil come upon thee, thou shalt not know from whence it riseth;" and so in Zech. i. 15, "I am sorely displeased with the heathen that are at ease, for I was but a little displeased, and they helped forward the affliction." Therefore in the 18th verse, he sends four carpenters to cut the horns, that is, the power, that scattered Judah and Jerusalem. Go, then, and tell the angry world that all their plots and designs against the Church of Christ shall certainly come to nought, they shall never attain their end; the wisdom of Christ makes the wisdom of men vain in its deepest designs and highest pursuits. It was a notable design of Haman's wife, "if Mordecai be of the seed of the Jews before whom thou hast begun to fall, thou shalt not prevail against him, but shall surely fall before him." It passed, it seems, for a known truth in those times (even among the heathen) that no power nor plot could succeed against the seed of God. This was Haman's ruin, and so it hath been to his betters; here

Pharoah perished and all his host, and so did Babylon and all her princes. "Jerusalem," God says, "shall be a cup of trembling unto all the people round about." (Zech. xii. 23.)

4. We may learn hence that Christ will, in due time, be the utter destruction of all his and his Church's enemies. "For he is the head over all things to the Church," (Ephes. i. 22.) "he rules in Jacob to the end of the earth; Selah." (Psa. lix. 10.) and his government over the world is directed against the enmity of the wicked to correct and restrain at present, and at last (when it will serve the interest of his glory no longer) to extinguish and destroy it. The Holy Ghost tells us in the 1 Cor. xv. 25, "He must reign until he hath put all enemies under his feet." The Church hath three grand enemies—Antichrist, Satan, and Sin.

(1.) Antichrist. He is a cruel enemy, a bloody enemy, but his date is almost out; there is a vial ere long to be poured out upon the throne of the beast, that will make it shake; he hath been in a consumption for some years, and his present seeming recovery is but a lightening before death, as is common in that disease. The Lord shall, ere long, consume him with the breath of his mouth, and destroy him with the brightness of his coming.

(2.) Satan—the great spoiler of the peace and comfort and communion of the Church with God, but what say the Scriptures? "The God of peace shall bruise Satan under your feet shortly." It is not long before he will bind him for a thousand years, so that he shall deceive the nations no more, and at last he will "cast him into the lake of fire, where the beast and the false prophet are," Rev. xx. 10.

(3.) Sin—the worst of all; an enemy to God, to Christ, to the Spirit of the Lord, to the soul. It wastes our graces, defiles our duties, debases our affections, degrades our sanctification, interrupts our progress in all ways of holiness. But Christ will not give up his kingdom until he hath destroyed sin; it is pardoned in regeneration, that it cannot condemn; it is mortified in sanctification, that it cannot reign; but it shall shortly be destroyed that it shall not be. " When this mortal shall have put on immortality, then shall that song be sung, The strength of sin is the law," &c. (1 Cor. xv. 56, 57.)

5. What an incentive to prayer should this be. No deliverance without it: the Jews could not be delivered out of Babylon without it. " Thus saith the Lord God, I will yet for this be inquired of by the house of Israel, to do it for them. I will increase them with men like a flock." And again, (Jer. xxix. 9, 10, 11, 12, 13, 14.) " For they prophesy falsely unto you in my name : I have not sent them, saith the Lord. For thus saith the Lord, That after seventy years be accomplished at Babylon I will visit you, and perform my good word toward you, in causing you to return to this place. For I know the thoughts that I think toward you, saith the Lord, thoughts of peace, and not of evil, to give you an expected end. Then shall ye call upon me, and ye shall go and pray unto me, and I will hearken unto you. And ye shall seek me, and find me, when ye shall search for me with all your heart. And I will be found of you, saith the Lord : and I will turn away your captivity, and I will gather you from all the nations, and from all the places whither I have driven you, saith the Lord; and I will bring you again

into this place whence I caused you to be carried away captive."

6. What an encouragement is here to all the Lord's people for faith and trust, and that is the most afflicted state of the church, that though she be as dead and in the grave, as dry bones in the open valley, yet God can breathe upon her by the spirit of prophecy, and cause breath to come into her, and she shall live. For " he hath the residue of the Spirit ;" (Malachi ii. 15.) therefore trust in the Lord at all times ye people.

SERMON IV.

" Therefore prophesy and say unto them, Thus saith the Lord God ; Behold, O my people, I will open your graves, and cause you to come up out of your graves, and bring you into the land of Israel. And ye shall know that I am the Lord.—Ezek. xxxvii. 12."

THE observation I have laid down from these words, is this—When the Lord comes to deliver his people out of their sufferings and oppressions, it will be in a wonderful manner.

It was so in the beginning, the redeeming of Israel out of Egypt, I have made out that to you. It was so in the instance of the text, redeeming the Church out of Babylon of old, I have made that out also in another discourse. And thus it will be to the end. The deliverance and salvation which God will work for his people in the latter day, shall outdo in greatness and glory, all the former deliverances that ever have been wrought for the Church. I promised to clear this in two instances.

(I.) In his redeeming his antient people the Jews and raising them out of their graves, in which they have lain now for sixteen hundred years.

(II.) In redeeming his present Church among the Gentiles, out of the power of antichrist, under which it hath been for twelve hundred years.

(I.) The redeeming and restoring the Jews, the old people of God, out of the present state of scattering and slavery wherein they now are, and from the blindness and judgment they are now under: and I shall proceed in this method,—

I. To show you that the present state and condition of the Jews is a state of great judgment.

II. That there is a time when they shall be redeemed and delivered from this judgment.

III. That this deliverance shall be wrought after a very wonderful manner.

IV. When this shall be accomplished, then answer the objections, and then apply it.

I. That the present state of the Jews is a state of great judgment, and that, whether it be considered outwardly or inwardly; with respect to their outward state, or their spiritual case.—

1. Consider them with respect to their outward state; and it is a state of very great judgment. What greater judgment than for a people to be unpeopled, to be destroyed at home and scattered abroad, and made a scorn and contempt, and byeword in all the earth! And this is the very condition of the Jews, that wretched people, to this very day.

(1.) They are unpeopled. They are not only (Lo-ammi) no people to God, but no people at all, politically considered; that is, they are no kingdom, no commonwealth, they are no more a nation.

(2.) They are a scattered generation of men and women, and that throughout the whole earth, therefore the apostle James writes to the twelve tribes in the dispersion, or that are scattered abroad.

Never were a people in the world so judicially scattered as they are. It was what God foretold to them, upon their first entrance into Canaan, that if they would be dutiful and fear God, and keep his commandments, he would then establish and settle them in the land, and bless them there; but if they forgot him, and waxed fat, and kicked, and turned away from his commandments, then he would drive them out and scatter them, and they should be plucked from the land, and the Lord would scatter them from one end of the earth to the other among all people. And this is their very present case; God hath fulfilled it to a tittle. There is not such a dispersed or vagabond people as the Jews are upon the earth. Christ told what would be the fruit of their killing the prophets, and despising the grace of the Gospel. " Your house is left unto you desolate." (Matt. xxiii. 38.) God's house, and your own houses, the temple wherein ye trusted, and your dwellings wherein ye sinned, both shall be destroyed, and you driven out. The Lord awaken us all by this ! It is ill resting in privileges, when God's Israel are made vagabonds in the earth. It is dreadful when the iniquity of sin and the severity of justice meet. Sin hath always been casting out. It cast the angels out of heaven, and Adam out of paradise, and Cain out of the Church, and Israel out of the land.

(3.) To add further to their judgment in this case, they are made the scorn and contempt of men ; and this is implied when God threatens to make them the tail, " Thou shalt be the tail, and a proverb, and a byword among all people." (Deut. xxviii. 44.) And this is made good to a tittle, for thus are the Jews to this day, they are a very common by-word : when you would describe a man in the most reproachful character, you say he is a very Jew, as much as to say the basest and the worst of mankind. They are a people despised of all nations, the offscouring and a curse.

2. Consider them with respect to their spiritual state, and that is a state full of judgment; for they are not only cast out of their land, but which is more dreadful, they are cast off from the Lord. God hath cast off that people. They are under all manner of spiritual judgments. All their privileges are lost; their eyes blinded, their ears stopped, their hearts hardened, they are cast out of the covenant, and the care of God. " I will not feed you : that that dies, let it die ;" (Zech. xi. 9,) and in the next verse, God saith "he will break his staff, Beauty, and cut it asunder;" by this staff, Beauty, the covenant of God is to be understood. " I took my staff, Beauty, and cut it asunder, that I might break my covenant which I had made with all the people." The covenant of God is called a " staff," to denote the strength and support it affords; and it is called " Beauty," for three reasons :—

(1.) Because it makes over God to be our God, which is the most beautiful object in heaven and earth.

(2.) It is called Beauty from the matter whereof it consists, namely, the holiness of its precepts, the excellency of its comforts, and the glory of its reward.

(3.) It is that which puts a beauty upon us in the ordinances it sets up, and the privileges it affords. The ordinances and the privileges of the covenant are the beauty of any people.

Now, for God to cut asunder his staff, Beauty, to break his covenant with his people and cast them out of covenant, certainly it must be the sorest of all judgments. So that it is most certain that the present state of the Jews is a most dreadful state, both inward and outward, political and spiritual.

3. Their judgment is greater than ever was inflicted on any people whatsoever, both for quality and duration.

(1.) For quality or kind, as for instance, to judge them for all the blood of all the saints and witnesses of God, that ever were shed from Abel's day to the day of their rejection; was not that a dreadful judgment, (Mat. xxiii. 35,) saith Christ to them, " Upon you shall come all the righteous blood shed upon the earth, from the blood of righteous Abel unto the blood of Zacharias," &c. To bring the utmost of wrath in this world upon them is a very great judgment, and this God did, 1 Thess. ii. 16, " Wrath is come upon them to the uttermost."

(2.) These judgments are very great in duration. They were under very great judgments in Egypt, and it continued a long time, but that was but two hundred and fifteen years. That of Babylon was a sore captivity, but that lasted but seventy years ; but this judgment they are and have been under, hath been upon them for sixteen hundred years already, and yet it continues still, and they must lie under it yet longer.

II. They shall be delivered and redeemed from all these judgments—from all outward judgments and from all inward and spiritual judgments. There is a time coming, and I believe, very near, when this poor people, this afflicted people of God, that belong to the covenant of God, shall again be restored and delivered, and become a people, and the greatest mercy and blessing to the world.

1. They shall be restored to their own land again.

2. They shall be called and converted to Christ.

They shall be restored to their own land, and so delivered from all the temporal judgments they now lie under, and they shall be converted to Christ and saved, and so delivered from all their spiritual judgments. It is of high concernment to us to understand this—

1. They shall be restored again to their own land. This is a great truth, though I know some will not own it. There are many that will not believe they shall ever be converted again; and many that do believe their conversion, will not believe that ever they shall return to their own land, and possess their own inheritance, and dwell again upon their holy mountain; but that such a thing shall be, seems to me most plain, and that

(1.) From their coming out of Egypt of old; for as I told you formerly, the deliverance of Israel out of Egypt was so contrived and designed of God, to be made the great pattern of all the after deliverances, that God will work for the Church. Now when God delivered Israel out of Egypt their deliverance was completed in Canaan—Egypt was the place from whence they were delivered, Canaan the place where they were settled. And so it shall be when God delivers them at last, he shall gather them from all lands, and settle them in their own land. The Scripture is full of this, " For the Lord will have mercy on Jacob, and will yet choose Israel, and set them in their own land, and the strangers shall be joined with them, and they shall cleave to the house of Jacob, and the people shall take them and bring them to their place, and the house of Israel shall possess them in the land of the Lord for servants, and handmaids, and they shall take them captives whose captives they were, and they shall rule over their oppressors." (Isaiah xiv. 1, 2.) Now I say this Scripture was never fulfilled yet; it had a partial fulfilment in their deliverance from Babylon, but never fully to this day, for

(I.) How did Israel in that redemption rule over their oppressors, and take captive those that had captived them ? I find many cannot reconcile this to their redemption out of Babylon, and therefore they tell us this was evidently fulfilled in a spiritual sense in the days of the Gospel, when the Apostles conquered a great part of the heathen world to obedience to Christ. But this cannot be the meaning of the text, for when the Gentiles are brought in, the Jews are cast off, nay, the apostle tells you that their very breaking off, was the taking in of the Gentiles. Through their fall, salvation is come to the Gentiles. The casting of them away is the reconciling of the world; and again, the branches were broken off, and thou (speaking of the Gentiles, the Gentile Church,) thou being a wild olive tree, wert grafted in *among* them, (so we read it,) but it is grafted in *for* them.

This is a Scripture to prove the church of Gentile Believers in covenant with God, for they are as really in Abraham's covenant, as ever the Jews were ; for the Jews were broken off, and the Gentiles, (the wild olive,) they were grafted in for them, and so with them partake of the root and fatness of the olive tree. It may serve then, for very great use in the great doctrine of the Covenant and the Baptism of believer's seed. But I return. If the Jews be cast off when the

Gentiles are brought in, then that cannot be the sense of the place instanced in, and consequently it must be meant of their return to their own land.

II. This return to their land, shall be such as they never yet had, for it shall be sweetened with a rest not only from sorrow and hard bondage, but from fear, and such a return as this, they never had to this day.

III. This return shall be when Babylon is destroyed, this to me, therefore, is a plain proof of the thing in hand.

(2.) You have an old prophecy that points to this very thing. " Rejoice, Oh, ye nations with his people, (that is, ye Gentiles with the Jews, for he had not a people in the world then but them,) for he will avenge the blood of his servants, and will render vengeance to his adversaries, and will be merciful to his land, and to his people." (Deut xxxii. 43.) These words are a part of that famous and last prophetic song of Moses, which he spake in the ears of all the congregation of Israel. Deut. xxxi. 30. And these are the last words of this song, and they plainly contain a prophecy of the calling and planting of the Jews in their own land in the latter day, and I think no other tolerable sense can be put upon them. They must be meant of the days of the Gospel, because the Apostle Paul applies this very prophecy to the Gospel days, " again he saith, Rejoice ye Gentiles, with his people." (Rom. xv. 10.) Now if it be meant of the days of the Gospel, it must be meant either of the first days of the Gospel, or the last; it cannot be meant of the first days of the Gospel, for the Jews were cast off, or the generality of them, when the Gentiles were taken in, and therefore how could the Gentiles rejoice with the Jews for this great mercy to Jews and Gentiles? Besides this is to be at a time of vengeance. " I will make mine arrows drunk with blood, and my sword shall devour flesh, and that with the blood of the slain, and of the captives from the beginning of revenges upon the enemy." (Deut. xxxii. 42.) And then it follows " Rejoice, O Gentiles with my people," &c. And so it points to the time when the fulness of the Jews and Gentiles shall both come in, for then God will destroy the enemies both of Jews and Gentiles ; for why are they called to rejoice together but because God will destroy him that hath been the common enemy of both ? and that is Antichrist which is intended in this place, " from the beginning of revenges upon the enemy," (so we read it,) but in the Hebrew it is, " with the head of the revengeful enemy," and then it plainly shows whose blood God's arrows shall be drunk with, to wit, with the head of the revengeful enemy ; and who is this revengeful enemy but Babylon? and who is the head of this enemy but Antichrist? So the meaning is this, Babylon shall fall, and Antichrist be destroyed. Then, not only the Gentiles, but the Jews also, shall be redeemed and restored, and so Jews and Gentiles shall be the Lord's together.

And this is what we read of as fulfilled. " And after these things, (that is, after the pouring out of the fifth vial upon Babylon,) I heard a great voice of much people in heaven, (that is in the church,) and in this heaven is heard a voice of much people, for now the Jews are come in, and mark what follows, they sang " Halleluiah ; Salvation, and glory, and power, and honour, unto the Lord our God." (Rev xix. 1.) Now what means this word " *Halleluiah*," here ? It carries much instruction with it. It is an Hebrew word, and

signifies " Praise ye the Lord." It is a word not used
in all the New Testament, but in this book of the
Revelation, and not in all this book, but in this chapter,
and in this chapter four times, in the first, third, fourth,
and sixth verses, and it is used in every place to express the Church's joy at the fall of the great whore.
It is a form not used till now; you find the church of
of the Gentiles often praising God, throughout the
whole book of Revelations, but we find not this " Halleluiah" till this nineteenth chapter : and the reason is
this, the nineteenth chapter is the exposition of the
sixth vial, and it is under that vial that the Jews are
converted, and therefore now this Hebrew word is in-
troduced into the Church's song, to shew us that now
the Jews being converted, the Jews and Gentiles shall
praise God together, and so Moses's prophecy is fulfilled, " Rejoice ye Gentiles with his people."

(3.) This return of the Jews to their own land, is
foretold as one of the peculiar blessings of the times of
Christ.   " And it shall come to pass in that day, that
the Lord shall set his hand again the second time to
recover the remnant of his people, that shall be left
from Assyria, and from Egypt, and from Pathros, and
from Cush, and from Elam, and from Shinar, and
from Hamath, and from the islands of the sea, and
he shall set up an ensign for the nations, and shall
assemble the outcasts of Israel, and gather together the
dispersed of Judah, from the four corners of the earth."
Isaiah xi. 11, 12. This is a plain prophecy of calling
them back again, but you will say, when shall this be ?

Mark the former verses 6th, 7th, 8th, and 9th. It
is when the wolf shall dwell with the lamb, and the
leopard lie down with the kid, and the calf and the

young lion, and the fatling together, and a little child
shall lead them, &c. This refers to the time that
shall succeed upon the ruin of the Beast, the peace-
able times of Christ's reign ; now mark ! In that day
it shall come to pass that the Lord shall set his hand
again the second time to recover the remnant of Israel,
that is the Jews.

" Thy people shall be all righteous : they shall inherit the land for ever," (Isa. lx. 21.) and verse 16.
" Thou shalt suck the milk of the Gentiles, and the
breasts of kings: for thou shalt know that I am thy
king, the mighty one of Israel." " Write all the words
that I have spoken to thee in a book ; for, lo, the days
come, saith the Lord: that I will bring again the captivity of my people Israel and Judah, and I will cause
them to return to the land that I gave to their fathers,
and they shall possess it." (Jer. xxx. 2.) Can any
thing be more plain than this is ? it cannot be rati-
onally thought that this promise had its full accomplishment in their redemption from Babylon, for that was
only the redemption of Judah, the two tribes, not the
redemption of Israel, the ten tribes, for though the
two tribes returned, yet the ten tribes never returned
to this day, but the promise is to bring back the captivity of Israel and Judah, that is the twelve tribes.

One upon this place saith, it seems not probable
that the Jews shall return again to their own land,
because, saith he, it is very hard to give an account
where the ten tribes are. A strange reason of a
learned man, as if the fulfilling of the promise de-
pended upon his knowledge. Indeed, if God knew
not where they were, it were something, but if he doth,
it is no hindrance of the promise, though we do not.

And that God doth know, is plain from the 10th and 11th verse. " Fear not, O my servant Jacob, saith the Lord; neither be dismayed, O Israel; for, lo, I will save thee from afar, and thy seed from the land of their captivity ; and Jacob shall return, and be at rest, and be quiet, and none shall make him afraid ; for I am with thee, saith the Lord, to save thee." " Hear the word of the Lord, O ye nations, and declare it in the isles afar off, and say, He that scattered Israel will gather them," (Jer. xxxi. 10,) that is, into their own land. " I will set up one shepherd over them, even my servant David ; and he shall feed them, and my servant David shall be a prince over them ; I the Lord have spoken it." (Ezekiel xxxiv. 23.) This is spoken of Christ, and it refers to the time, when he shall reign over the Jews. It is the same with what the Angel told Mary, " Thou shalt bring forth a son, and call his name Jesus ; he shall be great, and the Lord shall give him the throne of his father David, and he shall reign over the house of Jacob for ever ; and of his kingdom there shall be no end." (Luke i. 31.) This is a kingdom that Christ is to possess at the conversion of the Jews. So that here is a plain promise, nay, promise upon promise, of their settlement again in their own land, as a peculiar blessing of Christ's times. The Scriptures are very plain that prove this truth. (Zeph. iii. 9.) (Zech. xiv. 9, 11.) And truly the arguments to prove it, are very many.

(1.) The Jews shall be a nation again ; one part of their present judgment is to be unpeopled and destroyed as a nation. And therefore it is said, the children of Israel shall abide many days without a king, and without a priest, they shall be no people.

Their civil polity shall be wholly broken and destroyed, and that is what God threatens. " I will cause to cease the kingdom of the house of Israel." (Hosea i. 4.) This was fulfilled in the letter of it in the ninth year of Hosea's reign, for then the kingdom of Israel, after forty-one years tottering, was utterly broken, and so it hath continued to this very day. But yet this, no people, shall become a people again, a little one shall become a strong nation. " In that day, saith the Lord, I will assemble her that halteth, and I will gather her that is driven out, and her that I have afflicted, and I will make her that halted a remnant, and her that was cast off, a strong nation." (Micah iv. 6, 7.) Here is a plain promise of their being a nation again. And observe, this is in the last days, as in the first verse, " In the last days it shall come to pass, that the mountain of the house of the Lord, shall be established on the top of the mountains, &c."

Now if they shall be a nation again, then they must have a place, a land to dwell in as a nation. They cannot be a nation among other nations, and if they become a distinct nation, then they must have a distinct land, and what land so likely as their own land, which God had promised.

(2.) They shall not only be a people again, but a most renowned people, the greatest in the world for honour and glory. The poor Jews, who have been, and are to this day scattered in all nations, and scorned by all nations, shall shortly become the most glorious people in the world, and be had in the highest esteem in the world ; ten men shall take hold of the skirts of him that is a Jew, and say, " We will go with thee, for the Lord is with you." " Arise, shine ; for thy

light is come, and the glory of the Lord is risen upon
thee; for, behold, darkness shall cover the earth; but
the Lord shall arise upon thee, and his glory shall be
seen upon thee, and the Gentiles shall come to thy
light," &c. (Isaiah lx. 1, 2.)

(3.) It appears further, that they shall be again a
nation, for they shall be a Church to Christ. And this
I shall make out to you, when I come to the next
head to speak to their conversion.

(4.) The judgment that the Jews are under, is a
dispersion into all nations. They are scattered into all
the quarters of the world, East, West, North, and
South. And shall not their mercy be as great as their
judgment? shall not their restitution correspond with
their dispersion? therefore they must be restored to
their own land. The land of Canaan is theirs by a
special title, sealed by Heaven; and they are driven
out for their rebellion against God; therefore when
they shall repent and return to their obedience, what
hinders but they should return to their old inheritance?
" I will bring thy seed from the east, and gather thee
from the west; I will say to the north, give up; and
to the south, keep not back; bring my sons from far,
and my daughters from the ends of the earth." (Isaiah
xliii. 5, 6.) Now this shews that their gathering shall
be as universal as their scattering; but how will God
dispose of them? He tells you, he will feed them
with the heritage of Jacob their father. Now what is
the heritage of Jacob, but the land of Canaan, which
God in Gen. xxxv. 12, punctually promised as an
heritage to Jacob and his seed?

But why doth God call it the heritage of Jacob?
because the whole posterity of Jacob was in covenant

with God, and so had a share in that promise, but the whole posterity of Abraham and Isaac had not; for there were Ishmael and Esau both excluded and shut out of this land; therefore he calls it the heritage of Jacob. Now, as sin drove them out of Canaan, so when God pardons them, he will bring them again. " I will bring Israel again to his own habitation, and he shall feed on Carmel and Bashan, and his soul shall be satisfied upon Mount Ephraim." And then it follows, " In those days, and at that time, the iniquity of Ephraim shall be sought for, and the sins of Judah, and they shall not be found: for I, the Lord, will pardon them." (Jer. l. 19, 20.) Besides, I would ask, whether the threatenings of God denounced against Israel, and the promises of God made to Israel, shall have the same kind of accomplishment, and fulfilling or not? if not, then we make the mind of God un-intelligible, though revealed, and his word cannot be understood; and if they shall have the same kind of fulfilling, then how can it be, that when the threat-enings of God have been fulfilled literally, the pro-mises should be fulfilled only typically? This is just as if you should say some promises made to England are fulfilled, because they are made good to India; the Jews and Gentiles are spoken of in a contradistinc-tion, and the promise made to one is not to another. I could multiply Scriptures that speak plain to this truth of Israel's return. I know nothing so frequently insisted on by the prophets in the book of the Old Testament, but I need look no further than this chapter; for the restoring the Jews to their own land in the latter day is the great thing ultimately intended in opening their graves, and raising them again; that it is immediately meant of their coming out of Babylon, I grant; but I say the Holy Ghost had a design upon a far greater redemption than that was, and this is plain to be seen, by observing some particulars in this prophecy.

(1.) The bones are said to be very many, and they are said to be an exceeding great army, now this could not be intended only of the Jews, that came out of Babylon; for though they were many, yet not *very many* in the language of the Holy Ghost.—When Cyrus proclaimed a liberty for them to return, the whole of them was not 50,000, and these cannot be called *very many;* if they be called a great army, yet it cannot be called an *exceeding* great army, for time was, when the army of the Jews was ten times as many.

(2.) The expression in the 11th verse shews it to have a farther look than to the Babylonish Captivity, for there the Holy Ghost doth explain the Bones to be meant of "the whole house of Israel." Now the whole house of Israel was not in captivity in Babylon, for the ten tribes were captivated by the Assyrians, there were only two tribes carried into Babylon, therefore this must have a further extent, than the Jews in Babylon, for though they be sometimes called Israel, yet no where " the whole house of Israel;" that is never used but when it takes in all the twelves tribes—therefore the Holy Ghost in saying here, these bones are the whole house of Israel, doth thereby point us to such a resurrection of the bones, as shall contain the whole twelve tribes, the whole house of Israel.

(3.) This truth is further evident from the (9th verse,) where the prophet is commanded to prophecy to the four winds. Now this answers to the present dispersion of the Jews, which is said to be unto the four quarters of the earth, and the calling upon the four winds to breathe upon the dry bones, is to put life into the whole house of Israel, and to raise up those that are scattered through the whole world.

(4.) This appears from the noise of the shaking that is to make way for the rising of the bones, as I prophesied, there was a noise and behold a shaking and the bones came together, bone to his bone; there was a shaking at their deliverance from Babylon, but that did not make so much noise, but when the Roman, and Turkish empire shall be shaken, and broken, Oh! what a noise will this make all the world over, when the Throne, and the power of the Babylonish Beast shall be destroyed. The vials are to be poured out on the river Euphrates, that is upon the Turkish Empire, to dry up the waters, to waste his people and strength, that the way of the Kings of the East may be made.

(5.) It appears yet plainer, from the 14th and 15th verses of this prophecy; where the Jews owning and acknowledging Christ for their Lord is foretold.

"And ye shall know that I am the Lord, when I have opened your graves, and brought you out of your graves," (that signifies their redemption), "and shall put my spirit in you, and ye shall live," (that signifies their conversion.)

Now that this looks beyond their redemption out of Babylon, is most plain, from the next prophecy after this, which is nothing else but an explanation of this of the bones, by the metaphor of two sticks made one, to shew that Israel and Judah shall be for ever united together under Christ. I will make the stick of

Ephraim and Judah one stick, and they shall be one
stick in my hand, that is when they come under my
government. And this is when the fore-mentioned
things shall come to pass, when they shall be gathered
out of all nations, and settled in their own land, and
converted to the Lord; which three things, you have
again asserted by the Holy Ghost, in the following
parts of the prophecy to put it out of all doubt.

1st. That they shall be gathered out of all nations.
(ver. 21.) I will take the children of Israel from
among the heathen, and will gather them on every side,
and bring them into their own land, which is the

2d. And I will make them one nation in the land,
upon the mountains of Israel; and he adds in the
25th verse, they shall dwell in the land that I gave
to Jacob my servant, wherein your Father's have
dwelt; and they shall dwell therein, even they and their
children, and their children's children.

3d. They shall be converted to the Lord; that you
have in the 23rd verse, they shall not defile themselves
any more with their Idols, nor with any of their transgressions; then it follows, I will cleanse them, so shall
they be my people, and I will be their God. Here is
their conversion, which is further confirmed from the
26th verse. I will make an everlasting covenant with
them, and I will set my sanctuary in the midst of
them for evermore.—Which is not meant of their
worldly sanctuary, but a gospel sanctuary, a glorious gospel temple that shall never be destroyed, as their
first and second temple was.

So then, it evidently speaks of the glorious time of
Christ's kingdom in this world, therefore it is said in
the 24th verse, " David my servant, shall be king over

them, and in the 25th verse, my servant David shall be prince over them for ever, that is, the Lord Christ, who is called David often in the prophets, so that here is enough in this chapter to give light unto this truth, that the poor vagabond Jews shall yet be gathered and planted in their land, and be a glorious people, a people to God for ever, which brings me to the

2nd thing which I did purpose to have insisted on. For as they shall be restored to their land, so shall they most certainly be called of God, and converted to Jesus Christ, but of this another time.

Give me leave now to speak a word of application; you will say, what doth such a doctrine as this of the Jews returning to their own land concern us, what is it to us whether ever they return or not? I answer, this doctrine is very instructive and teaching to us, and especially in these four or five things.

1. It shews us what a wonderful efficacy there is in the electing love of God; not one of the objects of it shall ever miscarry. The Jews are a great proof of this; though they have been as wicked a people as ever lived in the world, who murdered their Lord—an abominable, wicked, grinding, deceitful people, yet God will not utterly cast them off; though he cast them out, he will not cast them off, because God hath a seed among them, that must be converted. The election shall obtain, though the rest are blinded and hardened. So we may see here reason to admire the electing love of God, what the virtue of it is through all ages and times.

2. This doctrine is of great use to confirm our faith in the great attribute of God's faithfuless, both to his people, and to his promise.

F

(1.) To his people. What an instance is this here before you! Here is an old people of God, that once were so, but have been cast off for one thousand six hundred years together, and yet such is the love of God to their fathers, that he will not utterly reject them, for they are beloved for their fathers sakes.

(2.) "God will ever be mindful of his covenant." (Psa. cxi. 5.) God had of old, made a covenant with Abraham, and Isaac, and Jacob, that he would be their God, and the God of their seed after them, and of their seed's seed for ever. Now God having once promised the fathers, no infidelity of the seed can frustrate the promise of God, for the gifts and callings of God are without repentance.

Oh, the faithfulness of God! well might the prophet say, "it is like the great mountains." Not a promise God ever made, but it shall be fulfilled, though never so old, or never so little understood. Thus he keeps covenant to a thousand generations.

3. We may learn from this return of this people to their own land, what use to make of lesser blessings, and do not let us slight them, for they are the fore-runners of greater mercy.

(1.) Great mercies are always a security for less. If God save Lot from Sodom, he will not deny him a Zoar, and mark the reason, is it not a little one? "He that hath given us Christ, how shall he not with him freely give us all things?"

(2.) Less mercies are a preparation for greater. They are like John the Baptist, not Christ, but the fore-runner of Christ. As when God is in a way of judgment, he proceeds gradually from less to greater, and doth advance by degrees, like fire that smokes and then burns and flames out.. It is first a little wrath, and then great wrath, and then wrath to the utmost; therefore we should tremble whenever God comes out in a way of judgment, for when he begins, he will make an end, if repentance and humiliation do not stop him in the way. Hence that of Moses to Aaron, " go quickly and make atonement, for there is wrath gone out from the Lord, the plague is begun." It is good to meet God betimes, in a way of judgment. Thus it is also when God is in a way of mercy, little mercies make way for greater. If once the dry bones come together, he will put sinews and flesh upon them, and then cover them with skin, and put breath into them, and make them stand upon their feet and live. If once the Lord gathers Israel, he will sanctify them, if he plant them in their land, he will convert them, and if he sanctify them he will save them, so that the way to Canaan, is the way to a better country, that is to Heaven. Thus love heightens the dispensation, therefore the kingdom of God is compared to a mustard seed, the least of seeds, but of mighty increase. Grace is in the beginning small, but in the end great.

4. Let us all have faith in this truth, that the poor Jews shall be converted; let us believe for a people that cannot believe for themselves. Doth God require us to preach it ? Then he requires you to believe it. " Hear the word of the Lord, oh ye nations, and declare it in the isles afar off, and say, He that scattered Israel will gather them and keep them." (Jer. xxxi. 10.)

5. From this truth we are called of God, to the duty of prayer for the poor Jews. Oh, pray for them that cannot pray for themselves. The Apostle James

saith, " The prayer of faith shall save the sick." I will carry it further, The prayer of faith shall save the dead. The Jews are a dead people, dead and dry bones, and cut off; now the prayer of faith shall save the dead, shall awaken the great God to put on his power and might to redeem and restore this poor lost people. For when the Lord builds up Zion, he will regard the prayer of the destitute. It is our duty to pray for them; I shall give you three motives to this.

(1.) Conscience of this duty will mightily quicken our cries against Antichrist; will set an edge upon faith in prayer for the removing the cursed stumbling block of Rome, for it is their idolatry that is the great stumbling block to their conversion. I know not wherein you can shew more of a public spirit, or do more for Christ and his kingdom by any thing in the world than by this. Pray against Antichrist, both eastern and western.

(2.) This will be of marvellous advantage to the Gentile Church. For when the Jews return to their land, then they shall return unto their Lord too, and this the apostle calls "life from the dead." (Rom. xi. 15.) If the casting them off be the reconciling of the world, (the casting off the Jews was the means of bringing in the Gentiles, and the reconciling of the whole world,) what shall the receiving them be, but life from the dead? You shall reap great benefit by it. You shall be one church with them, you shall have that light in the mysteries of God, which now you have not, for a great light shall then break out.

(3.) This is one thing that doth prepare the way for the Lord. Every mountain shall be laid low, therefore, Babylon, the great mountain, must fall ; every valley shall be filled, therefore the valley of dry bones shall be filled up. This is preparing the way of the Lord, that so all flesh may see the salvation of God. Oh, pray that the graves may be opened, that this people of God may arise, and return to their own land, and so become the people of God.

SERMON V.

" Thus saith the Lord God, behold, O my people, I will open your graves, and cause you to come out of your graves, and bring you to the land of Israel." Ezek. xxxvii. 12.

I gave you this doctrine from those words, that when the Lord comes to deliver his people out of their oppressions and sufferings, it will be in a wonderful manner; I have shown you that this hath been the way of God in all ages; in redeeming Israel out of Egypt; in the instance in the text of redeeming them out of Babylon, and it will be thus to the end of the world. The great deliverance God works for his church shall be with wonder. And I shall make use of this instance of the Jews to clear this at *this* time.

I have shewed you that the present state of the Jews is a state of great judgment; great outward judgment, in being unpeopled and cast out of their land; great spiritual judgment, in being unchurched, and cast off from the Lord.

I am upon the second thing propounded, that they shall be redeemed and saved from all these judgments, both outward and spiritual judgments. They shall be restored to their country and covenant; they shall return to their land, and they shall return to the Lord.

Now the first of these I have spoken to at large last time, that they shall be restored to their land, and I proved it by Scripture and argument. I am now to speak to the

2. That the Jews shall be converted to the Lord. They shall not only be brought into Canaan but brought to Christ. I shall premise some things to give light to what I intend.

(1.) That by the conversion of the Jews to Christ, we must not understand it of any one part of that people that are distinguished into two kingdoms, the ten tribes and the two tribes, but must take it of the whole body of the people.

(2.) That their conversion must be considered either with respect to the inchoation or completion of the work; for there will be a deal of time between the beginning and the completing of it. I proceed now to prove that they shall be converted, not only brought to Canaan, but to Christ. Now I shall clear the truth of this,

I. From the Scriptures, which are full of this truth. " The children of Israel shall abide many days without a king, and without a prince, and without a sacrifice, and afterwards shall the children of Israel return and seek the Lord their God and David their king, and shall fear the Lord and his goodness, in the latter days." (Hos. iii. 4, 5.) Here are three expressions that signify their conversion. They shall return and seek the Lord and David their King, and shall fear the Lord and his goodness. They shall return; it is not a political but a spiritual return that is here

meant; not a return to their land, but to the Lord.
A return by a sincere repentance, for right repentance
is often expressed by turning and returning. No man
truly repents of sin that doth not turn from sin and
return to God. Therefore to shew that they shall
sincerely repent, he expresses it by returning, and to
shew it shall be real, he adds, they shall seek the
Lord their God, and this implies very much in it.
Sometimes seeking the Lord is only to express the
duty of prayer, but here it is more comprehensive. It
implies an imploring of his favour in the pardon of
sin, and a renouncing all false worship, and returning
to the true worship, this is seeking the Lord. "They
shall ask the way to Zion with their faces thitherward."
And then this is added here, they shall seek the Lord
their God, which relative term, so full of sweetness,
may have a double reference, either to what is past or
what is to come.

1. To what is past, and so their God points them
back to their old relation, that is to him who was
once the King of the Jews, Abraham's, Isaac's, and
Jacob's God; and so their God, or,

2. It may refer to what is to come, they shall
seek the Lord who now seeks them, and is ready to be
their God.

Again, to set out the truth of their conversion to
Christ, he adds, they shall not only seek the Lord
their God, but David their King. This is not David
the son of Jesse, for he was dead and rotten long
before this promise was made; nor can it be Zerub-
babel, for this is spoken of a time that is to be two
thousand years after his time. There is nothing
plainer than that by David is meant the Lord Christ.
He is often called David in the Scriptures. "They

shall serve the Lord their God and David their King;"
that is Christ. (Jer. xxx. 9.) "I will be their God
and my servant David a prince among them." (Ez.
xxxiv. 24.) And, "My servant David shall be their
prince for ever." (Ezek. xxxvii. 24.) Now who can
this be but Christ? What David is a prince for ever,
but he that was David's Son and David's Lord? and
is therefore called the root and the offspring of David.
He is his Root as God, his Offspring as man des-
cending from him. That by David, is meant Christ is
plain; we find David himself calling Christ by his own
name. " For thy servant David's sake turn not away
the face of thine anointed." (Psa. cxxxii. 10.) Here
David begs mercy for David's sake. Now David
never used to beg mercy for his own sake, we often
hear him begging for God's mercy's sake, for his truth
and goodness and righteousness sake, but never for
his own sake. And truly this makes many of our
commentators think that David was not the pen-man
of this psalm; but this is cutting the knot that may
be easily untied, for it is David begging mercy for
the sake of David, the Christ. But why is seeking
David added to their seeking the Lord? It is to
teach us a great truth in which, the very marrow of
the Gospel lies, to wit, that none can seek God aright,
but in and through Jesus Christ. He is the way to
the Father. No man comes to the Father but by
him. They that seek the Lord their God must seek
David their King.

But why is Christ called David their King? This
is to point to us the glory of Christ in that day, when
the Jews shall be converted. The kingdom is then to
be the Lord Christ's, not only, " De Jure," " of right,"

for now it is so, but " De Facto," for Christ shall then have actual possession. The great thing that the Jews opposed Christ in was his kingly office, "we will have no king but Cæsar :" but in that day they shall own him for their rightful Lord and King, and none else. But when shall this kingdom of David begin? he tells you it shall be in the latter days, that is in the days of the Messiah, and in the last of those latter days; and if so, then it is evident that this Scripture was never fulfilled, and therefore a promise of God that is yet to be accomplished, the same with that, (Luke i. 32.) " And the Lord God shall give unto him the throne of his Father David, and he shall reign over the house of Jacob for ever, and of his kingdom there shall be no end." Jacob was the father of the twelve tribes, so that the house of Jacob over which Christ shall reign is the whole seed of the Jews. Now when was this promise ever fulfilled? What is there like it in the world? Some say at Christ's Incarnation; but that cannot be, for then the generality of the Jews rejected and denied him. Some say it is meant of a spiritual kingdom, which cannot be, for this is called the throne of his Father David, and that was a throne over the Jews, and what throne hath Christ over the Jews, who reject and disown him to this very day? But this is spoken of a time when Christ shall so be a King as he never was before. The Jews shall own him as such. They shall say, " The Lord is our Law-giver and Judge, he shall save us." And this is spoken of the time when Jerusalem shall be a quiet habitation. I say there never was such a day in the world, nor shall be until the sound of the seventh trumpet. " And the seventh angel sounded, and there were great voices in heaven, saying, the kingdoms of this world are become the kingdoms of our Lord and his Christ, and he shall reign for ever and ever." (Rev. xi. 15.) How many evidences are there in this one Scripture now opened to prove the truth of this doctrine of the conversion of the Jews. " They shall return and seek the Lord their God and David their King, &c."

Another Scripture to prove this is in Ezek. xlvii. in the beginning, there you read of a temple and waters issuing from under the threshold of this temple, and the increase of this water, and their healing virtue. This temple some will have to be the temple that was built after the return of the Jews from Babylon ; but this cannot be; here is a river said to issue from under the threshold of this house, but there is no such thing affirmed of the temple at Jerusalem.

The meaning of this is, that there shall be a mighty effusion of the Spirit according to that of Joel. It is true that there hath been something of it already, but that is but little to what is intended in this prophecy. In John, (chap. 7,) you have mention made of " living water," and this (it is said) spake he of the Spirit. It is then, the spirit that is meant by these waters, but not the Spirit alone, but the Spirit accompanied with the word and ordinances; therefore 'tis said, these waters issued from under the threshold of the Temple.

Now there are three things I take notice of concerning these waters.

(1.) They are healing waters. The Jews are as a dead sea, as a stinking lake that nothing can heal till these waters come—and the eighth verse gives some countenance to this, for they are said to issue out towards the East Country; and to go into the sea, and being brought into the sea, the waters shall be healed, &c.—Here is a dead sea made to live. Or the sea may note a multitude of people converted to Christ: and these sanctuary waters healing the sea, intimates a mighty conversion both of Jews and Gentiles in that day, for it is said, there shall be a great multitude of fishes. (verse 9.)

(2.) And to confirm this they are said to be waters of life; not only living waters but waters which make to live, which give life; and that not only here and there, but wherever they come. Every thing that liveth, wherever the river cometh shall live; that is, they who before lived a natural life shall by the coming of these waters live a Spiritual life. They did live only by a soul living in them, they live now by Christ living in them. Not like the waters of Babylon which issue from Antichrist's seat, which are poisonous and killing wherever they come, so that it is said every living thing died in that sea, but these waters of Babylon shall be all dried up, and there shall be no more sea. (Rev. xxi. 1.) The Church shall no more hang up her harps and weep by these waters of Babylon, but shall stand by the waters of the Sanctuary having the harps of God in their hands, and shall sing the song of the Lamb in their own land.

(3.) These waters are said to run two ways, in two streams, for it is said, (verse 8,) these waters issue out toward the East Country, there is one stream, and they go down into the desert, there is another stream, and therefore called two rivers, (verse 9,) as it is in the Hebrew and the margin of the Bible.

It imports abundance of Grace both to Jews and Gentiles, therefore it is said, (verse 10,) their fish shall be according to their kinds, exceeding many. Many among the Jews and Gentiles shall that day be turned to the Lord.

This is another Scripture that doth plainly and fully prove the conversion of the Jews.

I might add many Scriptures more, but I pass them, and come to a

II. Argument.—I would argue this truth from the wonderful preserving of this people, of the Jews, as a distinct people from all nations for so many hundred years. Though the Jews have been dispersed into many Countries, scattered among all nations, yet they have never been mixed with any other nation to this day. It is not so with any other nation in the world. Others become one people with those where they live, but the Jews keep their own customs and manners and remain Jews; they are not English in England, nor Spaniards in Spain.

Now this is a wonderful thing that God should for so many hundred years scatter a people in judgment among other nations, and yet preserve them from mixing among any; this shews some great design of God, that he will call them again and make them a people to himself.

III. If the vail that is upon them shall be taken away, then they shall be converted to Christ. (2 Cor. iii. 14, 15.) "Until this day remaineth the same vail un-taken away in the reading of the old Testament, which vail is done away in Christ. But even unto this day when Moses is read, the vail is upon their heart; nevertheless when it shall turn to the Lord, the vail shall be taken away." What vail is this? There is a double vail.

1. A vail upon the object, a vail upon Moses, that is upon the Law of Moses.—There is a Temple and altars and sacrifices and washings, all these are Christ in virtue and significancy, only under a vail; now the poor Jews are not able to see Christ through this vail; they cannot see Christ in the burnt offerings, and peace offerings and their washings; the cloud is so dark that the Sun of Righteousness is quite hid from them.

2. There is an internal vail, and that is blindness and hardness of heart. Never any people of so stupid a conscience, and so hardened against Christ, as the Jews. They will not believe that the Messiah is come or that Jesus is He, though they might see it in many things. For the Sceptre and Lawgiver are departed from Judah, which were not to depart until Shiloh came; therefore Christ must be come, yet they will not own it.

That word also hath been fulfilled that a Virgin should conceive and bear a son. Christ was to come before the destruction of the second Temple, and this is destroyed, yet will they not believe; and the reason is, the vail is upon their heart to this day. O! the hardness and blindness of these poor Jews! But shall this vail abide always thus? No, for when it shall turn to the Lord, the vail shall be taken away. For this vail is not to be always upon them, their blindness is great and sad, but it is but partial. (Rom xi. 25.) "I would not brethren that you should be ignorant of this mystery, that blindness in part is happened to Israel, until the fulness of the Gentiles be brought in." Where is the mystery of this? Not only that blindness is happened to Israel, which is indeed a great thing, that the only seeing people should become blind and be cast off, this made the Apostle cry out "O the unsearchable judgments of God ! But this is not all the mystery, it is no less a mystery that this blindness which is happened to Israel is but partial, and not final. It is to last but till the fulness of the Gentiles be brought in—when the seventh Angel shall sound his trumpet, then this mystery of God shall be finished.

IV. If there be a time when the Jews shall be convinced of their sins, especially of their sins against Christ, and shall obtain pardon, and forgiveness, and healing, then they shall be converted ; but such a time there is, that they shall be convinced of their sin against Christ. " They shall look upon me whom they have pierced and mourn." (Zech. xii. 10.) " Behold he cometh with clouds, and every eye shall see him, and they also which pierced him, and all kindreds of the earth wail because of him." (Rev. i. 7.)

" Then shall all the tribes of the earth, or of the land, (that is the land of Israel) mourn. (Matt. xxiv. 30.) But shall they mourn, and not be comforted ? No. "I will restore comfort to him, and to his mourners." (Isa. lvii. 18.) And the foundation of this comfort shall be in the pardon of their sins. And if their sins shall be pardoned then they shall be converted, for justification and sanctification are inseparable. Wherever he comes by blood, he comes by water. Where he justifies, there he sanctifies. You have both together. " There shall come out of Zion the deliverer, and shall turn away ungodliness from Jacob."

V. If God will renew his covenant with them, and take them again into covenant, then they shall be converted. That they are at present cast out of covenant, is evident. As to the Ten Tribes, saith God, "Call their names *Loammi*, for ye are not my people, I will not be your God;" there are the Ten Tribes cast off, and it is as clear of the two tribes from Zech. xi. 10. "I took my staff beauty and cut it asunder, that I might break my covenant which I had made with all the people; and it was broken in that day." Therefore you read of their being broken off. (Rom. xi. 17.) But they shall be taken into covenant again, for though God hath cast off the Jews, yet he hath not cast off his covenant, therefore God promises to renew his covenant with them, and make them partakers of all covenant blesings. " I will make a new covenant with the house of Israel and Judah, I will put my law in their hearts, and write it in their inward parts. I will be their God, and they shall be my people." (Jer. xxxi. 31, 33.)

This is the very same covenant with the old covenant made with Abraham, but it is called a new covenant because of a new manner of administration. Now if God will take these Jews into covenant then they shall be converted.

VI. If Christ shall have a glorious tabernacle among them, and bring them into a glorious church state, then they shall be converted. Now it is evident that God shall have a glorious church among the Jews in the last day.

" It shall come to pass, in the last days, that the mountain of the Lord's house shall be established on the top of the mountains, and all nations shall flow unto it." (Isa. ii. 2.) I will set my sanctuary in the midst of them for evermore." (Ezek. xxxvii. 26.)

Now the Jews are no church, they are without a priest or Ephod, &c., yet the time is at hand, when God will erect a glorious church among the Jews, as ever was. Their ministry shall be very spiritual, for then God will sit as a refiner to purge the sons of Levi, that they may offer to God an offering in righteousness. The members of this church shall be very holy and spiritual. " Thy people shall be all righteous." "There shall be no more a Canaanite in the house of the Lord for ever ; " (Isa. lx. 21.) that is, there shall not enter into this church any thing that defiles. Mere civility and morality, and outward profession goes a great way now to make a church member; but then it will not do, for God saith, in that day no stranger uncircumcised in heart, shall enter into my sanctuary. O what a blessed time ! what a glorious church will that be ! Such as never was in the world for holiness and glory ! And if the Jews shall be brought into so glorious a church state, it follows that they shall be converted to Christ.

III. I come now to prove that the deliverance of the Jews, the old people of God out of their graves, and bringing them to own and believe in Christ, shall be brought about in a wonderful manner. And this will be evident in the character the Scripture puts upon this deliverance. This work of God in delivering and saving his people is called a mystery. The mystery lies in this, that " this blindness is a partial not a perpetual blindness, but till the fulness of the Gentiles be brought in, and then all Israel shall be saved." (Rom. xi. 25.) The conversion of the Gentiles was once a mystery and if the Gentiles' conversion be called a mystery, well may the Jews, for the Gentiles were not converted from so great sins as the Jews shall; the Gentiles were never made to share in so great grace, as the Jews shall.

You read of a threefold mystery to be finished.

(1.) There is the mystery of the resurrection of the dead. "Behold I show you a mystery. We shall not all sleep, but we shall be changed."

(2.) There is a mystery of Antichrist, called a mystery of iniquity.

(3.) There is the mystery of the calling and bringing in of the Jews. This is called the mystery of God, to show what a wonderful work it will be.

Again,—It is made more wonderful than any deliverance that ever God wrought for them before. God hath wrought wonderful deliverances for that people formerly; he hath not dealt so with any nation, yet this salvation shall be such as shall outdo them all.

The deliverance from Babylon, was a wonderful deliverance, but that was but a type of this; what a wonderful deliverance was that out of Egypt, he showed them marvellous things in the land of Ham, dividing the sea and making them a way through, cleaving the rocks for water for them, and sending them bread from Heaven in the wilderness. But God will do greater things than these. Therefore it is said, "The days come that they shall no more say, the Lord liveth who brought up the children of Israel out of the land of Egypt; but the Lord liveth who brought up the children of Israel from all countries, whither I had driven them, and they shall dwell in their own land." (Jer. xxiii. 7.)

"Remember not the former things, neither consider the things of old, behold I will do a new thing in the earth." (Isa. xliii. 18.)

This then shall be more wonderful than any former deliverance, for

They are under a more sore dispersion than before. In Egypt they were in one country, and in Babylon under one Government, but now they are driven into all countries, scattered over all the earth. Now the bringing a people together out of such a dispersion and scattering is more wonderful than the deliverance out of Egypt.

Again, this is more complete and full than any former deliverance. Then a deliverance is complete, when it is once for all and for ever. But that from Egypt was not, for they had many bondages after ; but when this comes, they shall never be in bondage more.—" Then shall no stranger pass through her any more." " The saints of the most high shall possess the kingdom and reign for ever." (Dan. vii. 18.) This is called a resurrection from the dead, and this hath always been reckoned among the greatest wonders.

Now the Jews are under a two-fold death.

(1.) A death of affliction and suffering, for misery is a living death, and therefore the Scriptures call great sufferings death. And if sufferings be a death, great sufferings are a great death, and long sufferings, a long death ; then how great a death hath been upon them !

(2.) They are dead in sin, and that is death indeed. Of all deaths that is the most deadly ; affliction is a death that kills the body, but sin is the death of the soul.—And this is the case of this poor people, dead, and dead again. Now what a wonderful resurrection will that be, when God shall raise this poor people from both deaths at once. " O my people, I will open your graves, and cause you to come out of your graves, and put my spirit upon you and ye shall live;" pointing at both these deaths,—are ye dead in affliction? I will open your graves; are ye dead in sin? I will put my spirit upon you, and ye shall live. Here is not only a political, but spiritual resurrection, and to have political and spiritual thus joined together is a great mystery.

God will not only work this deliverance which shall be wonderful in respect of the work itself, but shall be wonderful in the way, and manner in which it is done. It shall be done at once. It is not so with other nations: when did God ever convert a nation at once? but when the time of the Jews conversion comes, it shall be at once. So that as the work is wonderful, so the manner is wonderful. " Before Zion travailed, she brought forth." (Isa. lxvi. 7, 8.) Here is a great and sudden salvation foretold which God will work for his people. It is said in the Revelations, that the woman being with child travailed crying, being in pain to be delivered, that is, the Gentile converts. But here is a being delivered without pain. And this the prophet speaks of as a wonderful thing, the earth being made to bring forth in a day, and a nation being born at once.

And the means that bring this about, are wonderful. The first means of their conversion, shall be a sign from heaven; by the appearing of Christ. " Then shall appear the sign of the Son of man in Heaven, and then shall all the tribes of the earth mourn." (Matt. 24.) Some understand this of the wonderful manifestation of Christ in order to the Jews conversion,

and Rev. xi. 19, may give some light to it. It is
said there, that " the temple of God was opened in heaven, and there was seen in the temple, the ark of the
covenant; by this ark Christ is to be understood."
Now the ark of the testament is seen in heaven at the
sounding of the seventh trumpet. Then shall Christ
visibly appear, and at the beginning of this trumpet
shall the Jews be converted. So that it seems that
the conversion of the Jews, whenever it shall come to
pass, will not be effected only by the ordinary means of
preaching the Gospel, but by some wonderful vision
from heaven. And that which seems to confirm this
notion, is the manner of St. Paul's conversion. God
seems to set up St. Paul's conversion who was a Jew,
for a type and pattern of their conversion. " For this
cause, saith he, I obtained mercy, that in me first
Christ Jesus might shew forth all long suffering, for a
pattern to them, who should hereafter believe on him
to life everlasting." Why doth Paul say, that in me
Christ might shew a pattern ? it must refer to the
manner of his conversion, which began by a bodily sight
of Christ. A vision from heaven converted Paul.
Christ thus appeared to him, to convert him, that he
might be for a pattern of God's grace, and of the manner of God's working upon the Jews ; for it is not to
the Gentiles, they are not called after this pattern ;
but it is to them that should hereafter believe, that is
the Jews, that did not believe now, but abode in unbelief, but hereafter they should be brought in, and be
brought in, in this manner as St. Paul was brought in,
viz., by a sign from heaven. And this makes the
manner of their conversion wonderful, though their
conversion may be completed by the gospel, yet it

shall be begun by a light from heaven; " they shall look to me whom they pierced and mourn." " Behold he comes in the clouds and every eye shall see him and they also which pierced him."

Besides it will be wonderful, as being contrary to expectation. That which comes to pass contrary to faith and hope and expectation is very wonderful. How few believe and look for the salvation of the Jews. Yet there is no one truth, more abundantly attested by Scripture, a thing spoken of by all the prophets.

Again, it will be wonderful because of their great averseness, and unpersuadableness to own Christ to be the Messiah. There are none so hardened against Christ as the Jews are. It is easier to convert a Heathen or Mahometan to Christ than a Jew, therefore their conversion will be very wonderful.

IV. But I shall come now to some application of this truth. Is it so that the Jews shall be so wonderfully converted and brought home to Christ? Then let us consider what is our duty incumbent on us from this great truth.

1. It behoves us to search into these things, and labour to understand them. Paul calls the conversion and salvation of Israel, a " mystery, and he would not have us to be ignorant of it." (Rom. xi. 25.) And indeed it is a great mystery that ever such a people as this, should be owned of God. A people that put away the gospel from them, that killed the prophets, and persecuted the Apostles, that murdered and killed the Lord Jesus and his followers. Now that such a people, so vile, and sinful, and blind and hardened, and cruel, should ever be converted to Christ, and become the Church and people of God in the world, is a wonderful

thing. And indeed there be many mysteries depend upon it. The fulness of the Gentiles is a great mystery, and that depends upon it. The breaking out of light in the evening is a great mystery, and that depends upon it. It is therefore a blessed thing to understand this mystery.

Again there is a promise, that they that study them shall understand them. Daniel is commanded to shut up and seal the word to the time of the end; and then many shall run to and fro, and knowledge shall increase, therefore mark the command in Rev. xxii. not to seal but to unseal; " seal not the sayings of the prophecy of this Book for the time is at hand." The nearer these things are to accomplishment the greater light will God give to the understanding of them.

Besides we do not know how to pray without this knowledge ; God hath nothing else to do in this world, but to make good his word. Time shall end, and the world shall be no more, when once God hath fulfilled his word. Now if we do not understand these things, how can we suit our prayers to the designs of God ?

We may fall short or shoot over or wide, if we do not understand these things.

And therefore to profit in this knowledge, labour

(1.) For sincerity of heart and uprightness of your whole walk with God. " The upright in the way are his delight," and to these he reveals his mind. " Who is wise, and he shall understand these things." (Hos. xiv. 9.) Daniel was greatly beloved, and what great discoveries did God make to Daniel. John was the beloved disciple, and what revelations did God make to John of all things that should be to the end of the world ! " Thus the secret of the Lord is with them that fear him." (Psa. xxv. 14.)

(2.) Again, there must be a diligent use of all means designed to this end. Knowledge comes not only by immediate Revelation, and inspiration, but by a wise comparing the word and the works of God together. Therefore—

(3.) Study the word of God. This gives light.— It was Daniel's practice.—He understood by books the number of years that he would accomplish concerning the desolation of Jerusalem; and then he set himself to pray. We cannot direct our prayers aright in this matter, if we do not understand these things.

2. And to this add another duty, it is not enough to understand it, but we must believe it—God hath said it, and therefore we ought to believe it. " Behold, O my people, I will open your graves," &c. And the gospel is express and plain. " The receiving of them shall be life from the dead," (Rom. xi. 15,) and the 26, " And so all Israel shall be saved, as it is written, there shall come out of Zion the deliverer and shall turn away ungodliness from Jacob, &c."

3. And if you believe this, then have bowels for them. Let them be the object of our pity and prayer; never any needed it more, for they are the most miserable people in the world, whether you respect their sins or judgment. Their sins are of all the greatest, and their judgments of all the saddest, not only outward and temporal, but inward and spiritual. No mind so blind, no will so obstinate, no heart so hard, as the poor Jew's. And this hath been their case for many ages

together. They have no Christ, for they have re-
nounced him, they have no God for there can be no
God without Christ.

And if you have bowels to pity them, then pray for
them. Beg earnestly of God to hasten their conversion
follow the example of the great Apostle, " My heart's
desire, and prayer to God for Israel is, that they may
be saved." What God makes the matter of his promise,
we ought to make the matter of our prayer. Now
God hath promised that the Jews shall be converted
therefore, let us pray that God would make this
promise good, and hasten it in his time.

I would press the duty by one argument, and that
is this. This duty of prayer for the conversion of the
Jews ought to be on our heart, because of the great
peace that will issue thereupon. Peace is a sweet thing,
—it is a blessing all court and desire,—it is a blessing
God hath bestowed upon us after a long and expen-
sive war, and we are called this day to bless God for
this peace, and blessed be God that hath wrought peace
for the nation.

But let us not stay here.

The peace of Christ's times, is better than the peace
we have now. God hath returned our Prince in peace,
but what will it be when the great Prince of Peace
cometh. God hath made him an instrument to settle the
nation. O ! what will it be, when Christ shall come
to settle the nation ! When Christ's kingdom shall
come and be set up in the world, it will be other peace
than this, more universal and more durable. There
are three things will make it such. Righteousness,
Love, and Union.

(1.) Then shall be times of great righteousness, for it

is the character of the new heaven and earth, that in them dwells righteousness, (2 Peter iii. 13.) Truly how there is but little righteousness, but then there shall be much. " Thy people shall be all righteous." Then shall be righteous rulers. No throne of iniquity to establish iniquity by a law. All civil government in that day, shall be administered in righteousness. " I will make her Officers peace, and her Exactors righteousness." Princes shall be righteous Princes; Judges shall be righteous Judges. " Judgment shall run down like water, and righteousness like a mighty stream." And when this righteousness thus takes place, that must needs be a place of peace. Oh ! what a blessed world of peace will that be, peace with righteousness ! " The fruit of righteousness shall be peace."

(2.) Then shall be times of great love and affection. Never such a world for love as shall be in the days of the Jews' conversion, for then shall be a great effusion of the spirit, and one of the fruits of the spirit is love ; not only love to God and Christ and the truth, but to all saints, to all that love God. The Apostle makes a defect of this grace in the church, an evident character of a carnal frame, wherever it is. " Ye are yet carnal, whereas there is envying and strife and division, among you, are ye not carnal?" He appeals to their own consciences, who knew that these were the manifest marks of the flesh. But in that day these shall cease. No hurting or destroying in all the Holy mountain. The devil with his cloven foot is got into the churches of Christ, and he makes sad work there, and that is the reason there is so little love. But then all this shall cease, for

(3.) Then shall be a time of great union, and that both in judgment and affection, one heart and one way : and the holiness of that day shall heal all the wounds which are now made by the pride and darkness of men's spirits; and the present rents and divisions shall then end in a blessed union. Now we are at that pass, that the people of God speak just as if there was a confusion of languages, but then they shall be of one lip, and one language, and a pure one too. " Then will I turn to the people a pure language, that they may call upon the name of the Lord, and serve him with one consent." " In that day there shall be one Lord, and his name one." Is not his name one now ? Yes, in itself, he is a God of truth, that is his name ; but while there be different ways of profession and each party entitles Christ to his particular way, one saith, "here is Christ," and another, " there is Christ." But in that day there shall be no more of this, for then shall the Lord be one, and his name one ; that is, all shall be united in the same mind, and shall own God in the same truth and way of worship, and so his name shall be one. There shall be such a unity in God's people in judgment and affection and practice, as shall cause all names of distinction to cease; for then Jews and Gentiles shall be one, one in affection, one sheepfold under Christ, all brought into one body under Christ one shepherd, and have one hope, and one God and one heaven at last. O, what a blessed union shall that be ! and the time that will abound with such love and union, must needs be a time of blessed peace. In Psalm lxxii., which is a Psalm of Christ's kingdom and reign, it is said,—" In his days shall the righteous flourish, and abundance of peace, as long as the moon endures." Then shall not only be peace, but abundance of peace.

Peace with man we have in part now, no more war. But then shall be peace for ever, " they shall beat their swords into ploughshares, and their spears into pruning hooks, nation shall not lift up sword against nation, nor shall they learn war any more." There shall be peace from persecution and sufferings. "Princes shall no more oppress my people." (Ezek. xlv. 8.) " Violence shall no more be heard in thy land." Therefore in Rev. vii. 9, 10, you read of a great multitude of all nations, standing before the throne, clothed in white robes, and palms in their hands, and they cried with a loud voice, saying, " Salvation to our God." Here are three things, that set out the great peace, that shall be in Christ's times—they are clothed with white, in token of peace,—with palms in their hands in token of victory,—and they sung salvation, in token of peace and safety.

Oh ! what a blessed time will this be ! But you will say will this peace last ? yes. It is not like a peace with France, that a treacherous person may break upon the next occasion.—No ! this is a lasting peace ; " for in his day (that is in Christ's day,) shall the righteous flourish, and abundance of peace so long as the moon endureth;" and " of the increase of his government and peace there shall be no end."

TWELVE SERMONS

ON THE

FEARFULNESS OF FALLING INTO THE HANDS OF

THE LIVING GOD.

SERMON I.

" It is a fearful thing to fall into the hands of the living God."—Heb. x. 31.

THE Apostle having, in the foregoing part of this epistle, been exalting Christ above Moses, and the Gospel worship above the Mosaical, and having thereupon been pressing them to faith in Christ, and a constancy in the profession of the Gospel; he proceeds by way of motive, to shew them the danger of Apostacy, and of contempt of the Gospel, from the heinous nature of the sin, and the severity of the punishment due thereunto, and that of all sinners God would be most severe in judging Apostates: and having done this, he winds up his arguments with an elegant expression, which puts a great emphasis upon what he had been urging in this matter, and that in the words of the text: " It is a fearful thing to fall into the hands of the living God."

In the words before the text, the Apostle gives us a distinct account of God's dealing with man, under the law and under the Gospel, and the difference between the one and the other in 28 and 29 verses. " He that

despised Moses Law died without mercy, of how much
sorer punishment shall he be thought worthy, who
hath trodden under foot the Son of God, and hath accounted the blood of the covenant, wherewith he was
sanctified, an unholy thing, and hath done despite to
the Spirit of Grace." Here the sin of apostacy is set
out as the highest offence against the gospel imaginable; and as the offence is, so also is the punishment;
for here is the greatest punishment threatened against
it: the offence is described in three particulars; tread-
ing under foot the Son of God; accounting the blood
of the covenant an unholy thing; and doing despite to
the Spirit of Grace. The punishment threatened is
not positively expressed, but comparatively described;
and the comparison is between the punishment of sins
under the Law of Moses, and the law of Christ; and
as sins against the Law of Christ are greater than sins
against the Law of Moses, so is the punishment. The
punishment for the breach of Moses' Law was corporeal,
but the punishment for the breach of Christ's Law is
spiritual and eternal; he that broke Moses' law fell into
the hands of a dying man, suffered a temporal death;
but the offence against the gospel brings a man to fall
into the hands of the living God, and so brings him
under eternal death; and this he calls a much sorer
punishment, because the hands of a living God are
infinitely heavier than the hands of a dying man. So
that the words of the text, are brought in by way of inference from what goes before; as if the Apostle had
said, seeing matters stand thus, that gospel sins are
such great sins, therefore let a man look to it; let him
take heed to himself, and consider what he doth, when
he neglects Christ, and slights the tenders of gospel

grace, " for it is a fearful thing to fall into the hands of the living God.

In which words there are three parts.

1. A description of God with respect to the present case, he is the living God.

2. The event of their sin, with respect to this living God, that is, falling into his hands.

3. The nature of it, in the general, the Apostle tells you it is a fearful thing.

There are several observations deducible from the words, (1.) That God is a living God. (2.) That God, this living God, is a God of justice and powerful vengeance, for that is meant by his hands. (3.) That all such as neglect and despise the Gospel shall fall into the hands of this living God. (4.) That property of God, which is the chief object of the faith, and hope, and comfort of believers, is an eternal spring of dread and terror to impenitent sinners, he is the living God. (5.) The dread of the wrath of the living God should prevail upon all that make a profession of the Gospel, to hold fast their profession without declension.

These are all truths of great concernment, but I shall not insist upon these distinctly, the words are in themselves an entire proposition, and I shall consider them as such, and in speaking to them, I shall observe this method.

I. Speak somewhat to this epithet that is given to God, the living God, what the import of it is.

II. Open the notion of falling into his hands.

III. Demonstrate the truth of the text, that it is a fearful thing to fall into the hands of the living God.

IV. To whom it is a matter of such dread.

V. Give you the reasons of the point, and then

VI. Apply it.

I. The term that is given to God here, "the living God," of whom this is spoken, and then, in what sense he is the living God.

1. Of whom this is spoken, "the living God." Who is this title given to in the text? this is applied to God both essentially and personally. *Essentially*, as comprehending each person in the Godhead, the Father, Son, and Holy Ghost, as one God, are called the living God. " My soul thirsteth for God, for the living God." (Psa. xlii. 2.) " We preach to you that you should turn from these vanities to the living God, who made heaven and earth, and all that is therein. (Acts xiv. 15.) " Ye turned from idols to serve the living and true God." (1 Thess. i. 9.)   Now this is spoken of God, not with respect to his personality, but his essence, and so takes in all three persons.

Sometimes this epithet is ascribed to God as *personally* considered, and so it is applied distinctly to each person, to Father, Son, and Spirit.

(1.) Sometimes it is meant of the Father, and intended of Him only. " Thou art Christ, the Son of the living God." (Matt. xvi. 16.) " We believe and are sure that thou art that Christ, the Son of the living God. (John vi. 69.) That must be meant of God the Father.

(2.) Sometimes it is meant only of Jesus Christ, the Son of God, and applied distinctly to him. " We trust in the living God, who is the Saviour of all men." (1 Tim. iv. 10.) And who is this but the Lord Christ?

(3.) Sometimes it is applied to the Holy Ghost, and intended particularly of him. "You are the temple of the living God." (2 Cor. vi. 16.) This is meant of the Holy Ghost, the third person in the Godhead, as appears by comparing it with (1 Cor. vi. 19.) "Know you not that your body is the temple of the Holy Ghost?" in one place you are the temples of the living God, in the other you are the temples of the Holy Ghost, so that the Holy Ghost is the living God. Thus you have the title of the living God given to all the three persons in the Godhead. But in the text I conceive it is used with respect to God, not as the first person only, nor as the second or third, but with respect to all, Father, Son, and Spirit; and therefore it is to be understood in this place, of God essentially, and that in an absolute sense, God as God.

2. In what sense is God said to be the living God?

(1.) In opposition to idols, such as the heathens worshipped. The Psalmist tells us what dumb and dead idols they are. "They are the works of men's hands, they have mouths, but speak not; eyes, but see not; ears, but hear not; hands, but handle not; &c." (Psa. cxv. 4, 5, 6, 7.) Here are two things that put a great contempt upon these gods.

1st. They are made gods, the work of men's hands, it is like to be but a sorry God, that is made by a sorry man; if God make man he becomes a living creature, but if man makes a god, it is like to be but a dead God.

2nd. They are gods with senses, and yet without sense; ears, and yet hear not; eyes, and see not; mouths, and speak not; and what a pitiful God is that which hath all

senses, and yet without any sense ; a blind, deaf, and
dumb god, must needs be a dead god. (Jer. x. 14.)
"His molten image is falsehood, and there is no breath
in them, but the portion of Jacob is not like them,
he is the living God."   ver. 10—16.

(2.) He is the living God originally, as having life
in himself, nay, God not only hath life, but he is life ;
we cannot so properly say that he hath life, as that he
is life, for it is his very essence. The life of God is
the living God; the life of man is another thing, from
man,—it is the bond that knits body and soul
together. But life and God are one, and he is so
both, " a parte ante," and " a parte post," whether you
look backward to what is past, or forward to what is to
come.

1st. Look backward to what is past, and so he is
the living God. He hath always been the living
God : no time can be assigned for the beginning of his being. If we look back we can go no
further than the date of the creation—there time
begins ; " In the beginning God created the heavens
and the earth," in the beginning of time. If we look
further back, we shall lose ourselves in the abyss of
eternity, for all before time is eternity. God did not
begin to be, when he made the world, for as the world
that was made must have a maker, so he that made it
must have a being before it.

2nd. Look forward to what is to come, and so he is
the living God, he is without end. He always was,
always is, and always will be what he is, " for in him
there is no variableness nor shadow of turning." (James
i. 17.) Ye read of mortal gods, " that shall die like
men." (Psalm lxxxii. 6, 7.) But God cannot die—
can eternity expire ? his Godhead is an eternal God-

head, and therefore as he is said to be from everlasting as to his beginning, so he is said to be to everlasting as to his duration. " From everlasting to everlasting thou art God." (Psalm xc. ii.)   The life of God is from eternity to eternity, he would not be God if he were not the living God, therefore the Apostle elegantly saith of him.   " He only hath immortality." (1 Tim. vi. 16.)   How comes this " only " in ? are there no beings immortal but only God ? are not angels immortal ? is not the soul of man immortal ? True ! but they are not immortal as God is, they are not immortal by nature, but merely by gift and grant. It is as easy for God to strip them of it, as to invest them with it; nay, it is impossible but that they should perish, if God should withdraw the power from preserving them, which he exerted in creating them; so that they are not immortal of themselves, but by dependance on divine influences.   It is not essential, but by donation, so that the immortality of saints and angels, is but a precarious thing.   But God is immortal of himself; He is immortality, fixed in his own being, none gave life to Him, and none can take it from Him : and in this sense it is that the Apostle says, " He only hath immortality," and thus He is the living God, as having life originally in himself.

(3.) He is the living God communicatively, as giving life.   There is no life any being partakes of, but what is derived from the living God, " he gives to all, life and breath and all things."   (Acts xvii. 25.) Therefore he is called the fountain of life. " He is the fountain of life." (Psalm xxxvi. 9.)   He doth not say of this or that life, but of all life, the life of vegetation in plants, the life of sense in brutes, and the life of reason in man, the life of grace in saints on earth, the life of glory in saints in heaven, all these lives are in God, who is the fountain of life. All the powers in heaven and earth without God cannot give life ; art may imitate living things, but there was never any artist could make things live ; a painter may make the picture of a man, but he cannot put life into it. No, it is the living God, who is the only life-giving God.

(4.) He is the living God, with respect to his eternal power, whereby he is able to avenge the sins of men, and this is the special reason why he is called the living God in the text. He that is the fountain of life, must needs be the spring of power. His power must needs be eternal, because his life is eternal, and this is that which puts a terror on all the attributes of God, which are employed against sinners. His power, his justice, his wrath, would not be so dreadful if it were not the power, the justice, the wrath of the living God ; and as God's life is a continued act in himself, so it being attributed to him with respect to his wrath upon sinners, it doth import his continued hand therein without intermission or cessation ; as the soul is immortal in the duration of it, and as the stain of sin is eternal in the nature of it, so whilst God lives, and thy soul lives, thou must bear the punishment of it, if thou fall into his hand.

You see in what sense God is said to be the living God ; now that he is thus the living God, I might make out by divers mediums. He is the living God.

(1.) In that he is said to have "life in himself." (John v. 26.) "The Father hath life in himself," that is, it is in him originally and radically, and therefore eternally ; he that hath life in himself, and from himself, cannot cease to be; what he never received, he can never lose; he that hath life in himself cannot cease to be, for he doth necessarily exist, and what doth necessarily exist, must exist from eternity.

(2.) His perfection proves his eternal being, he could not be infinitely perfect, if he were not eternal; nothing more inconsistent with infinite perfection than a finite duration; being infinite, nothing can be added to him, or taken from him.

(3.) It is evident in that he is the first and supreme cause of all things. " I am the first and the last, the Alpha and the Omega." (Rev. i. 11.) Now that which is the first, cannot begin to be, for then was not that the first, and it cannot cease to be, for then it were not the last: if God be the first cause of all things, he must be before all things, and therefore from eternity.

(4.) It is evident that there is no such thing as succession in the life of God; his essence knows no such thing as past and to come, and therefore the name that he makes himself known to Moses by, is, " I AM," that is his name; it is not, "I was," for that would intimate as if he now is not, what he was once; nor is it, "I will be," for that would intimate as if he is not yet what he shall be; God hath nothing now which he had not before, nor shall he have any thing hereafter, which he hath not now; if there was any succession in God, he could not be the eternal " I AM." (John viii. 58.) "Before Abraham was I AM:" he hath an eternal duration, he hath all at once, and possesses all things altogether. There is no time past, present or to come with him, and if God be always I AM, then he must be without all succession, for all succession supposes motion, and all motion presupposes a cause, and an effect. Whatever is moved from no being, to a being, or from an imperfect to a more perfect being, has a succession, now God hath nothing in him to be perfected, and therefore he is not capable of any higher degree of being.

(5.) It is evident that he is the living God, in that his dwelling is in eternity. " Thus saith the high and lofty one, that inhabiteth eternity." (Isaiah lvii. 15.) If God inhabit eternity, he must needs be the ever-living God, his dwelling house is eternity, into which none ever did, or can enter but himself. It is true the angels inhabit glory, but they cannot properly be said to inhabit eternity, because there was a time when they were not.—The saints are said to have a "house eternal in the heavens." (2 Cor. v. 1.) But yet the saints cannot be said in glory to inhabit eternity, because they are but finite creatures, though they are glorified creatures. It is proper to none but God to inhabit eternity, therefore he is the living God. In this the life of God differs from the life of angels and the souls of men; the angels are living angels, and glorified spirits are living spirits, but there was a time when they were not so; though their being shall never cease yet there was a time when their being began; duration of being among creatures differs from their being, for all creatures may cease from their being if it be the pleasure of God; therefore they are not durable in essence; and though angels and the souls of men may be said to be everlasting as a perpetual life is communicated to them by God, yet that cannot be called their own eternity, because such a duration is not simply necessary or essential to them, but depending upon the pleasure of another; but now God is his own eternity; the eternity of God is nothing else but the duration of God. " Thou art the same, and thy years shall have no end." (Psalm cii. 27.) If eternity were not in the essence of God, there would be somewhat which were not God, necessary to perfect God, therefore eternity is essential to his being and life.

But here may an objection be made, is not the life of God measured by days and years, and what comes under the measure of time, is a bounded being, and hath but a finite duration? I answer, it is true the Spirit of God doth in Scripture set out the life of God by days and years, which are the measure of finite beings, but we are to look upon his so doing as divine condescension to comply with the narrowness of our capacities, that thereby we might be fitted to form such conceptions of God, as our finite understandings are capable of reaching, but we are not to conceive that God is bounded in his being, or measured by time, or that there is a succession of days and years in the life of God. How often is God described in Scripture as having human parts, as hands and eyes, and the like. Shall we therefore suppose him to be comprehended in a body and parts as man is? This would be most absurd, but these are only to help our conceptions of God's glorious nature and operations, and so it is in this matter; therefore things spoken of God after the manner of men, must be so understood as becomes his nature and being, which is every way perfect; and therefore though days and years are ascribed to God, yet it is in such a way and manner, as that his eternity is pointed at even in

those measures of time. (Job. xxxvi. 26.) says Elihu,
" Behold God is great and we know him not, neither
can the number of his years be searched out:" his years
are of such a number, as that they are innumerable,
therefore the years that are not expressible, express
the being of God : this speaks infiniteness and eternity, for we may easily search out the number of the
years, of all the creatures in the world, yea, the
years of the angels in heaven may be numbered,
but we cannot search out the number of God's
years.   " The heavens shall wax old, like a garment,
as a vesture shalt thou change them, and they shall be
changed, but thou art the same, and thy years shall
have no end." (Psa. cii. 26, 27)   Mark here, the
world hath its years, and God hath his ; the years of
the world wax old, but God is no older than he was
before the world was ; he is called " the Ancient of
days," yet his days do not make him ancient, years make
no change in God, but he is for ever the same, therefore
it is said, " Thy years have no end."   His life must
needs be eternal, whose years have no end.

II. Thus you see in what sense God is the living
God, and the demonstration of it, that it is so ; I come
now to the second thing to be opened, and that is of
falling into the hands of God.

1. What is meant by, the hands of God ?

2. What is meant by falling into his hands ?

1. What is meant by the hands of God ? this phrase
as applied to God is metaphorical, and must be so
understood ; for as God hath no years properly, so he
hath no hands ; as his being is not measured by time,
nor is it comprehended by parts and members ; as he
lives without years, so he works without hands ; there

is a figure in the words, which is when God doth as it were stoop to us, in expressing heavenly mysteries to our capacities, under human metaphors which are suited to our understandings. Others call it by a metaphor which signifies that that which is properly agreeable to the creature, is by some similitude transferred to God; and this is very common in Scripture to speak of God after the manner of men, and by bodily things to set out the spiritual life of God; the Scriptures often use these kinds of figures, because they are so much proportioned to our senses; therefore the Casuists say, " Divine light never descends without a covering;" thus God is said to have eyes and ears. (Psalm. xxxiv. 15.) Now God hath neither eyes nor ears ! but by these things he signifies to us his omniscience, that he knows all things ; he is said to have bowels, in (Jer. xxx. 20.) God hath no bowels, but the expression is to set forth the tenderness of God's nature and condescension; he is said to have a face, (Psa. xxxi. 16.) to set forth his love and grace ; thus God is sometimes said to have feet. (Psa. lxxiv. 3.) "Lift up thy feet to the perpetual desolations ;" which is to denote his speed and swiftness, to succour his Church in distress; and thus he is said to have hands, as in the text. Now the hands of God signify very variously in Scripture;

(1.) Sometimes by it is meant the Spirit of God. " The hand of the Lord was with them (speaking of the apostle's ministry), and a great number believed," (Acts xi. 21.) a mighty presence of God's Spirit by their ministry, converting many. So it is said of Ezekiel, " the word of the Lord came to him, and the hand of the Lord was upon him." (Ezek. i. 3.)

(2.) Sometimes the hand of the Lord signifies a right to dispose of things and persons, and so it is said of Herod and Pilate, about the crucifying of Christ, that "they did whatever his hand and counsel determined to be done ;" intimating that there was a divine disposal in making Christ an offering for sin : so the word is used, where David saith, (Psa. xxxi. 15.) " My times are in thy hand," that is, at God's disposal.

(3.) Sometimes the hand of God, notes the power of God. " Thy hands have made me and fashioned me." (Job x. 8.)   So (Gen. xlix. 24.) " the arms of his hands were made strong by the hand of the mighty God of Jacob;" that is by his power; and indeed the hand of God doth more frequently in Scripture signify the power of God, than any thing else, for the hand is the emblem of strength and power; to put a thing into the hands of another, is to put it into his power; so that grant of God to Satan is to be understood. (Job. i. 12) " Behold (saith God to Satan) all he hath is in thine hand," and it is often used so. (Isa. lix. i.) " The Lord's hand is not shortened, that it cannot save," his hand is not shortened, that is, the power of God is no ways lessened or abated : now as the hand of God is put for the power of God, so it is taken three ways in Scripture : there is his protecting hand, his chastening hand, and his revenging hand.

1st. His protecting hand, by which he doth preserve and secure his people from all hazards and dangers. " No man is able to pluck them out of my Father's hand." (John x. 29.)   The preserving of grace calls for the hand of God as much as working grace; no less power is seen in preserving it, than in the first

planting it. It is this hand of God that breaks
the violence of temptatation, that breaks the power
of Satan, and bruises him under our feet; this
it is, that breaks the power of indwelling lust; this
kills the reluctance of the flesh against the spirit : as it
was a mighty power that brought your soul into a
state of grace, so it is the same mighty power that
preserves you in that state." (Eph. i. 19.)

2nd. There is his correcting hand, by which God
doth chastise for sin; this is the hand that lay so
heavy upon David. (Psa. xxxii. 4.) " Day and night
thy hand was heavy upon me." It was the correction, the chastisement of God that was heavy upon
him, and this chastising hand of God is sometimes
more immediate, and sometimes more mediate; sometimes more immediate, when God afflicts by himself
alone, without the appearance or intervening of second
causes, and that may seem to be intended by Satan,
where he saith to God concerning Job, " Put forth
now thine hand, and touch him," deal with him in an
immediate way, and thou shalt see what he is, he will
curse thee to thy face. God doth sometimes send an
affliction in such an immediate way, that man cannot
see which way it comes ; therefore it is called creating
of evil ; creation is out of nothing, when there is
nothing out of which it is made ; so God oftentimes
creates an evil, bringing it upon a man when there is no
appearance of second causes, but it comes immediately
from the hands of God, like that in Job xx. 26. " A
fire not blown shall consume him," an immediate dealing of God upon his conscience. Sometimes these
chastisements are more mediate, yet it is God's hand,
though the creature's hand only be seen ; yet it is God's

hand that is felt; and so it is the hand of the creature in, the hand of God, and so Job owns it; " the Lord gives, and the Lord takes away." It was the Sabæans that robbed him, but he saw the hand of God upon the hand of man, the Lord takes; so David prays : (Psa. xvii. 13, 14.) " Deliver my soul from the wicked, which is thy sword, from men which are thy hand." Wicked men are God's sword ; though they cut, it is God strikes ; they are the rod of correction in the hand of God.

3rd. There is the revenging hand of God, the hand of his wrath, by which he doth execute judgment upon sinners, without remedy, and without mercy; and this is the hand that the text points at. " It is a fearful thing to fall into the hands of the living God." It is not meant of his protecting or chastening, but his revenging hand ; the first is sweet and comfortable, the second is bitter, but profitable, but the last is neither comfortable nor profitable, but amazing and fearful. It is a fearful thing to fall into the hands of the living God.

Thus you see what we are to understand by the hands of God, his revenging hand, his wrath upon impenitent sinners at the last day.

2. What is meant by falling into his hands ; as hands are ascribed to God by way of metaphor, so this expression of falling into his hands, must be taken metaphorically too, and the metaphor is taken from one that falls into the hands of his enemy that lays in wait for him, or it may be taken from a poor debtor that owes more than he can pay, and cannot look his creditors in the face, but shrinks from corner to corner, but is taken at last; such a thing as this is falling into the hands of God; now man goes on in his sin

securely, and God is quiet and lets him alone, and they speak peace to themselves in sin; but when God's hand takes hold of judgment, (Deut. xxxii. 41.) "then he will render vengeance to his enemies, and reward them that hate Him," he will then right himself upon sinners for all the wrongs they have done him all their lives long. Now this expression of falling into the hands of the living God, is not to be so understood as if sinners were not in his hands now already; for thus all are in his hands, all are under his power; but this falling into the hands of God, in short implies three things.

(1.) Having to do with God immediately,

(2.) Necessarily, and

(3.) Eternally.

(1.) Immediately, and that in a twofold respect:

1st. Without a Christ to mediate for us.

2nd. Without an instrument to convey his wrath to us.

1st. Without Christ as mediator. The privilege of every believer in the great day of judgment is this; he hath a Christ to plead for him, to stand by him, to manage his cause, and interpose between him and the severity of God's justice. Matt. x. 32. "He that confesses me before men, him will I confess before my Father which is in heaven," I will own him for one of mine; this is a blessed thing to have a mediator at God's right hand, when we appear before the bar of God: but what will become of unbelieving sinners, that have to do with God immediately, that must appear there without a Christ! they have slighted him here, and then he will deny them; so that sinners in that day shall fall into the hands of God immediately.

2nd. God will be the executioner of his own wrath in that day; he will never more use the ministry of the creatures to inflict his wrath, but he will do it by himself. We read of unquenchable fire, and fire and brimstone, outward darkness, which is nothing else but the wrath and vengeance of God; here God makes use of second causes, and acts by instruments and means, and these are terrible when the wrath of God is conveyed by them; but alas! the wrath of the creature is not to be compared with the wrath of God himself; the soul of man is of a vast capacity, and can take in more than all the creatures can convey, either of good or evil. No creature goodness can fill the soul of man; it is not in the power of all the creatures of the world to satisfy the soul. If it should drink up the rivers of all created good at one draught, this could not quench its thirst; nothing can fill the soul of man, but God himself; a boundless appetite cannot be satisfied with a finite good: and as no created good can satisfy him, so no evil from the creature can fill the soul; as the soul is the receptacle of more good than is found in all the creatures; so it is capable of more misery and anguish than all the creatures can inflict upon it; therefore God will in the eternal world no more use the ministry of creatures, but will do all by his own hands; God can make the least creature a judgment, even lice and flies, if they come upon God's errand upon earth, they are dreadful; but God, hath infinitely more wrath than the creature can contain; God cannot by creatures (to speak reverently) put forth all his wrath; but when the sinner falls into the hands of the living God, then he hath to do with God alone, with God immediately; "Who knows

the power of thine anger !" (Psa. xc. 11.) You may
guess a little at it by what the prophet saith. (Nah.
i. 5, 6.) " The mountains quake at him, and the hills
melt, and the earth is burnt up at his presence, yea,
the world, and all that dwell therein ; who can stand before his indignation ? who can abide in the fierceness of
his anger ? his fury is poured out like fire, and the rocks
are thrown down by him." What a dreadful thing
is it to have to do with God immediately, and this is
implied by falling into the hands of the living God.

(2.) It implies having to do with God necessarily;
he cannot escape nor shun him ; you read of them that
cried unto the rocks and mountains to fall upon them,
and cover them from the wrath of God, but they could
not help them ; they must necessarily have to do with
God, and that is intended by the Apostle, where he
saith, (speaking of the eternal state of saints and sinners in the other world,) "God shall be all in all;" a man
hath to do with God only in the other world. In heaven
God is all in all to the saints ; in hell God is all in all to
those souls in misery; falling into the hands of God
implies having to do with him necessarily.

(3.) It implies having to do with God everlastingly,
for he is the living God, and if you fall into his hands,
you must be the eternal prisoner of his wrath ; as long
as God lives you are miserable, and damned, and undone ; for he is the living God, and as long as God
lives, so long the sinner shall live under the weight of
his wrath and vengeance ; for God holds the sinner in
life to that end, that he may bear his wrath as long as
he is the living God ; God lives for ever and therefore
the believer's heaven shall be for ever, and because he
lives for ever, the sinner's hell shall be for ever. His

being the living God, is matter of as great terror to them that hate him, as it is comfort to them that love and fear him; a mortal man cannot extend punishments beyond this life, when they have killed the body, they can do no more. (Luke xii. 4.) We are mortal and therefore cannot suffer long here ; and they that trouble and persecute us are mortal, and therefore they cannot make us suffer long here, but the life of God is eternal, and therefore he can punish us eternally; so Christ saith of him. " He can cast body and soul into hell for ever."

O ! that you would seriously consider this ; that God is a living God; think of this when thou art about to sin,—this is done in the sight of the living God, I must appear and give an account of this before the living God; It would be an awakening thing if we would but let this thought dwell in our minds, that God is a living God, and that you must have to do with this living God for ever, either in heaven or hell. Nothing is so dreadful to a soul under wrath as to consider that God lives for ever; it is that which puts a terror into all those attributes that are engaged against the soul ; the justice of God and the wrath of God are terrible, and the power of God which makes them so, is made more terrible by its being eternal. It is his power that makes his justice terrible, and eternity that makes his power dreadful. The eternity of hell makes hell more dreadful than his power ; his power makes it sharp and smarting, his life makes it everlasting, and everlastingness is the sharpest sting in hell's misery. As none can convey good with such a perpetuity, so none can inflict evil with such a lastingness as the living God, therefore it is a fearful thing to fall into the hands of

God, because it is into the hands of the living God;
and O ! that God would persuade sinners to consider
these things ;   O ! that you would be awakened :   these
things are of great use for conviction, if God makes us
so wise as to lay them to heart.   Dare therefore to
live in sin no longer, for if you die in those sins, you
must have to do with God immediately, for then there
will be none to interpose, no Christ to save you ; you
must have to do with God necessarily, for God in that
state is all in all ; and you must have to do with God
eternally, for he is the living God.

SERMON II.

" It is a fearful thing to fall into the hands of the living God."—(Heb. x. 31.)

I come now to give you some demonstration of this truth; that to fall into the hands of the living God is a very fearful thing, and I will make it out by a variety of demonstrations.

I. From that which is the chief subject of this misery, and that is the soul of man. When a man falls into the hands of the living God, it is the soul that is the chief subject of this misery; and I shall speak to this gradually in *six* things.

1. That the soul of man being by nature a spirit, and spirit of an intelligent order, and a spirit assimilated to God in its subsistence and faculties, and bearing his image, it must for that reason be very sensible of all the impressions of God upon it, and of all the weight of his wrath; the eye is not so sensible when touched, as the spirit of a man is of the least touch of God's indignation. It is that which doth immediately wound the soul, and a wounded spirit who can bear? wounds in the flesh are tolerable, because they are without, but inward wounds, which touch the spirit of a man, they are unsufferable; who can bear them?

2. The soul is capable of the greatest good, or the greatest evil.

(1.) It is receptive of more goodness than is in all the creatures in the world ; all present comforts are too little to fill it, for the desires of the soul are boundless, and how can bounded enjoyments satisfy boundless desires ?   Nothing but an infinite good can fill the soul of man.

(2.) It is receptive of more evil and misery, than all the creatures under heaven can put into it, therefore no sufferings of any kind from a finite hand can make a man truly miserable.   The soul is made for God, and made to be filled only with God, and that either in a way of love and blessedness, or in a way of wrath and vengeance : all that is called blessedness in heaven, all the pleasures of that state can never fill the soul without the immediate presence and enjoyment of God there : so in hell, all the miseries of that state can never fill the soul with evil ; they cannot destroy the well-being of it, and this is the reason why Christ bids us not to fear man in the height of his wrath and rage, because they can only kill the body ; if they could kill the soul as God can, then they were to be feared as God is, for that is the very reason why Christ once and again calls us to fear God, because he can cast body and soul into hell.

3. Inferior spirits to him who is the Father of Spirits, can greatly vex, and trouble the spirit of man ; when Saul had but one evil spirit from the Lord sent to him, how was his soul terrified, though in the midst of the enjoyments of a kingdom ; and though Paul had been rapt up into the third heavens, and had such ravishing views of the glorious objects there, as con-

firmed his faith, and highly fortified his spirits; yet at the buffetting of one angel, how is he distressed and disturbed, that he is not able to bear it? But Christ tells him for his support, that his grace should be sufficient for him. Now if it be so terrible to be vexed and set upon by spirits that are but creatures, what is it to fall into the hands of that Great Spirit, who is God over all? These spirits have nothing to do with us beyond this world; they are the rulers of the darkness of this world, and there their power ends. When Christ gives up his kingdom, then the damned spirits shall rule no more. In the eternal state we are in the hands of God; and if it be so terrible to be in the hands of these infernal spirits, what is it to fall into the hands of the living God?

4. These souls that fall into the hands of the living God fall into them in sin, and so are made the everlasting subjects of wrath and misery; sin makes them vessels of wrath, by fitting them for destruction. (Rom. ix. 22.) Take a barrel, and it will burn as it is wood, but if it be full of pitch or any combustible matter, it will burn more readily; it is sin that makes hell so hot; it is sin that kindles wrath, and wrath is a devouring fire.

5. The wrath of God in the future state falls chiefly upon the soul; though body and soul both shall be subjects of God's wrath; in that day both shall bear their parts in suffering; as they have sinned together, so they shall suffer together; but yet the soul bears the greatest part of God's wrath, having been the greatest instrument in sin.

6. In that state of the soul, all the affections that are renovating and refreshing shall utterly cease, and

those affections that serve to heighten our torment shall be drawn forth. There are in the soul some affections that do greatly relieve and support a man in the utmost misery, as joy, delight, and hope; when these are kept up in act, they bring in a great deal of delight and support under the most burdensome evil in the world; but when the soul falls into the hands of the living God, these affections cease; Hope, that perishes, joy and delight are cut off for ever, but on the other hand, those affections are drawn forth, which do greatly aggravate the torment; the soul shall then be filled with grief and sorrow, with weeping and wailing for ever. In that state the eyes of the soul shall be always waking to behold their misery. This then is one demonstration of this truth, that it is a fearful thing to fall into the hands of the living God. It is evident from that which is the chief subject of this misery, the soul of man. No misery equal to soul misery—no sufferings to soul sufferings; "now is my soul troubled," saith Christ, and that was the greatest of all his troubles.

II. That it is a fearful thing to fall into the hands of the living God is evident from hence, that the withdrawings of God from the souls of believers here in this world are so dreadful: let God but hide his face, and withdraw from his people, and suspend the wonted discoveries of his love, and it is as an hell to the soul, and if so, what is it to feel the weight of the whole of his wrath to eternity?

Let me in speaking to this, shew you,

1. What this withdrawing of God is.

2. Lay down some conclusions concerning this withdrawing from believers here.

3. Make it out that, to be under these withdrawings of God is a very dreadful thing, and then to fall into the hands of God must needs be so.

1. What is this withdrawing of God? It must not be understood of his divine presence in the common and general notion of it; for there is no coming or going, no approaching nearer or drawing farther off, in regard of that. There is an immensity in the divine essence; in this sense God is every where present, in all places, in all persons, in the wicked as well as the good, as much in hell as in heaven; hence that of David, (Psalm cxxxix. 7, 8.) "Whither shall I flee from thy presence? If I ascend up into heaven thou art there, if I make my bed in hell, thou art there;" God is as much in one place as another; if a man were in the highest heavens, he is no nearer to the essence of God than in the lowest hell: God cannot withdraw this presence of his, from any creature for one moment; for he were not God if he were not every where; therefore when God is said to withdraw and hide himself, or to desert a soul, it must have no respect to his essence at all, for when God embraces us in the arms of his mercy, his essence is no nearer us, than when he hides his face from us; and therefore this withdrawing and hiding of God from a soul refers to a more special and peculiar presence, to wit, the presence of his grace, his quickening or comforting presence, and such a withdrawing is that of God from his people, and these are either absolute or limited, either in appearance or reality.

Sometimes God withdraws his gracious presence absolutely and really, and no believer can be the object

of this his withdrawing; thus he forsakes the fallen
angels, and thus he forsakes reprobate sinners : but no
believer can be thus forsaken, God may seem to withdraw absolutely, but it is but in appearance ; a soul may
draw sad conclusions as Asaph did, that " God hath
cast him off for ever," (Psa. lxxvii. 7.) But it cannot be,
for the soul that says it, will see cause to unsay it
again, as Asaph did (xth verse,) " this is mine infir-
mity." But then there is a limited withdrawing of God
which is personal and momentary, and in this sense,
God may be said to withdraw from his own people: concerning these withdrawings, I would hint *four* things.

(1.) Sometimes it may be, but as it were so ; as there
is a real withdrawing of God, so there is a seeming
withdrawing. God may be really present when he
seems to be absent; he is many times near us, when
we know; it not, so saith Job, " Lo he goes by me,
and I see him not, he passes on, but I perceive him
not." (Job ix. 11.) Thus Mary seeks and weeps
for Christ, and cries out, " they have taken away my
Lord, and I know not where they have laid him."
(John xx. 13.) And yet Christ at the same instant
was just behind her ; God may be nearest to us when
we think him farthest from us.

(2.) There is a withdrawing of God which respects
only outward comforts ; spiritual influences may be
great, when yet the stream of common mercies may
be dried up ; God many times when he gives least of
the world, gives most of himself, as when the Israelites'
dough was spent, God gave them bread from
heaven.

(3.) There is a withdrawing in regard of spiritual
mercies, and thus God doth sometimes withdraw from

his own people, but then it is more as to comfort, than as to grace. He strengtheneth grace, even when he withholds comfort; our Lord Christ was without the comforting presence of God when he cries out, "Why hast thou forsaken me?" but he was not without his strengthening presence; when he withdraws from the soul, he draws the soul after him, and so he is most in power, when least in appearance.

(4.) There is a forsaking or withdrawing of God as to grace, God doth not only take away his comforting presence, but sometimes in a great measure his quickening presence too. David by the manner of his prayer seems to have lost both these. (Psa. li. 11.) "Take not thy Holy Spirit from me," it implies he had lost his quickening presence," and in verse 12, "Restore unto me the joy of thy salvation," there is his comforting presence. Now when God is said to withdraw his quickening presence, we are to understand it chiefly of such graces as are accessary, rather than such as are absolutely necessary; there are some graces which are for his well-being, and some for his being. Now the quickening wherein a believer's well-being lies may be lost in some measure, but that wherein his being consists cannot be lost; there are some graces which are for the sweetening his way, and some for securing his end; now the quickening of God may be withdrawn from the former when not from the latter, this is the withdrawing of God that is of all the saddest, that can befall any believer in the world, when God withdraws his quickening presence.

2. Now let me premise some conclusions about this withdrawing of God; I do it for the understanding and quieting of believers, lest they should be dejected

at what I shall hereafter speak. There are *eight* conclusions I would lay down about God's withdrawing from his own people.

(1.) That the special approaches and peculiar influences of God which he doth at any time vouchsafe to the soul of any of his, they are pure acts of his will, and are so to be received; they are not natural and necessary, but voluntary and free: his essential presence is necessary, and therefore common to all; but his gracious presence is an act of his will, and therefore the privilege of some only.

(2.) These withdrawings of God from the soul are not to be understood as to the abating of his love, but the suspending the acts of his love; when we say God withdraws and hath forsaken us, it is not meant that he hath taken away his love; the love of God lies either in intention or execution, either in willing good or in working good; now when God withdraws, he doth not cease to will good, for that he cannot do any more than deny himself; when he hath once taken a soul into union with himself, he wills good to that soul to eternity. Now when he is said to withdraw, we are to understand it of the acts of his love, he loves us though he does not show it; God's love may be shut in, but the believer can never be shut out, the believer is still the object of God's love, though he suspend the acts of his love.

(3.) This withdrawing of God from the soul is not of what is necessary to his being, only to his well-being; a believer may want that of God which is convenient to his state, but he shall never want that which is necessary to life; he may be deprived of that without which he cannot have comfort and peace, but he can never be deprived of that without which he cannot live; though he may want that which may make his way comfortable, yet he shall never want that which shall make his end safe ; that word is as stable as heaven itself, " he holds our souls in life," the influences of his good spirit may be restrained, but the presence of his spirit can never be recalled, for this is one of the gifts of God that are without repentance.

(4.) Under the highest divine influences, we cannot be sure of their continuance ; God hath given us no such assurance that our communion shall last always without any interruption, for that were to secure us, that we should never sin, or to leave himself without liberty to shew his dislike of sin when we commit it; for though God hath said, " I will never leave thee, nor forsake thee," that respects the constant continuation of our union, yet it does not warrant the constant enjoyment of our communion, it makes sure to us the support of his grace, but not the comforts of his presence.

(5.) In what degree soever God doth at any time withdraw himself from his people, yet as it is never total without some secret support, so it is never final without some hopes of a return ; it is but for a season, and that season is short; it is " in a little wrath," and that little wrath never lasts long. The sun may set upon a believer's comfort, but it will rise again. Our provocations may make God depart, but if they do, his own compassion will cause him to return.

(6.) These withdrawings of God are consistent with the highest measures and most eminent degrees of grace. Who fuller of grace than the Lord Christ ?

but yet his communion with God was suspended, he was under these withdrawings himself. It is the privilege of saints on earth, to have a perfect lasting union, but it is the privilege of saints in heaven, to have a perfect and lasting communion.

(7.) It is possible that a believer may lose the presence of God, though under the exercise of fear and care to preserve it. Was not this Job's case? " The thing which I greatly feared is come upon me, I was not in safety, nor had I quiet, yet trouble came." (Job iii. 25, 26.) What trouble was this? not only outward trouble, but it was the loss of God's presence which was a thousand times greater trial; and in ver. 23, " Why is light given to a man whose way is hidden?" and God doth this sometimes by pure prerogative, to show us that our privileges are not of merit, but of grace.

(8.) As the presence of God may be lost under the saints' fears and cares to preserve it, so it may not presently be found again, notwithstanding his diligence to recover it; was it not so with Job? " O that I knew where to find him?" (Job xxiii. 3.) Ay, but what means doth he use? all manner of means, as is implied in the 8th and 9th ver. " Behold, I go forward, but he is not there, and backward, but I cannot perceive him; on the left hand, where he works, but I cannot behold him, he hideth himself on the right hand, that I cannot perceive him;" he spared no pains to seek him, but yet he could not for the present enjoy him. This is one of the exercises God is pleased to put his people upon; he hides himself that he may be sought, and yet sometimes when he is sought, he will not presently be found: and this by way of conclusion to prevent misgiving thoughts in any weak Christian, by what I am now to say, I come now

3. To make it out that these withdrawings of God are very bitter things, a heavy burden, a great affliction. Nothing in the world can befall a child of God so afflicting as the withdrawing of God. As communion with God is a good that sweetens all our troubles, so the loss of it is an evil that clouds all our comforts; the loss of another mercy is but a particular evil, it is but blowing out our candle at noon, where we have light enough without it; but the loss of this is like the setting of the sun, by which we are left in the dark, and have no light; no enjoyments can ever make up the loss of God's presence, all other comforts are but creatures, and what are all creatures to be laid in the room of God! It is not the presence of an angel that can stop the fountain of tears, which the absence of Christ sets open. "They have taken away my Lord." No sorrows to a child of God like the loss of communion with God; this I shall make out in five things.

(1.) In that a believer doth account all the communion he hath with God for the present, but a degree of unhappiness and misery, because it is imperfect; and if it is his misery not to enjoy God so much as he would, what is it not to enjoy him at all? If he complains when he is at the stream, what will he do when the stream is cut off? This is the main of a believer's unhappiness, that he hath neither a full nor a fixed state of communion with God in this world; what a sorrow then must it be to lose that little, and to be deprived of his communion with God?

(2.) The general sense of believers evinces this

truth, for they have ever accounted it the sorest affliction, next to the sin that caused it, to lose God's presence ; no affliction so heavy to a true believer, David
accounted it so, so did Asaph, and Heman; and this
appears by their behaviour when under it.

(1st.) It occasions very unbecoming thoughts of God,
as if he were utterly gone, and would never return
more, as if he had shut up his loving kindness in utter
displeasure, and was become cruel, and while the soul
thinks it so, the anguish of his spirit is as great as if
it were so. Dejection of spirit clouds the understanding, and causes such apprehensions of God, as fill the
soul with terror.

(2nd.) It causes desperate thoughts concerning ourselves, as if all was rotten and naught; " My state is
a lost state, my profession is dissimulation ;" I have
been a close hypocrite, and now the righteous God hath
found me out; now I am past hope : will God shew
mercy to the dead ? shall his loving kindness be made
known in the grave ?"

(3rd.) It sometimes causes a believer to speak very
hardly and unbecomingly of God. Oh ! how hardly
did Job speak of God, when this was his case. " Know
now that God hath overthrown me, and hath compassed me with his net, behold I cry out of wrong,
but am not heard, I cry aloud, but there is no judgment ; he hath fenced up my way that I cannot pass,
and he hath set darkness in my paths ; he hath destroyed me on every side, and I am gone, and mine
hope hath he removed like a tree ; he hath also
kindled his wrath against me, and accounted me for
his enemy." (Job. xix. 6.) What dreadful things
these are to be spoken of God by a good man ? What
a sad reflection doth he make upon God's justice ?

(*4th.*) Sometimes it stirs up in believers, dreadful passions, as fear and trembling, so "Fear came upon me, and trembling, which made all my bones to shake." (Job. iv. 14.) "When I remember God, I am afraid, and trembling takes hold of my flesh." (Job xxi. 6.)

(*5th.*) Sometimes it works a fearful despondency, and brings down the soul to the very brink of despair. "I am free among the dead, like the slain that lie in the grave, whom thou rememberest no more; thou hast laid me in the lowest pit, in the darkness of the deep. I am shut up, I cannot come forth." (Psalm lxxxviii. 5, 6.) Now see what the carriage of the believer is under the withdrawings of God, and this shews what a bitter thing it is; and it must needs be thus afflicting, for how can a man that knows what the comfort of God's presence is, but be filled with trouble and terror at the hiding of God's face?

(3.) This withdrawing of God is that which turns living hopes into killing fears. "I thought God had been my God, but now I am dealt with as an enemy: I did hope my interest in God had been sure, but now He writes bitter things against me." How sad must the case of that soul be, where hope dies and fear lives.

(4.) This withdrawing of God from a believer is not only itself a burden, but it makes other things a burden too. Is not the sense of the guilt of sin a burden, where it is sensibly felt? it is a very heavy one; this is the fruit of God's withdrawing, for then the soul is made to turn in upon itself with dreadful reflections, and then sins repented of and pardoned, appear to the soul as if they were unpardoned, and had never been forgiven. The soul is as if pardoning grace had never reached him. (Job. xiii. 26.) "Thou makest me to possess the sins of my youth." The sense of all his sins from his childhood recurred upon him, and he bore the burden as though they had never been forgiven. Though when God pardons sin, he never doth remember it more, yet he gives us occasion to remember it often; though he never revokes a pardon, yet he often revokes the sense of pardon; though a believer never loses his forgiveness, yet he may lose the sense of it, and in that sense, those sins which have lost their commanding strength, may appear to have in them great condemning strength; the guilt of sin may possibly lie as heavy upon the conscience, as if it had never been pardoned. Again, hardness of heart is a burden to every believer; it is a great burden, a heavy burden, that he can have no ease under it; this is another fruit of the withdrawing of God, for when he withholds his quickening presence, the heart must needs grow harder. (Isaiah lxiii. 17.) "Why hast thou hardened our hearts from thy fear?" God hardens no man's heart positively, that is, by infusing any evil quality or disposition, that was not there before; but God may do that to a believing soul, upon which hardness of heart will insensibly grow upon it. He may withdraw his Spirit, his quickening presence, and influence; he may leave a man to himself, and to the lust of his own heart, and this must needs work to a great degree of hardness, and thus God doth sometimes harden the heart of his own children, that is, he doth withdraw and suspend his influence, and so a hardness grows upon the heart; and must not this be a dreadful burden to a child of God, to be as if sin were never pardoned, and as if he was given up to hardness of heart?

(5.) It is a very wounding thing, it makes sad wounds in the spirit and conscience of a believer. No wounds like to wounds in the conscience, they are such as none but God can cure; if the body be in misery, external means may help; in nakedness, raiment; in famine, bread; but when the soul is in distress, who, or what can relieve it? It is out of the reach of every arm but God's, there is nothing can wound the spirit of a man but the arrow of God, and nothing can relieve a wounded spirit, but the comforts of God. There are three things in God which wound the believing spirit in this case very sore, and they are His goodness, His greatness, and His eternity.

(1st.) His goodness, this is a wounding thing to a soul under God's hidings. The greater sense a deserted soul hath of the goodness of God, the deeper is the wound that is caused by his withdrawing. The soul draws very bitter conclusions out of that attribute, which is a fountain of comfort to others. " Unhappy I! that these streams of grace that flow so freely to others, should be shut up from me. How vile and sinful must I be, whom goodness itself rejects. Were there in me any thing of God's image, surely he would have regard to the work of his hands, for when are the works of the righteous cut off? Were I a child of God, sure he would have the bowels of a father!" thus the sense of God's goodness makes the wound of his withdrawing from the soul very deep and smart.

(2nd.) Another thing which helps on the misery is the sense of his power and greatness. In this world the more men are clothed with power, the more we court their favour, and dread their frowns. " The wrath of a king is like the roaring of a lion," that is, it is very terrible and dreadful; and how dreadful then must the wrath of God be, who is so great as that there is none like him, and whose power there is none can withstand: He disposes of life and death at pleasure, therefore how miserable must that soul be, that looks upon itself as forsaken of that God, in whose favour is life, whose frowns are the foretastes of hell and death. All the world cannot comfort a soul in this case, till God speaks it comfort. Tell a prisoner that is going to be tried for his life, his case is good, and he will certainly be acquitted, "Alas!" saith he, "it is not what you say, but what will the judge say;" so tell a soul thus distressed under God's hidings, "be of good comfort, your case is good, this cloud will be over, and heaven will be the end of all;" "Oh!" saith he, "that God would say so to me,—let my sentence come forth from his presence."

(3rd.) Another thing which fills the believer with dread under the withdrawings of God, is His eternity; to be cast off by a dying man is not much, but to be rejected by the ever-living God is dreadful. His eternity is that which puts a sweetness into his love, and makes the burden of his wrath intolerable. O! what a dreadful thing it is to lose God for ever! that God that lives for ever, and is the ever blessed God, this God hath forsaken me! O! this makes a wound indeed, and such a wound as no hand can cure, but that which made it. And can a soul be thus wounded by the withdrawings of God, but it must needs feels unspeakable anguish and sorrow. It is that which turns his sunshine into darkness. Whatever is any ways grievous doth now stand forth in its most astonishing appearance, and shews itself with a terrible greatness:

now sin is sin indeed, and guilt is guilt indeed, and
death is death indeed, and hell is hell indeed, and
the soul is even borne down under the sense of it, and
is ready to take up David's complaint, (Psalm. lxxxix.
2.) " I sink in the deep mire where there is no
standing, I am come into deep waters, where the
floods overflow me." Nothing looks so like judgment
as this. In other things the Christian combats with
the creature, but in this his contest is with God. So
that by all this it appears to be a very terrible thing
to be under the withdrawings of God in this world;
and if so, O ! then do but consider what it is to fall
into the hands of the living God. To be under these
withdrawings of God is consistent with his love, but
none fall into his hands hereafter, but the vessels of
wrath. If God hide his face now, it is but for a
moment, but if you fall into his hands, it is for eternity. These are rods in the hand of love, but the
others are scorpions in the hand of vengeance: these
are anger mixed with mercy, but those in hell are
judgment without mercy. And that is a second demonstration which doth clearly evidence the truth of
this, that if it be such a dreadful thing for a believer,
one of his own children that he loves as himself, to be
under the withdrawings of God for a moment here,
what is it for a sinner to fall into the hands of the
living God for ever !

SERMON III.

"*It is a fearful thing to fall into the hands of the living God.*" (Heb. x. 31.)

I HAVE been opening the words to you, and shewed you in what sense God is called the living God, in opposition to idol gods; he is the living God *originally*, having life primarily in himself; the living God by way of *communication* of life; he is the living God with respect to his *eternal power*, whereby he is able to avenge himself for sin, and that is the reason why he is called the living God. I shewed you what is meant by the hands of the living God; there are various senses in Scripture, but in this place his hand denotes his power, and so you read in Scripture of the protecting hand of God; "None shall pluck them out of my hand;" of the correcting hand of God; "day and night thy hand lies heavy upon me;" of the revenging hand of God, and that is the hand in the text, "It is a fearful thing to fall into the hands of the living God."

I shewed you what is meant by falling into his hand. It implies three things:

I. Having to do with God immediately, as every sinner in that state shall.

II. Having to do with God necessarily.

III. Everlastingly.

I have given you the demonstration of this, that to fall into the hands of the living God is a fearful thing. I did demonstrate it to you,

I. From that which is the chief subject of this misery, and that is the soul of man. When a man falls into the hands of the living God, it is his soul that is the chiefest sufferer.

II. From hence, that the withdrawings of God, even from the souls of believers in this life is so dreadful. Let God but withdraw from his people a little here, suspend the influences of his grace, and it is a hell to the soul; I shewed you what this withdrawing of God is, and gave you several conclusions about it, and then made it out, what a dreadful thing it is to be under the withdrawings of God, the greatest misery that can befall a believer in this world; this I made evident to you by five things.

1. In that a believer accounts his imperfect communion with God here a misery.

2. The common notion and general sense of believers evinces this, and it sufficiently appears by their carriage and behaviour, when God withdraws.

(1.) It occasions hard and unbecoming thoughts of God.

(2.) It occasions desperate conclusions concerning themselves.

(3.) Sometimes it occasions them to speak hardly and unbecomingly of God.

(4.) It stirs up dreadful passions, as fear and trembling.

(5.) It sometimes works a fearful despondency of soul.

Thus the behaviour of believers under God's withdrawings, shews it to be a dreadful thing.

3. This is that which turns living hopes into killing fears.

4. It is not only a burden, but makes other things a burden too.

5. It is a very wounding thing, it makes sad wounds in the spirit and conscience of a believer, and such as lie out of the reach of all medicines, that no hand can cure, but that of God himself: and if it be such a terrible thing for a believer to be under the withdrawings of God for a moment, what is it to fall into the hands of the living God for ever? I come now to

III. Demonstration; the fearfulness of this falling into the hands of the living God, will be evidenced from that terror which sinners themselves many times feel under the sense of God's wrath in this world. God doth sometimes give them some tastes of his wrath here in their souls, and it becomes very dreadful when it is so, and this I take to be the fire not blown, which Zophar speaks of, (Job xx. 26.) " A fire not blown shall consume him." What fire is that but the wrath of God? When this fire burns, it kindles such a flame in the conscience, that a sinner cannot bear the burning thereof. It is worse than Nebuchadnezzar's fiery furnace, when seven times heated. Never any have been so scourged and tormented as those that felt these burnings of conscience within; God doth sometimes in this life, let in his wrath into the soul of sinners, as a present rebuke for sin, as he doth put joy into the heart of believers in an immediate way, by the " light of his countenance." (Psa. iv. 6.) What is this light of God's countenance upon a believer, but the irradiation and discovery of his love in an immediate way; so when God punishes for sin, he doth the like by way of discovery, filling the soul with terror, from the immediate stroke of his wrath; it is not such a sort of punishment as falls wholly upon the flesh in pain and smart, but such as is internal, which falls upon the spirit of a man. This many times upon sinners hath so much of the wrath of God in it, that it becomes intolerable, cannot be borne; so it was with Judas, the wrath of God entered into his soul, and filled his conscience with terror, and he could not bear it, but hangs himself to be rid of his burden; there is not a livelier emblem of the torments of hell in this world, than a conscience filled with God's wrath; so it was to Cain, and that made him cry out, "my punishment is greater than I can bear;" this was it that made poor Spira cry out, "I feel the wrath of God upon my soul, and I am in hell already;" of all the miseries that are incident to the wicked in this world, there is none like these distresses of conscience, being tormented wtth the sense of immediate wrath; and yet these distresses in their utmost extremity, if compared with what the miserable sinner feels in hell, are but like sipping of the top of that cup the dregs whereof are reserved to the eternal state. (Psalm lxxv. 8.) "In the hand of the Lord there is a cup, and the wine is red; it is full of mixtures, and he pours out the same (here in this world,) but the dregs thereof all the wicked of the earth shall wring them out, and drink them." It is but the top of the cup that is tasted of now, but the utmost bottom of this cup of fury is reserved for hereafter. Whatever of the wrath of God sinners at any time feel here, is in comparison of what is to come, but as the flame of a candle to a fiery furnace. This may be another demontration of this truth, that it is a fearful thing to fall into the hands of the living God. If the inchoation of hell be so dreadful here, what shall the consummation of it be hereafter? if the first fruits be so bitter, what shall the full crop of divine vengeance be? Now you feel a little touch of God's finger, but then you fall into his hands.

IV. It is further evident from the sense Christ had of this wrath of God, when he as our surety fell into the hands of the living God, for Christ did not only suffer in his body a cruel painful death, but he suffered in his soul too, and indeed the sufferings of his soul, are the soul of his sufferings; they are the greatest part of what the Lord Christ underwent, therefore speaking of Christ, (Psalm xxii. 14.) He cries out, " My soul is melted like wax, it is *melted* in the midst of my bowels;" and Christ tells his disciples, (Matt. xxvi. 38.) " My soul is exceeding sorrowful even to death;" and (Luke xxii. 44.) " He was in an agony, and sweat drops of blood which ran down to the ground." Now what is it that thus wrought upon the Holy soul of Christ, that should make a man in perfect health and strength, in the vigour of his days, in such a dreadful agony, to sweat drops of blood, whence came it? We do not read of any devil let loose to torment him, for they are tormented at his presence; we read of no other angel that had any commission to torment him, nor is there any reason to think, that the fear of a bodily death now approaching, was that which forced these drops of blood from him, for then he had discovered more weakness than many martyrs; his nature was sure as strong as theirs to bear it, had not his sufferings had infinitely more in it, than any of the martyr's sufferings; the martyrs suffered as great outward sorrow as Christ did, and that with courage. But alas! Christ's was another kind of death than theirs. He suffered under the weight of his father's justice, and his great conflict was with the wrath of God; Christ standing for us and in our stead, did suffer under a vindictive dispensation of God's wrath, for he was made a curse for us; the curse that was due to our sin, was transferred from us to him, who became our surety. (Gal. iii. 13.) "Christ hath redeemed us from the curse of the law, being made a curse for us," so that there is a great difference between the death of martyrs, and the death of our Redeemer. Christ in his death, conflicted with sin, and wrath, and hell, with enemies whose force was never broken before; there was a curse in his death, but the curse was taken out of theirs. Christ did not only conflict with a temporal, but an eternal death; this, the martyrs knew they were delivered from. Christ endured the torments of hell in his sufferings, the martyrs felt nothing of that, for Christ had freed them from it. Christ's death had infinitely more in it than the death of all the martyrs ever had; all the soldiers in the world could not have drawn out one doleful cry from his blessed lips, had not the wrath of God drawn it out; he fell into the hands of the living God. "Awake, O sword against my Shepherd, against the man that is my fellow," therefore he is said "to be smitten of God, and afflicted." (Isa. lxiii 4.) So that our Lord Christ had to do with the wrath of God in his soul, and this made him to cry out, "My God, my God, why hast thou

forsaken me?" He doth not say to his friends or disciples, why have ye forsaken me? but why hast thou
my God, forsaken me. What a deluge from heaven
fell upon this our ark, of which Noah's was a type!
It must be more than a finite breath that thus melted
his holy soul in the garden. One drop of the wrath
of God is infinitely more bitter than all human wrath
and revenge can be. It is clear there was a negative
hand of God in denying Christ the comfortable presence which was due to him, an holy person by the
covenant of works, and could not be denied to his
humanity as it was united to the second person in the
Godhead, had he not been in another capacity upon
the cross, and not precisely as the Son of God. If the
wrath and justice of his father did not immediately fall
upon him, how could he be said to satisfy his father's
justice? The fire which consumed the sacrifice upon
the typical altar, came down from heaven, and so did
the wrath of God which consumed our sacrifice, therefore it is said, " it pleased the Lord to bruise him."
(Isa. liii. 10.) Now then, if the wrath of God was so
dreadful to the Lord Christ himself, as to put him
into such an agony, what will it be to the undone sinner in the great day? Our Lord Christ endured it but
for a time, but the sinner falls into the hands of the
living God, and must bear it to eternity; if it was so
heavy upon Christ, how will it be upon the damned?
What will become of them that slight this blessed
Redeemer, and have no part in his death, no benefit
by it, because they tread it under foot? If Christ died
to this end, that God might with a salvo to his justice,
pardon believing sinners, what will become of those
that do not believe in him? The death of Christ will

be a bitter consideration unto unbelieving souls, to consider what wrath Christ himself underwent, when he stood in the stead of sinners. If he suffered so much that stood in our stead, what must they suffer when they stand in their own stead, and must bear their own guilt? "If these things be done in a green tree, what shall be done in a dry!" if he drank so deep of this bitter cup, dost thou think thou shalt escape? What will become of you that neglect so great salvation? You that make light of the threatenings of God, and cannot believe that God will be so severe against sinners as the Scriptures speak, and ministers tell you, do but see the justice of God against Christ, and tremble at unbelief. Did he sweat under the wrath of God drops of blood, and dost thou make light of it? Did it stagger him, and will it not confound thee? God hath once indeed accepted a sacrifice for sin, but if any man sinfully refuses this Christ, "there remains no more sacrifice for sin, but a certain fearful looking for of judgment and fiery indignation that shall consume the adversary."

V. It is evident that it is a fearful thing to fall into the hands of the living God from that judgment which God will pass upon every soul in the great day. Let me a little shew,

1. What this judgment is.

2. That such a judgment there shall be.

3. What the nature of this judgment is.

1. What this judgment is, though it hath various senses in Scripture, yet it is most usually put to signify the proceeding of a righteous God in the last day with saints and sinners; and this judgment is a judicial act of God, which he will exercise in the last day by

Christ, both upon angels and men, pronouncing the elect blessed, and making them sharers in his glory, and pronouncing the wicked cursed, and condemning them to eternal misery.

2. That there shall be such a judgment as this is most plain and evident, if you consider these six things.

(1.) The unerring testimony of Scripture; the Scriptures are the perfect revelation of the mind of God, called the word of truth; whatever is contained in them is of undoubted verity, whatever is foretold in the word shall most certainly come to pass, as all things hitherto in their appointed seasons have done. The Scriptures foretold of Christ's coming in the flesh some thousands of years before he was born, and it came to pass accordingly. " In the fullness of time God sent his Son." It foretold his dying for sinners, and bearing the wrath of God for us, and it came to pass accordingly. It foretold the casting off of the Jews, and the coming of Antichrist, which is now come to pass, and whatever it hath foretold that is yet to be accomplished, shall certainly be made good. Now there is nothing in this Scripture, that it doth more plainly foretell and forewarn us of, than of a judgment day coming. It makes it as sure as death. " It is appointed for all men once to die, and after this the judgment;" nay, it makes it more sure than death, for all shall not die; the Apostle saith, " We shall not all die, but we shall all be changed." (1 Cor. xv. li.) They that are found alive at the coming of Christ, shall not die, but though they shall not die, yet they shall all be judged, nay the Scripture foretells what we shall be judged for, for our works. " He will judge every man according

to his works." (1 Pet. i. 17.)   Aye for our words.
(Matt. xii. 36, 37.) "I say unto you, that every idle
word that men shall speak, they shall give account
thereof in the day of judgment, for by thy words thou
shalt   be   justified,   and   by   thy   words   thou
shalt be condemned."   Aye, we must give an account
of our very thoughts.   (Rom. ii. 16.)   "God shall
judge the secrets of men," the most close and secret
sins that we have done at any time, shall all come into
judgment, "there is nothing covered, that shall not be
revealed, nothing hid that shall not be known."
(Matt. x. 26.)   The Scriptures foretell what the rule
is that God will proceed by, in judging in that day.
(Rom. ii. 12.)   "As many as have sinned without
law, shall be judged without law, and as many as have
sinned in the law, shall be judged by the law."   But
what shall be done to them that lived under the gospel? They shall be judged by the gospel. (John xii.
48.)   "The word I have spoken, the same shall judge
you at the last day."   It is evident then, that there
shall be a judgment, for the word of God hath plainly
foretold it.

(2.) The justice and righteousness of God makes a
day of judgment to be a thing of necessity.   This
righteousness of God is an attribute that is equally
infinite with his other attributes; now God will glorify
every attribute.   His other attributes have had their
day.

The power of God had a day when he made the world;
he made all out of nothing by the word of his power.
Creation work is said to shew forth his eternal power and
Godhead.

The love and mercy of God had a day when he
redeemed the world in giving Christ to die for us, then

was love and mercy made visible, "God so loved the world, that he gave his only begotten Son, that whosoever believes, should not perish, but have everlasting life." (John iii. 16.)

The patience of God hath had his day. It is the time of man's life here, that is the time of God's patience, wherein he bears with sinners, and their crying provocations, and doth wait for their repenting and returning, and believing. All the time we live, and are on this side the grave, is so much taken off from eternity, for God to exercise his patience towards sinners in; the life of man is nothing else but the season of God's patience, wherein he waits upon him, and calls to him to believe and repent, and secure the interest of his soul.

Now then shall the other attributes of God have their day, and shall not the justice and righteousness of God have a day too. How else shall his righteousness be made known and made manifest. It cannot be known in this world, the wicked prosper, and the righteous are afflicted. Is this righteousness? therefore a day of judgment is highly necessary, for that is "the day of the revelation of the righteous judgment of God." The justice of God makes this necessary both with respect to believers and sinners.

1. With respect to believers.

(1.) That the wrongs they have undergone and sustained in this world may be righted. You know the interest of religion is a very suffering interest here, and they that own it, and will adhere to it, must expect to share in the reproaches and sufferings of it. Sometimes they suffer from Satan, sometimes they suffer from wicked men, sometimes they suffer in their names, and sometimes they suffer in their persons, sometimes in their possessions : now is it reasonable that the righteous God should always suffer this ? Is it consistent with his justice to let his people be run down in the world, and never vindicate them ? You cannot think so—there is a time coming wherein God will do them right. (2 Thess. i. 4, 5.) "The persecutions and troubles you endure is a manifest token, (mark it) of the righteous judgment of God ;" that is, it is an evidence, a sign, a witness, that there shall be a day, wherein God will set things right ; when we see the righteous suffering such injurious things causelessly from wicked men, and they in the mean time go unpunished, they go on and prosper, we may well take this as a token of judgment, how else can we vindicate the righteousness and wisdom of God in governing the world ? When Solomon saw so much corruption in private communities, and so much unrighteousness gotten into the seat of justice, what doth he infer from thence ? but that surely a day will come wherein there shall be a more righteous administration of things. (Eccl. iii. 16, 17.) All these unrighteous judgments shall be judged over again, and the Apostle puts this upon the righteousness of God. (2 Thess. i. 6.) "It is a righteous thing to recompense tribulation to them that trouble you, and to you that are troubled rest with us." It is a righteous thing with God to give his people rest, and to bring the wicked into trouble. This tribulation to the wicked, and rest to believers, is the fruit of God's righteousness ; he will right his people in every kind ; if their persons have been dishonoured and despised, God will vindicate them ; if they have been condemned for a generation of hypocrites, God will in that day manifest their sincerity before all the world.

2. A day of judgment is necessary that believers may receive the glory which is prepared for them from the foundation of the world, and purchased for them at the cost of Christ's blood; heaven is the believers's due, his right, I do not say by virtue of any works done by him, no, the apostle disclaims that, (Tit. iii. 5.) "Not by works of righteousness which we have done," but it is due by virtue of God's promise; a believer stands firmly entitled to the promises, and he may claim boldly whatever is contained in the promise, for it is an engagement upon God; there is nothing more just than that a righteous God should make good his promise; so then if I believe and have closed with Christ and have ventured my eternal all upon the promise of God, I may lay claim to heaven as my just due, because God hath promised heaven to every true believer, "he that believes shall be saved," and shall not the righteous God make good his word? and besides it is a purchased possession, it cost the blood of Jesus, and he bought it for the believer's use and behalf; "for their sakes I sanctify myself," saith Christ. The great design of Christ in the flesh in all he did and suffered was to bring many sons to glory; therefore a day of judgment is absolutely necessary with respect to believers, that they may receive the inheritance that God hath prepared, and Christ hath purchased at so dear a rate as his own blood.

(2.) A judgment day is necessary with respect to sinners, here "all things come alike to all, one event to the righteous and to the wicked, to him that sacrifices, and to him that sacrifices not; as is the good so is the

sinner, and he that swears as he that fears an oath."
(Eccle. ix. 2.)   What a strange administration of
things is this, if there be not a future state! therefore
there must be a day wherein God will set these matters
right, and a difference put between one and the other,
though not now.   Now the wicked devours the man
that is more righteous than he, and yet God is said to
hold his peace, here "the wicked are not in trouble as
other men" (Psalm lxxiii. 5.)   "Therefore they set
their mouths against heaven, and they say how doth
God know?" therefore there must be a reckoning to
come; here " they prosper in the world, and have their
good things in this life : their belly is filled with this hid
treasure, where waters of a full cup are wrung out to
his people ;" therefore there must be a day to set matters
right; here sinners take advantage of the patience of
God to sin with the greater courage; because God
doth not strike the sinner immediately, therefore their
heart is fully set in them to do evil, they set light by
Christ here; therefore if there be a righteous God, there
shall be a day of judgment.

(3.) There is that in the conscience of every man
that proves this; the apostle speaking of the gentiles
saith, "their consciences bearing witness, and their conscience excusing or accusing within themselves."   In
doing evil they accuse, in doing good they excuse, and
this proves a judgment, for the judgment of the conscience is with respect to the judgment of God; "if our
hearts condemn us," saith the apostle, " God is greater
than our hearts, and knoweth all things."   It is said
" when Paul reasoned of righteousness and judgment to
come, Felix trembled," (Acts xxiv. 25.)   Why did the
doctrine of the judgment to come make him tremble?

Because his conscience filled him with terror at the remembrance of that day.

(4.) That there shall be a judgment day is evident from the resurrection. That there shall be a general resurrection of the body from the grave we all believe. (Dan. xii. 2.) " They that sleep in the dust shall awake, some to everlasting life, and some to shame and everlasting contempt." It is as plain as words can make it ; (1 Cor. xv. 22.) " As in Adam all die, so in Christ shall all be made alive." It is not meant of universal redemption, as the Arminians pervert it, but it is meant of the universal resurrection, as the context proves it. The resurrection of the dead is an article of our creed, and it is made by the Apostles, one of the fundamental articles of the christian religion, (Heb. vi. 2.) Now the resurrection of the dead doth necessarily infer a day of judgment, for if there be no judgment day, what do the dead rise for? It is in order to judgment, " that every man may receive according to the things done in the body." (2 Cor. v. 10.) Therefore the body must be judged as well as the soul; John saith in the representation of the last judgment, (Rev. xx. 12.) " I saw the dead small and great stand before God," how can they stand before God, but in a resurrection state? and what do they stand before God for, but to be judged according to their deeds? The Apostle gives you a full proof of this, (John v. 28, 29.) " For the hour is coming in which all that are in their graves shall hear his voice, and come forth, they that have done good unto the resurrection of life, and they that have done evil to the resurrection of damnation." Why is it called a resurrection of life and damnation. but because of the judgment which at the resurrection shall pass upon every one, either to life or damnation ?

(5.) The present condition of Christ makes this day of Judgment necessary ; Christ is now an advocate for us with the Father, he is gone to heaven to transact for us at the right hand of God by his intercession, and must Christ be always at that work ? Must he be always interceding to God for us ? Shall he never put off his priestly garments ? Yes, the scripture tells us, " the time is coming, when Christ shall deliver up the kingdom to God the Father," and when is that? when doth he give up the kingdom ? when the judgment is past ; He must judge the world first, for the Father hath committed all judgment to the Son, and one end of this judging the world by Christ is, that they, that would not bow to him might be broken by him ; that they, that would not submit to the golden sceptre of his grace, might feel the iron rod of his power ; you read what the sentence shall be at last, " Those mine enemies that would not that I should, reign over them, bring them hither and slay them before me ;" and when his enemies are subdued, then his mediatorial kingdom is ended, for he must reign till he hath put all his enemies under his feet ; therefore the present condition of Christ makes a judgment necessary.

(6.) I might evince this from the faith of the people of God ; there hath not been one saint upon the earth from the begining of the world to this day but hath believed a judgment to come. This I could prove from Adam, from Enoch, from Noah, from David, and from all the Old Testament saints. And would God have fixed the faith of his saints in all ages upon a thing which could not be? I tell you it cannot be, and if there be no judgment, then, (as the Apostle saith of the resurrection of Christ,) "is our preaching vain, and your faith is vain." It is most evident therefore that there shall be a judgment.

3. I come now to speak a little to the nature of this great and last judgment, to bring it home to the demonstration that it is a fearful thing to fall into the hands of the living God.

(1.) It is universal, none can be exempted from it, "before him shall be gathered all nations." (Matt. xxv. 32.) Jews, Turks, Heathens, Christians, all nations, (Rom xiv. 10.) "we shall all stand before the judgment seat of Christ;" we shall, the apostle here includes himself, and all believers, to shew us that saints shall be judged as well as sinners; first, Christ shall judge the saints, then as assessors with Christ, they shall judge the rest of the world. (1 Cor. vi. 2.) "Know ye not that the saints shall judge the world?" not by an equal authority and commission with Christ, but as the present approvers of his righteous proceedings; "I saw the dead small and great stand before God." The greatest princes on the earth shall stand at the bar of Christ, as well as the poorest peasant. No man shall be excused from the trial of that day, neither ministers nor people, young nor old, godly or ungodly, all must receive their final doom, no shifts or indirect means can shift off, or bias that judgment, there is no hiding of sins from God. You may hide them from men and the devil, but not from God. Men may say now as they did. (Ezek. ix. 9.) "The Lord hath forsaken the earth, and the Lord seeth not," but then it will appear otherwise; when there came but one guest that had not on a wedding garment, how soon did Christ find him out? "He knows vain man, he seeth his wickedness, will he not consider it?"

(2.) It is certain, "you yourselves know perfectly that the day of the Lord comes as a thief in the night." (1 Thess. v. 2.) The word of God is not more positive and full in the fixing any one truth in the book of God than this. Jesus Christ would never have revealed, and the prophets and apostles would never have preached it, had it not been a thing of the greatest certainty. Nay it is made so by the very oath of God. "As I live, saith God, every knee shall bow to me." God hath sworn it. "Every one of us shall give an account of himself unto God."

(3.) It is sudden; it approaches apace, the apostle saith so. (Phil. iv. 5.) "The Lord is at hand." (James v. 8.) "The coming of the Lord draws nigh," and our Lord Christ speaks of it, as at hand, (Rev. iii. 11.) "Behold, I come quickly," and (Rev. xxii. 20.) the last words of Christ, and those with which he seals up the canon of Scripture are, "surely I come quickly," therefore it cannot be long before Christ comes to judgment.

(4.) It is impartial, he is said to "judge without respect of persons," (1 Pet. i. 17.) God forbad acceptation of man's person in judgment, that is to esteem one person above another, or carnal advantages or by ends; and "there is no respect of persons with God," the enemies of our Lord justified him in this, that he regarded not the person of men, and in the great day, there shall be no esteem of one above another. Every man must stand or fall, as the merit of his cause is.

(5.) It is a strict and just judgment. He hath appointed a day wherein he will judge the world in righteousness, there shall be no wrong verdict given. Now is the time of God's forbearance and suffering with sinners; now he rules the world with patience, but then he will rule in strict justice. No persuasion or bribery can take place at God's bar. These may do much with corrupt man, but they will not do with the righteous God. Righteousness is said to be the girdle of his loins, and he will never put off that girdle; no man shall there suffer wrong; "shall not the judge of all the earth do right?"

(6.) This judgment is final and peremptory, there is no appealing from it, if matters go against you: here, you may be cast in one court, and find relief in another, but there is no appeal from that bar. The sentence of that day is conclusive and binding for ever. If God then binds guilt upon the soul, it shall lie there to eternity; here God may bring a judgment upon a man and remove it again, but there the judgment of that day shall never be removed, but it shall lie upon the soul for ever. The present wrath of God may be reversed, for God deals here in a way of grace; but there, every man shall be in his final state, and God will deal with him in the way of justice. It shall be judgment without mercy and without remedy. He that is happy in the sentence of that day, will be happy for ever, and he that is miserable then, is miserable for ever; if any man die in his unbelief and impenitence, he is as sure to perish as ever he was born. "For the Lord Jesus shall be revealed from heaven with his mighty angels in flaming fire, taking vengeance on them that know not God, and obey not the gospel of our Lord Jesus Christ, who shall be punished with everlasting destruction from the presence of the Lord, and from the glory of his power." (2 Thes. i. 8, 9.) This is the nature then of the great judgment day, and if there be such a day of judgment as this, so universal, so certain, so impartial, so sudden, so strict and just, so peremptory and final, then it is sufficiently demonstrative that, "It is a fearful thing to fall into the hands of the living God."

SERMON IV.

---

*" It is a fearful thing to fall into the hands of the
living God."*—(Heb. x. 31.)

I have in speaking to those words, shewed you,

I. In what sense God is the living God.

II. Opened the notion of falling into his hands, what
is intended by it.

III. Demonstrated the truth of this scripture, that
it is a fearful thing—I evinced it,

I. From that which is the chief subject of this misery;
the soul of man.

II. It is evident, in that the partial withdrawings of
God from a believer in this life are so dreadful.

III. From the terrors that sinners many times feel
under the sense of God's wrath in this world.

IV. From the sense Christ had of this wrath of God,
when he as our surety fell into the hands of the living
God.

V. From the dreadfulness of that judgment, that
shall pass upon every soul in the great day.

I now come to shew you,

IV. To whom it is such a fearful thing to fall into

the hands of the living God; if you respect the notion more largely, as having to do with God in a state of eternity, so it is not a dreadful thing to all, for to some it is a matter of comfort. It is so to all that believe, to all that are in union to Christ by faith, and it must needs be so, for,

I. It is such an union as that by it, a man's state is fundamentally changed, so that he is no more a child of wrath.

II. It is an union fixed in the blessed state of justification, and the forgiveness of sins.

III. By virtue of this union, he hath a right to all the blessings of the covenant.

IV. This is that which gives great boldness in the day of judgment.—But if you consider this falling into the hands of the living God in another sense than this is, than barely having to do with God in a state of eternity, and that is falling into the hands of an absolute God, that is a fearful thing; and this is that which is intended in the text, having to do with God alone, with God without a Christ, this is dreadful. This was it which that good man so dreaded when he cried out. *Nolo Deum absolutum.* "Let me not have to do with an absolute God," with God alone, with God out of Christ, for this is to have to do with the power and wrath of God, when there is nothing in God himself, nothing in his word, nothing in his promises, nothing in his institutions, which should oblige him to shew mercy or mitigate punishment. Now in this sense, none fall into the hands of the living God, but they that live and die in their sins. They, all they, and none but they, are the subjects of this misery. All men since the fall are " by nature children of wrath."

(Eph. ii. 3.) But there is a way, found out by the wisdom and grace of God, to escape it, and therefore we are called to flee from the wrath to come, and that is by believing in the Lord Jesus Christ; this is the great, the only remedy which God hath set up, by which his wrath may be avoided, and there is no other. " He that believes on the Son, hath everlasting life, but he that believes not the Son, shall not see life, but the wrath of God abides on him," and that for ever, for he falls into the hands of the living God, and this is the case of all sinners, such as live and die in the neglect and contempt of the grace of the gospel ; God hath, in rich grace, set Christ to be a Redeemer, and the great design of the gospel is to bring us to Christ, that we may be sharers in the benefits of redemption. Now he that slights and sinfully rejects the offers of Christ, and the grace and mercy purchased and tendered by Christ in the ministry of the gospel, he doth by his own act sinfully exclude himself from all hopes of mercy, and so falls into the hands of the living God, and there remains to him then " nothing but a certain fearful looking for the wrath and fiery indignation that shall consume his adversary." Oh ! therefore how dreadful then is this sin of unbelief, though we make so little of it ! How miserable is the state of every soul, that lives and dies in this sin ! His damnation is unavoidable, he must perish, and why ? Because he hath no interest in the great mediator. Christ is the middle person between us and God, to screen us from the wrath of God, who is a consuming fire. Now the unbeliever hath no Christ, he might have had him, but he would not; he neglected him, refused and despised him ; now therefore he will reject him, and he shall fall into the hands of an absolute God.

V. Let me give you the reasons of this truth. Why it is such a fearful thing to fall into the hands of the living God.

1. Reason, shall be with respect to those attributes of God which make it so fearful. The attributes of God are all of them eternal like himself, and those attributes must produce suitable acts. Power shews itself in acts of power; mercy in acts of mercy; justice in acts of justice; and these must have suitable objects; for though the immanent acts of God, such as abide in him, of which number are his secret decrees, do not necessarily require the pre-existence of any object, yet his transient acts must necessarily suppose some object upon which they are terminated. Now as there are no creatures besides angels and men which are capable of merit and demerit, and consequently of rewards and punishments, so there are no creatures else that are immortal, and so capable of eternal happiness or misery. There are some attributes of God, which though they are in their nature eternal, yet they are but temporary in their use and exercise, such as patience and long suffering, whereby God bears with sinners and delays to execute the judgments threatened, gives warning before he strikes, and sends lesser judgments to prevent greater, and by these things, waits to be gracious, these are the exercises of his patience and long-suffering to sinners. But in the next world all these shall cease, God will then wait no longer, and bear with sinners no more. "I have a long time been still and refrained myself, now will I destroy and devour." (Isa. xlii. 4.) Neither sinners

nor saints shall ever share in the patience of God in the other world : not the saints for they cannot need it, they shall never sin more, nor provoke God more, and therefore shall need the exercise of his patience no more, but shall be in the full fruition of his love and goodness; nor shall sinners share in it in that state, they have sinned away the patience and mercy of God by abusing it, and so are fallen into that condition where there is no room for the exercise of it. There shall be then an exercise of such attributes only, as shall make the sinner's case dreadful. I shall instance in (Three) the Omniscience, the Power, and the Justice of God.

(1.) The omniscience of God. That is one of the attributes by which God knows all things, the great attribute by which he knows all things. " His understanding is infinite." (Psa. xclvii. 5.) It is one of the names of God. " The Lord is a God of knowledge," it is spoken there to give check to the pride of vain man, that is so apt to be puffed up with his own light and knowledge and attainments, Alas ! what doth man know like God ? As it is said of the essence of man, compared with the essence of God, it is nothing, less than nothing and vanity ; so it may be said of the knowledge of man in respect of the knowledge of God. Who can search the infiniteness of God's understanding ? He knows more than all the men in the world, more than all the angels in heaven. Knowledge is the root of wisdom, as wisdom is the flower of knowledge. God is described with " seven eyes," (Zech. iii. ix.) which is to set out the perfection of his knowledge. It is an universal knowledge for it reaches to things past, present, and to come.

1st. He knows all things past. No duty or good

work the believer ever did, but God remembers it.
Therefore it is said, "a book of remembrance was written
for them that fear the Lord," (Mal. iii. 16.) to intimate
they are continually in God's eye. On the other hand,
not a sin the carnal sinner ever did in this world in all
his life time, God remembers it as if it were but now
committed.   This is that which Job intended, (Job xiv.
17.)   " My transgression is sealed up in a bag, and
thou sewest up mine iniquity."

How could Moses that was born two thousand years
after the world was made, have given such a distinct
account of the life of Adam, the circumstances of Cain's
murder and the like, if God had not revealed them ? and
how could God have revealed them if he had not known
them ? Nay without this knowledge of things past, he
could not be a governor of the world.   He could not
reward virtue according to his promises, nor punish sin
according to his threatenings.

2nd. He knows all things present, there is nothing
hid from him; " all things are naked and open to the
eyes of him with whom we have to do." (Heb. iv. 13.)
Nay actions are not only known to him, but thoughts
too, the most secret imaginations, the most inward
contrivances, the closest inventions are all in the view
of God. This is one of God's peculiars, from which
all creatures are shut out.   " What man knows the
things of a man, but the spirit of man which is in him ?"
There is no angel good or bad, that can know thy
thoughts or mine.   It is an incommunicable property
of the divine Omniscience. The devils do not know
our thoughts, they may guess at them by our actions,
but thoughts merely as thoughts cannot be known by
any but God himself. Indeed one man may know the
heart and thoughts of another by revelation, as Elisha

did, what was in Gehazi's heart. But we cannot know them without revelation. " The heart is deceitful above all things, and who can know it ?" You have the question put, and none can answer it but God. " I the Lord search the heart and try the reins." Now then if God knows all things, all our actions and thoughts, then he must needs know all our sins, whether they are more open or secret, " there is no darkness, where the workers of iniquity can hide themselves." (Job. xxxiv. 22.) If God did not know all sin, how could he permit it, or order it, or punish it, or pardon it ? What is sin but the transgression of the law, and the law is the revelation of the will of God, and that will is the rule of righteousness ; and shall God make his will the rule of righteousness, and not know when it is fulfilled or transgressed? It is our imperfection to be ignorant of the nature of any thing ; and can there be thought to be such a defect in the understanding of God ? There is not one motion of lust in us, nor one sin acted by us, but it is known to God. " Doth not he see all my ways, and count all my steps ?" saith (Job. xxxi. 4.) How can any action of man be con-cealed from God, who makes darkness light before him? How could he be a righteous judge of the world, if he did not know all the sins of man ?

3rd. God knows all things future, and that shall at any time come to pass. As nothing can actually be, without his will giving it existence, so nothing can be future without his will designing it shall be. This is a knowledge which distinguishes the true God from all false deities, and proves him to be God indeed. (Isa. xli. 22.) " Let them shew us what shall happen, or declare the things that shall come hereafter, that we

may know they are Gods." Where had the prophets
their skill in foretelling things to come? It could not be
natural, for then others might have had it as well as
they; it must be from divine revelation, and so the Jews
acknowledge. Who could have foretold the seven
years famine in Egypt? The captivity of the Jews in
Babylon for seventy years? The coming of Christ in
the flesh thousands of years before he was born? the
calling of the Gentiles, and the casting off of the Jews?
None but a God could know this. God must needs
know all things future, because he knows his own
decrees and will; God sees all things by his effecting
will, as having decreed to produce them: by his
permitting will, there is nothing in the world
but what God hath willed to be; not an action
to be done, but he hath willed it to be by his
permission: or else we may say that things come to
pass whether God will or no, or that he doth not
know it; but this cannot be, " for known unto God are
all his works;" God knows all things as if now present.
Upon this account things that are to come, are spoken
by God with respect to God, as if they were present.
(Isa. ix. 6.) "To us a child is born, to us a son is
given," and yet it was a long time after, before Christ was
born; so (Isaiah liii. 4,) " He hath born our griefs, and
was wounded for our transgressions," and yet this was
to be done long after; God foreknew that Judas would
betray our Lord, and therefore speaks of it as a thing
done already.

He foreknows all the sins sinners would commit, and
that they are at present averse from committing.
When the prophet told Hazael what he would do when
he was king, that he would burn their houses, and slay

their young men, and rip up the women with child;
What? said Hazael, " is thy servant a dog that he
should do this?" (2 Kings viii. 12.)   Hazael did not
think himself so vile and base, but the Lord (saith the
prophet,) hath shewed unto me that thou shalt do so.
That such a perfect knowledge as this should be ascribed to God is highly reasonable,

For,

(1.) This knowledge is most essential to the perfec-
tions of God, if God be all-wise he must be all-knowing,
for knowledge is the foundation of wisdom; a creature
can be no more wise without knowledge, than active
without strength.   Now God is said to be the only
wise God, therefore he must be an all-knowing God.

(2.) Whence hath man that measure of knowledge
that he is endowed with? Is it not from God? What
a great measure of it had Solomon, but it was all received from God: now see how the Psalmist argues,
(Psalm xciv. 9, 10.) "He that framed the eye shall he
not see, and he that teaches man knowledge shall he
not know?"   Can we think that he that enriches the
creature with knowledge from time to time, should
not have a fulness of it in himself?

(3.) There is that in every man that gives a great
evidence of this, for why doth conscience check a man
at any time for the most hidden and secret closet sins?
Why doth it [accuse] and gnaw for such sins, as none in
the world are privy to but himself? Doth not this bear
witness to the Omniscience of God? Those fears and
terrors in the conscience do evidence that there is one
above us that understands all our secrets; this self-
judging in a man's own conscience, for such things as
none in the world can charge him with, doth plainly

prove that there is one greater than our consciences, that knows all things. What need a man's conscience trouble him, if no one could know his sin but himself? But every man's conscience preaches up a God, and tells him that there is a God that knows all things.

(4.) How could we suppose God any ways fit to govern the world without this knowledge? If God directs every thing to its proper end, then he must know the nature of it, and its fitness to reach that end, for which it is intended. The Divine Providence is conducted by Divine Omniscience; " your heavenly Father knows that you have need of these things." Suppose a blind man should drive a chariot, he could never direct it in the right road, and if God were ignorant of the things under his conduct, he would not be fit to rule the world.

(5.) He would not be fit to judge the world at the last day, for right judgment is to proportion the punishment to the crime, therefore it is necessary in order thereto, that the crime be exactly known. Two may commit the same kind of sin which may be in every way alike, in regard of outward circumstances, and yet the sin in one may be far greater, and have much more guilt in it than the other. It may proceed from viler principles, and from more corrupt ends, from a heart more invenomed against God, and these do very much aggravate a sin. Now therefore if God had not a knowledge of our hearts, our principles, our ends, and of the whole bent and disposition of our minds, how could he pass a right judgment? Among men, justice is painted blind, not blind with regard to the offence, but the offender: blind so as not to regard one more than another, but not so as not to distinguish the nature of one crime from another; therefore it is necessary God should know all things, the most hidden things of the heart, secret thoughts and secret principles, secret aims and ends; therefore he tells us, (Jer. xvii. 10.) "I the Lord search the heart, and try the reins, to give to every man according to his ways, and according to the fruit of his doings." Now as this Omniscience of God makes him fit to govern the world, so the great reason why it is made known to us is to awaken us to duty.

The other attributes of God have been more discovered, and made to shine forth more than this of his Omniscience. The creation of the world is a rich display of the power of God. The harmony of the creature wonderfully sets out the wisdom of God. The sending a Redeemer sets out the mercy of God. The great sufferings of Christ upon the cross set out the justice of God. But what doth set out his Omniscience in proportion to the other attributes? There hath been some discovery of it in those gripes of conscience which some have felt, but yet when these inward terrors are not felt, this attribute of Omniscience is little believed, sinners in favour of their lusts will not own it, they say, how doth God know? can he see through the thick darkness? (Psa. x. 11.) " He hath said in his heart, God hath forgot, and he hides his face and will never see;" therefore there must be a day when there shall be a judgment, and such a judgment wherein his Omniscience shall be made manifest to all, in bringing to light the hidden things of darkness, and making manifest the counsels of the heart. It shall then appear that God knows all that ever we have done, all the sins that ever you committed, sins of

thought, of word, of deed, sins against the law of
God, sins against the gospel of God, sins of omission,
and sins of commission, sins of ignorance, and sins of
knowledge, open sins and secret sins shall all be told
and made manifest, neither is there any thing hid that
shall not be made known; and thus the exercises of this
attribute of God in that day will make the sinner's
case dreadful, for then God will be a judge and a
witness too, and he will witness according to truth.
He is called "a swift witness." (Mal. iii. 5.) It is his
own Omniscience that makes him so; God doth not
need to call for other evidences as judges now do, but
by a light in himself, he shall [*enlighten*] the consciences of men, to see and own all the sins they ever have
done.   As God doth now know all, so it shall then be
made manifest to the sinner, that he doth know it.   He
"will convince them of their ungodly deeds." (Jude xv.)
Oh! the conviction of that day, not like present
convictions here, which are few, and seldom, and sometimes slight: it may be God is pleased to take hold
of one here, one is convinced at this word, another at
that; some sit all their days under the powerful preaching of the word, and yet are never convinced of their
sins, and their lost estate, but go on in their lusts, but
that will be a day of great, of full conviction.   Such a
day as never was, such as wherein all their sins shall
be set in order before them, and they shall have a full
view of all that ever they did. Oh! this Omniscience of
God will appear a terrible attribute in that day, though
now many deny it; for,

  1*st*. Why else do many forbear to commit that sin
in the view of man, which they dare do in the sight of
God. The presence of a child will hinder us when the

eye of God cannot restrain us. Is not this a practical denying of God's Omniscience?

2nd. Why do men mock God in duty, and put him off with an outside worship? serve him with their lips when their heart is far from him? honour him with their lips, but keep their hearts for their lusts? Is not this a practical denial of God's Omniscience? as if God could be imposed upon by feigned lips and false pretences?

3rd. Why do men in their confessions of sin to God deal so falsely and partially and loosely? a plain ripping up of the heart to God puts a glory upon this attribute, it is as much as if the soul should say, "I know God knows all things, and therefore I will confess all to him;" but to excuse sin or to conceal it, or to transfer it to another, or in any way to extenuate it, is practically to deny God knows our hearts.

4th. Why do men nourish thoughts of sin, indulge secret lusts, and inward and speculative uncleanness? Many refrain from the overt acts of sin, that yet make no conscience of inward contemplative wickedness. what is the giving a liberty to our thoughts, but a practical denial of the Omniscience of God? The like may be said of neglect of secret duty. Now many deny the Omniscience of God, but then all shall know and own it; God will then bring all to light, reveal all hidden and secret sins. Not a vain word, not an idle thought, not a wanton glance, but it is more visible to God than any object is to us, even in the light of the noonday sun. Oh! what a poor shelter is secrecy to sinners. Can any thing be hid from God? What if man knows not thy sins, what if the devil and the angels know them not, so long as God knows them? What a fearful consideration is this to the dissembling hypocrite, and the vile sinner drest up in specious shows and sanctified appearances. For this all-knowing God judges not according to appearance. Omniscience will in that day rend off all veils, pull off all paint, and make every man appear to be what he is. We may take wolves for sheep, dross for gold, sinners for saints, and hypocrites for believers. But " God seeth not as man seeth, his eyes are not flesh like ours," (Job x. 4.) He can espy the treacherous heart of a Judas under a kiss, and the devil in Samuel's mantle. Woe to all hypocrites in that day. This Omniscience of God will be a fearful thing to them; so saith the prophet, (Isa. xxxiii. 14.) " Sinners in Zion are afraid, fearfulness hath surprised the hypocrites;" sinners in Zion are false members of a true church, therefore called hypocrites. This Omniscience of God must needs be a fearful thing to all such, to all that live and die in sin, and this will appear by two things.

(1.) This all-knowing God never forgets one sin, they are written as with a pen of iron, and the point of a diamond. " The sin of Ephraim is hid," not hid from God, but with God. (Deut. xxxii. 34.) " Is not this laid up in store with me, and sealed up among my treasures." So that not one sin shall be forgotten by God; we sin and forget it, the sins of our youth are forgotten, when we are grown up, and in old age; we forget the sins of riper years, but God remembers them all, the sins of your childhood and youth, riper age and old age: and this as it speaks great comfort to all believers, that this omniscient God knows all their graces and duties, doings and sufferings for Christ, and he will not forget one of them, so it speaks terror to all sinners, that God knows all their sins, their uncleanness and filthiness, and they shall never be forgotten, for they are recorded in heaven.

(2.) This all-knowing God shall be the all-judging God, for the eye of his Omniscience is to guide the hand of his justice. To what end should he take such an exact account of the sins of men, but in order to punish them? Sinners go on in their own sins and wickedness now, and God lets them alone, and they prosper, and therefore they think that God takes no notice of them. " These things hast thou done, and I kept silence," saith God? and what do they infer from the present silence of God? They "thought that he was altogether such an one as they." Because they forget their sins, they think God forgets them too, but, mark it, " I will reprove thee, and set them in order before thine eyes," and then it follows. "Now consider this, ye that forget God, lest I tear you in pieces, and there be none to deliver ;" consider what? This Omniscience of God. Whence is it that men are so daring, and impudent, and resolute in sinning, but because they never consider that God sees and takes notice of all they do? so saith David. " The proud hath risen against me ;" mind the reason, " they have not set God before them." What wickedness will not a man commit when the sense of God's Omniscience is blotted out. (Ezek. viii. 12.) " Son of man," saith God, " hast thou seen what the ancients of the house of Israel do in the dark, for they say, the Lord sees us not." That made them bold in sin, O ! that you would, but much, and often think of this all-knowledge of God. Keep the sense of it always upon your minds. Wherever you are, remember this, that God seeth you, and observes all your actions. This would be of admirable use for three great ends.

1st. It would be an excellent means to prevent much sin, and stir us up to the mortification of our lusts. What put Job upon making a covenant with his eyes against uncleanness? (Job xxxi. 1.) but what he saith, " Doth not God see my ways, and count all my steps ?" When thou art tempted with any sin, say with David, (Psalm xliv. 21.) " Shall not God search this out, for he knows the secrets of my heart;" Solomon prescribes this, as a sovereign remedy against uncleanness. (Prov. v. 21.) " Why wilt thou be ravished with a strange woman, and embrace the bosom of a stranger, for the ways of man are before the eyes of the Lord, and he ponders all his goings;" nothing like the sense of the Omniscience of God, kept up in the mind, to check the breaking out of lust.

2nd. It would greatly excite us to more care and diligence, and conscience in duty. What is the reason of all our omissions of duty, but because we have not a due sense of God's omniscience ? Did you but consider this, that God knows what you do, how you sanctify the sabbath, and how you pray and hear the Word, how you make it the rule of your practice, "When my body is coming to the ordinance, where is my heart ? both my body and soul are in God's presence." Did you but consider this, there would not be so much deadness in duty ; this would make our performances more vigorous, and our minds more watchful.

3rd. It would be an excellent means to sanctify our whole conversation, and make us more upright in the wholecourse of our lives ; therefore they are put together. "Walk thou before me, and be thou perfect" or upright. We can never be sincere with God, further than as we walk under the eye of God. This truth of his Omniscience is the foundation of all religion, and a powerful impression of it upon the mind is that which promotes the practice of all godliness. Who will regard the serving of God, that thinks that God regards not his service? he that thinks God doth not see him cares not how much he sins against him, nor how little he serves him. (Psa. cxix. 168.) " I have kept thy precepts and thy testimonies, for all my ways are before thee;" and when David presses Solomon to a close walking with God, the Omniscience of God is his argument. " And thou Solomon my Son, know thou the God of thy fathers, and serve him with a perfect heart; for the Lord searches the heart, and understands all the imaginations of the thoughts." Think often what an all-knowing God, God is. As he is too just to be bribed, and too holy to be mocked, so he is too knowing to be deceived, and let me tell you, till you come under an awful affecting sense of God's Omniscience, you can never come to walk close with him, nor be sincere in your obedience to him. The case would not be so dreadful with sinners, if it were not for this attribute. What end can we think God hath in so often declaring his Omniscience to us in this word of God, but in order to the government of our practice, and to convince us of a future judgment. As his justice, which consists in giving every man his due, could not be glorified, unless men were called to an account for their actions, so neither will his Omniscience appear in glory without a manifesting the secrets of the hearts of man. There must be a time for this, and no time so fit as that of the great judgment. And therefore pray do but think what a dreadful reckoning sinners shall have in that day of judgment, when the Omniscience of

God shall set before a sinner all the sins that ever he hath done, both in thought, word, and deed. If thou hast no right to the merit of Christ, thou shalt then be undone and lost for ever; for thou must fall into the hands of an absolute God, and he is a living God, and "it is a fearful thing to fall into the hands of the living God." Therefore dreadful will the case of sinners be in that day.

SERMON V.

" It is a fearful thing to fall into the hands of the living God."—Heb. x. 31.

I have opened the terms, and showed you in what sense God is the living God, I have opened the notion of falling into his hands, and showed you what it is; I have demonstrated the truth that it is such a fearful thing to fall into the hands of the living God, and have shown to whom it is such a fearful thing, and I have given you the reasons of this truth, why it is such a fearful thing to fall into the hands of the living God.

I. Reason, (which I am yet upon, which is a great reason), is with respect to those attributes of God which make it so dreadful. There are some attributes of God especially, which the sinner shall then fall under, which shall put so much terror into the case.

1. One is the Omniscience of God, that attribute of the Divine nature by which he knows all things, all things that either have been, are, shall, or can be. Without this, God would neither be fit to govern the world at present, or judge it hereafter, for then God

shall convince the world, and bring all things to light, even the hidden things of darkness, and make manifest the most secret evils, the very counsels of the heart, and God shall then sit judge upon all, and give to every man according to his works, and how can God possibly do this unless he be an all-knowing God? and this is one attribute of God, which makes it so fearful a thing to fall into the hands of the living God, because he is an all-knowing God.

2. I come now to another attribute of God, which makes the sinner's case dreadful in falling into the hands of God, for it is into the hands of a God of power. Whosoever falls into the hands of the living God, falls into the hands of an Omnipotent God. His very being supposes power; if you acknowledge a God, you must acknowledge him to be Almighty; If he be limited in his power, he must be limited in his essence, for power of acting is ever according to the nature of being, and either God is not infinite in his being, or if he is, he must have an infinite power in acting, for otherwise this would follow that there would be an inequality in the attributes of God; one would be greater than another : his wisdom greater than his power. He knows all things that are possible to be known, and if he cannot do all things that are possible to be done, then he is greater in understanding, than in the power of acting, which is absurd.

All the attributes of God are his very essence. His Power, and Wisdom, and Love, and the like, they are not qualities in God, as in a creature, but of the very essence and being of God; and therefore if any one attribute could be supposed to be greater than another, then in that attribute, God would be greater than himself in another attribute. If his wisdom were greater than his power, then seeing they are his essence, he himself would be greater in wisdom, than himself in power. But his power is as great as his wisdom. Among men, indeed, where these are but qualities, it makes no wonder; man may know more than he can do, and so be greater in understanding than in power: he may will what he cannot work, he may devise what he cannot perform; I say these things in men are but qualities, and therefore no wonder if they differ, and one be strong and another weak; but in God it cannot be so, because there are no qualities in God. Every attribute is his essence, and his essence being infinite, so must every attribute be, and so all be necessarily equal, for in things that are infinite, there can be no inequality; and the same may be said of his will, that is said of his knowledge and wisdom, for though the will of God, and the power of God are not really distinct in themselves, yet they are distinct in our conceptions. The will of God, determines, the power of God executes. The power of God, accomplishes the resolutions of his will. (Eph. i. 17.) " He works all things according to the counsel of his own will." So that the work of the divine power is to bring about the purposes of the divine will. His will is the supreme cause of every thing that is. All things come into being as God wills them. His power is as great as his will, for "he can do whatsoever he pleases." (Psa. cxv. 3.) Nothing can be absolutely perfect that is in any sense impotent, for weakness is an imperfection. Every thing is accounted more perfect by how much the more it hath of efficacy and virtue in it. They are the most perfect plants that are the most sanative, and have the greatest virtue to heal and cure. When God is declared to be unsearchable to perfection; he is set out by the title of Almighty. (Job. ii. 7.) "Canst thou by searching find out God? Canst thou find out the Almighty to perfection?" implying thus much, that the Almightiness of God is such a thing as cannot be fathomed or searched out, because it cannot be limited. As God might be said not to have a perfect liberty to will, if he could not will what he pleased, so he would not have a perfect power, if he could not do whatever he wills. This power of God comes under a two-fold distinction.

(1.) There is in it the power of authority and jurisdiction.

(2.) The power of strength and ability.

1st. The power of authority and jurisdiction: This is that power of lordship, which all the powers in the world are under as being from him. Every creature is God's subject, even the devils themselves are at his beck. It is so with the most inanimate beings: God bids the winds be silent and the seas be still, and how readily do they obey his voice? If God calls for a famine upon a sinning nation, how suddenly doth the earth become iron and the heavens brass? Flies and lice shall encounter thrones and kingdoms, if armed with a commission from this Almighty God. "All are thy servants," (Psalm. cxix. 91.) What the centurion said of his soldiers and servants, (Matth. viii. 9.) "I say to this man, go, and he goes, to another, come and he comes, and to my servant, do this, and he doeth it," is much more true of God. He hath a power and dominion over all the creatures, and a sovereign right to dispose of them at his own pleasure. Sometimes

he governs things according to the course of second
causes, working by them according to the innate
quality of natural motion. The motion of every
creature is ordered by the will of God, and acted by
the power of God. Sometimes he governs them in
an extraordinary way, above or beside nature. As
when he made " the sun to stand still in Gibeon, and
the moon in the valley of Ajalon." (Jos. x. 12.) Thus
at the word of God the sea divides for Israel to pass
over on dry land. He makes the earth open to
swallow up Korah and his companions. He shuts the
mouth of hungry lions. (Dan. vi. 22.) He commands
the fiery furnace not to burn, (Dan. iii. 25.) How
often in the New Testament do you find God putting
forth his power this way. As in the star that directed
the wise men to Christ. In the eclipse of the sun at
his death. In the fish that brought tribute to Peter,
and the like. No creature can evade the power of his
dominion, for all are at his command, (Isa. xlviii. 13.)
The angels, those inhabitants of the glorious world,
these do his commandments, hearkening to the voice
of his word. But all the creatures in heaven and earth
are acted by his sovereign power. (Psalm cxxxv.
6.) "Whatsoever the Lord pleased, that he did in the
heaven and earth, in the sea and all deep places." It
is so with all sickness, pain, and diseases. " Speak but
the word, and my servant shall be healed." (Matth.
viii. 8.) God's sovereign will and power gives law to
all. Now this is his power of dominion or sovereignty,
which the school-men make to consist in four parts.
In commanding, permitting, rewarding and punishing.

2nd. There is in God a power of strength and
ability, which is that whereby he can effect and bring

to pass whatever he pleases, this is called his Omnipotence and Almightiness. One observes, that God is called Almighty in more than seventy places in scripture. " I know thou canst do all things," saith Job; and Jeremiah, after he had been speaking of God's power in the creation, he adds, " nothing is too hard for thee." Sure nothing can be too hard for that God, who made such a world out of nothing, and he could have made a thousand for one, that he hath made. " With God all things are possible." When Sarah doubted of having a child in her old age, see how God rebukes her, (Gen. xviii. 14.) " Is any thing too hard for the Lord?" can any thing pose Omnipotence? And when Moses himself spake very unbecomingly of this attribute of God; as if God were not able to feed his people when they were in a strait, Moses saith, " shall the flocks and the herds be slain for them to suffice them? Shall the fishes of the sea be gathered together for them?" But see how God takes him up short in the next words, " Is the Lord's hand waxen short?" That God who is eternal without any limitation of time, is Almighty without any limitation of power. Consider here a few things.

1. Power: it is one of the names of God, (Mark xiv. 62.) " Ye shall see the Son of man sitting at the right hand of power," that is on the right hand of God. God and power are so inseparable, that they are put for one another. You do not know God at all, if you do not know him by this name, for power belongs to God. (Psa. lxii. 11.) " God hath spoken once, twice have I heard it, that power belongs to God." He heard it in the creation of the world, for by his power he made the world, and he heard it in his dominion, for by the

power of his providence he governs it. Or thus, he heard it in the making of the world, for that was done by a word, and he heard it in the redeeming of the world, for that was done by the word. Or, he heard it twice, that a double testimony might confirm the thing, and make it of the greatest certainty, that all might own his power; so that I say, you cannot have a right notion of God, if you do not conceive of him as a God of power, for it is one of his names.

2. Power is absolutely essential to the Divine nature, and that cannot be said of any creature; power is not essential to the creature. What power is in it is by derivation. In this sense "the powers that are, are ordained of God." (Rom. xiii. 1.) But power is in God originally, and he receives it of none, for it is of and from himself. Solomon tells us, (Eccl. viii. 4.) "In the word of a king, there is power." There is and there is not; he hath a power to command, but he hath not power to make his commands be obeyed. There may be authority where there is no power, and there may be power where there is no authority, they are distinct things; power is many times without authority, as in forcible invasion, where there is success and no right, and authority may be without power, as in a legal prince expelled by unjust usurpation; the right is in him but not the power. But both these are in God. He hath a power of dominion, and power to maintain his dominion. David was a great king, but he cries out, "I am this day weak, these sons of Zeruiah are too hard for me." But such is the power of God, so great and uncontroulable, so absolute, that none ever hardened himself against God and prospered. And power is not only essential

to the Divine nature, but it is more manifestly and visibly so, than any other attribute. It is true, Love is essential to God, so is Mercy, and Justice, and Wisdom and the like, but none of these attributes can be exercised in him without power. What is the Love of God without power, but fruitless good-will, that cannot bring good? What is Mercy without power, but ineffectual pity? What is Wisdom without power, but an useless contrivance? What is Justice without power, but a will to do right without a hand to execute it? All the excellencies of the nature of God would be of no signification, they could not exert themselves, nor make impressions upon the creature, without power. Therefore,

3. Power is the life of all God's other attributes, and gives activity to every perfection of his nature: there are two attributes of God that run through all the rest, his Holiness and his Power. Holiness is the beauty of every attribute, and Power is the life of them. Holiness is the beauty of his wisdom, Power is the life of it, whereby it accomplishes its designs without lett or hindrance. Holiness is the beauty of his justice, and Power is the life of it, whereby, he executes vengeance upon sinners. Holiness is the beauty of his mercy, Power is the life of it, whereby it succours us in our misery: no attribute can be exercised but by the exercise of power. This is the arm of the Lord which all the other attributes of God lay hold on, when they would appear in their glory.

4. Power is concerned where other attributes of God are not, and it acts where other attributes act not, and therefore is extended beyond them. Other attributes in God suppose an object in being, as the patience of God, there must be an object of that

patience; the justice of God, there must be an object
of that justice; and so of his mercy; but the power of
God doth not always suppose an object in being,
because it gives it a being: there would be no
object for patience and mercy, and justice, to
exercise themselves about, if the power of God
did not give them being, and when power doth
produce an object, it is not the object of all; a man
may be the object of God's patience and not of mercy;
or of mercy, and then justice shall not touch him, or
of justice, and then mercy cannot reach him. So that
the object of one attribute may be not the object of
another. But all are the objects of God's power; therefore " slow to anger, and great in power," are joined
together. (Nah. i. 3.) So (Rom. ix. 22.) "What if God
willing to make his power known, endured with much
long suffering, the vessels of wrath fitted for destruction." Patience is acted by power. It is this that
moderates incensed justice from taking present revenge
upon provoking sinners. " These things hast thou done,
(saith God to sinners,) and I kept silence." (Psal. l.
21.) " I have a long time held my peace, and have
refrained myself." (Isa. xli.. 14.) There is no greater
argument of God's power than his patience. It is
seen more in forbearing sinners, than in damning
them; for in the one, he hath dominion over the
creature, but in the other, he hath dominion over himself.
And therefore he gives this as a reason why he will not
destroy provoking Ephraim, " For I am God and not
man." So that you see his patience towards sinners
is acted by his power. Man in misery is the object of
God's mercy, but mercy cannot secure him, if the power
of God do not actuate his mercy. A guilty criminal is

the object of revenging justice, but his justice great and terrible as it is, would be nothing, though it had a right of sentencing, if it had not a power of executing, so that the power of God runs through every attribute. Nay, it runs through all conditions of the creature. When it lies in a state of nothingness, it is power which produces it into being, and when it is in the condition of a creature, power preserves it in that being; and when it is in its eternal state, power still preserves it in being. So that power runs through every state of the creature, which all the other attributes do not. A man may be in that state, though it is a sad one, as to be out of the reach of mercy, as in final impenitency; mercy gives him up, and will have no more to do with him, but power will have to do with him still. He that is in a state of damnation is cast out of the bosom of mercy, but he is in the arms of power; that sustains him in being, that he may be for ever miserable. Justice may cease to punish a creature, but power doth not cease to preserve him. The glorified saints in heaven are for ever out of the reach of God's punishing justice, but not out of the reach of power, for it is that which everlastingly maintains them in that blessed condition: Oh! how amazingly large and great is the extent of divine power! It reaches not only to the present state, but to eternity. It reaches from heaven to hell. It makes creatures everlasting creatures, that they may be for ever blessed in the enjoyment of God; and sustains others in being for ever, that they may be everlastingly miserable under the wrath of God.

5. This power of God is universal. It is not bounded and limited as the creature's power is; man can do some things, but there be many things he cannot do;

Angels can do much that man cannot, but God can do much, that neither man nor angels can. He can do all things, which they cannot do. Nothing can limit the power of God, but his own will. A limited power is a finite power. Unless his power be unlimited, he cannot be infinite. " I know," saith Job, " that thou canst do every thing." It is a great word and a great truth, but it must have respect to [*the Divine will in doing them,*] or to the things to be done.

(1.) God can do every thing that he will do. You must understand the necessary distinction of the power of God; there is the absolute and the ordinate power of God: the absolute power of God, is an ability to do whatsoever is possible to be done: his ordinate power is that which is guided and regulated by his will and decree. His absolute power is necessary, and belongs to his nature; his ordinate power is arbitrary, and belongs to his will. He is said to do all things by the counsel of his will; so that God can do many things by his absolute power, which by his ordinate power, it may be said, he cannot do, because he hath willed not to do it. As for instance, God by his absolute power could have prevented the fall of Adam, and the angels, but by his ordinate power he could not, because he willed not to do it. So that God will not do every thing that he can, but he can do every thing that he will.

(2.) When it is said God can do every thing, it must be considered with respect to the things themselves; that is, such things as are becoming God to do, for otherwise we may, and must say, there be some things God cannot do, because they are not becoming God to do, as for instance :

Some things that imply a contradiction; as for God to make an infinite creature, which he cannot do, for if it be a creature, it cannot be infinite, and if it be infinite, it cannot be a creature. Nothing can be infinite but God. There are some things utterly repugnant to the nature of God; God cannot grow old or die, it is repugnant to his power; for that which is mortal must cease to be powerful. Death would be a cessation of the divine power, but that can never cease; God remains for ever fixed in his own immutability. There are some things impossible to his attributes. He cannot lie, because it is against his truth. He cannot deceive, because of his faithfulness. He cannot forget, because of his omniscience. He cannot love sin, because it is against his holiness. Therefore, when it is said, God can do every thing, we must understand it of such things as are congruous to the holy nature of God, and becoming his holy will. He can do every thing that is just and good, fit for a God to do. God is good at any work that is good. Thus he can do every thing, and of whom can this be said, but of God. One man can do one thing, another another, a third more than both, but where is the man that can do every thing? Every calling hath its particular mystery, which a man of another calling is to seek to. It is well if every man can do one thing well. He that will be a doer at every thing, is no great doer at anything. But God can do every thing. As he is in being, so he is in working. As he is an universal good, so he is an universal agent. He can do every thing for us, as well as be every thing to us. He is mighty in strength. A man may be strong and mighty, but "mighty in strength" is a title becoming none but God. "I work and who shall let," (Isa. xliii. 13.) " He doth what he will in the army of heaven, and amongst the inhabitants of the earth," and this brings me to the—

6. This power of God is irresistible. "None can stay his hand, or say unto him, what doest thou?" (Dan. iv. 35.) " If he gives peace, who then can make trouble?" (Job. xxxiv. 29.) If he build up, who can pull down; if he take away, who can hinder him. The united strength and combined force of all the creatures in the world, are no match for his power. The four great monarchies of the earth, that made the world tremble, how are they broken by his power, and none could hinder him! How is the threatening of Christ made good against the seven churches of Asia, of removing their candlestick! All must down when God sets himself against them. No power nor plots can keep up what God will have down. Who hath resisted his will? for it is Omnipotent. The will of the creatures may be more extensive than their power, and their power too short to accomplish their will; but God's power is as great as his will, and therefore " his counsel shall stand, and he will fulfil all his pleasure."

7. The power of God is the fountain of all power. There is no creature but hath a power of acting according to its nature. How great is the virtue of the sun in its influences, and of every creature in their productions. Now all is derived from God. As he being the first being, must necessarily be the spring of all beings, and as he is the first good, he is the original of all good; so as he is the first power, he must be the fountain of all power.

8. It is power beyond all human conception. mark how the apostle sets it out, (Eph. iii. 20.) " Now to him that is able to do exceeding abundantly above all that we ask or think;" God is able to do what we ask or think; aye, to do all we can ask or think,—nay to do more,—to do abundantly, nay more,—exceeding abundantly above all that we can ask or think. What reason have we to acknowledge him Almighty, who hath a power of acting beyond our power of asking, or skill of contriving or conceiving. He is able to do infinitely more than ever he hath done or will do.

9. It is a power of infinite duration, therefore it is called "eternal power," (Rom. i. 20.) Now that which is eternal, can have no bounds. It is not limited by time, therefore it is of an infinite duration. His power can never be spent or expire. Nebuchadnezzar, that golden head of power, how soon was he turned to grass, with the beasts of the field, and became weak? The hand-writing turns Belshazzar's power into trembling. How soon is the power of the mighty cut off by the blast of God. But God's power never begins to be, nor ever ceases to be. It cannot languish or decay. It hath a spring which is everlasting. His lamp never consumes with burning, his strength is ever vigorous, without fading or decaying. " Hast thou not known, nor heard, that the everlasting God, the Creator of heaven and earth, fainteth not, nor is weary?" (Isa. xl. 28.) God's power is the same with his essence; he is the everlasting God, and therefore his power is an everlasting power.

Now then let us gather up these things to put a force into the notion of the text.

If the power of God be one of his names, and be

essential to the nature of God; if power be the life of all God's other attributes, and if it be concerned where other attributes of God are not; if the power of God be universal, and cannot be resisted, and is the fountain of all power; if it be beyond all human conception, and is of an infinite duration; this then gives you a sufficient reason for the confirmation of this truth, and why it is such a fearful thing to fall into the hands of the living God. It is because of his power, his Almightiness. It is a fearful thing to have to do with a God that is infinite in a way of wrath. Oh! what a word of terror is this to all Christless sinners that live and die in their sins! the power of God to all such is a dreadful attribute. Oh! that you would but consider it. Indeed to them that fear the Lord, that believe and repent, and live to God by obedience to his word, this power of God is a most comfortable attribute, and a great encouragement to believers. Therefore, (mind it) God when he would have Abraham to walk close with him, he reveals himself to him under the notion of an Almighty God. (Gen. xvii. 1.) "I am the Almighty God, walk thou before me, and be thou perfect." The Almightiness of God is a mighty argument to awaken the soul to obedience. The power of God is every way matter of comfort to a believer, for,

1. This power, great as it is, is made over to you in covenant, and is not that comfort? God in the covenant of grace makes over himself to a believer in every attribute. Is he a wise God? this shall be employed for your good. Is he a faithful God? this is for your comfort, he will never break covenant. His Almightiness is to save and preserve you. There

L

is nothing so strong, but God can overcome it.   This
is the blessed privilege of every believer, that God is
Almighty; thou art weak, but he is strong, thou art
feeble, but he is Almighty.   When fears and doubts
overtake a believer, then he may have relief by this
consideration, that God is Almighty.

2. It is comfort under the afflicting sense of
strong corruptions and lusts yet remaining in us. How
doth this fill the mouth of many a poor believer with
complaint! Oh! this sin, or the other lust. This was
Paul's trouble; " Whos hall deliver me from this body
of death?" but mark how he comforts himself, " I
thank God through Jesus Christ our Lord;" I cannot
subdue my sins, but Christ can.

3. It is comfort under the sad experience of strong
temptations. How is many a poor believer vexed with
Satan and his buffetings! How are they borne down
by temptations !   No rest day nor night.   But here is
comfort, Satan can do no more than God gives him
power to do.   God hath him in a chain, and he can
go no farther than he will suffer him, and God will not
suffer you to be tempted above what you are able,
but will with every temptation, find out a way for your
escape; therefore say with Paul ; " Most gladly
therefore will I glory in my infirmities that the power
of Christ may rest upon me;" his Almighty grace shall
support you.   " My grace is sufficient for you? " (2
Cor. xii. 9.) And his Almighty power shall deliver
you, for stronger is he that is in you, than he that is in
the world.

4. This is comfort under all persecuting powers,
let it be never so great, that God is Almighty. "Surely
the wrath of man will I restrain."

5. It is comfort in all distresses, whatever they be, for by his power he can and will make all things work together for good. It is comfort under weak grace. It is the complaint of many that their grace is weak. Aye, but God by his power will put strength into it, till he bring forth judgment unto victory. God can make the weakest believer stand. He shall be held up, for God is able to make him stand.

6. This is comfort under our doubts and fears, in the matter of perseverance in the ways of God. (John x. 28.) " My father is greater than all, and none shall pluck them out of my father's hand," and the Apostle tells us, (1 Peter i. 5.) " We are kept by the power of God through faith unto salvation."

But to the carnal unbelieving sinner this power of God is as dreadful as it is comfortable to others: for,

1. If God have such a power, then, hell and destruction are in his hand. " I live for ever, and I have the keys of hell and death." (Rev. i. 18.) Keys signify power. God hath the power of life, to save or to damn, they are at the disposal of this Almighty God, and do you think that God will have any to live with him but believers, and those that live to him? and who will he dispose of hell and damnation to, but impenitent sinners ?

2. This power of God (as I hinted before) runs through every attribute, and is that which puts a terror into all the attributes of God. I tell you his justice and wrath, and anger, would not be terrible, were it not for his power, but this power of God puts a terror into every attribute. He is an omniscient God that knows all your sins, and he is omnipotent, and able to punish you

for them. This is that which makes every attribute of God a terror to sinners. As they are clothed with his power, his justice is powerful justice, his anger powerful anger. "Who knows the power of thine anger." (Psa. xc. 11.) This power of God is a dreadful thing to sinners.

3. This power is engaged against all impenitent sinners that live in the contempt of the Gospel grace. (2 Thess. i. 8, 9.) " Christ shall come, in flaming fire, taking vengeance on them that know not God, and obey not the Gospel of our Lord Jesus Christ, who shall be punished with everlasting destruction from the presence of the Lord and the glory of his power." God will make his power glorious, in the destruction of every unbeliever.

4. It is a power that whenever the unbelieving sinner falls under it, he can never find deliverance from it. From thence there is no redemption, but he is held under the power of God in that state of wrath to all eternity. Men may slight the tenders of the mercy of God now, but they cannot avoid the stroke of his wrath then, or the reach of his arm. There is none can deliver out of his hand when once they come to hell. While sinners are in this world, Christ doth deliver them; and will deliver them. He saves to the uttermost all that come to God by him—he it is that delivers us from the wrath to come; but in that world there is none to deliver. When the soul hath to do with God in a way of wrath, none shall deliver him then. The blood of Christ is of no avail in the state of damnation, therefore pray hearken to the counsel of the Psalmist. (Psalm l. 22.) " Consider this, ye that forget God, lest I tear you in pieces, and there be

none to deliver." (Deut. xxxii. 39.) " See now, saith the Lord, that I am he, and there is no God besides me, I kill and I make alive, I wound and I heal, and there is none that can deliver out of my hand;" therefore it is a fearful thing to fall into the hands of the living God. O that you would think much of this attribute: meditate frequently and seriously on the power of God. It would greatly suppress sin, and promote the fear of God in your hearts, therefore take the counsel of our Lord himself, (Luke xii. 4, 5.) " I say unto you, my friends, be not afraid of them that kill the body, and after that have no more that they can do: but I will (saith he) forewarn you whom ye shall fear: fear him, which after he hath killed, hath power to cast into hell; yea, I say unto you, Fear him."

SERMON VI.

It is a fearful thing to fall into the hands of the living God.—(Heb. x. 31.)

I am shewing you that it is a fearful thing to fall into the hands of the living God, and to whom it is so, and I am now giving you the reasons of this truth, why it is so fearful a thing to fall into the hands of the living God. The reason I am upon, is with respect to those attributes of God, which make it so fearful. There are three attributes more especially which the sinner shall then have to do with, which will make his condition very dreadful.

(1.) One is the Omniscience of God. You will have to do with a God that knows all your doings, so saith the Apostle, " All things are naked and open before the eyes of that God with whom we have to do," of that God to whom we must give an account.

(2.) Another attribute is his power. The sinner falls into the hands of such a God as is Omnipotent. He is mighty in power, " I, even I, am he, and there is no God besides me; I kill, and I make alive, neither is there any that can deliver out of my hand." (Deut. xxxii. 39.) Again,

(3.) Another attribute of God, which renders the
sinner's case so fearful is, his Justice. He is a just
God. And this is that which makes the others so
dreadful, what is his omniscience if he be not powerful?
What is his power if he be not just ? Power without
justice may be unrighteously dispensed, and abused by
clearing the guilty, and condemning the innocent.
Solomon speaks of this as an evil under the sun. (Eccl.
iv. 1.) "Behold the tears of such as are oppressed, and
they had no comforter, and on the side of their oppressors there was power."

Power without justice degenerates into tyranny,
and authority unrighteously managed, is but wickedness established by a law, and this is what the
preacher then saw. (Eccl. iii. 16.) " I saw under
the sun the place of judgment, that wickedness was
there, and the place of righteousness, that iniquity
was there." What is meant here by the place of judgment, but the throne of princes, and the seat of judi-
cature, where justice ought to be impartially administered, but, saith he, wickedness was there, that is,
judgment was perverted, the guilty were acquitted, and
the innocent condemned. And what shall the people
do in such a case as this ? why even as the wise man
did, refer all to the judgment of God, who will set all
to rights when his time to judge is come ; (in the
17th verse.) " I said in mine heart, God shall
judge the righteous and the wicked." Men in their day
may make unrighteous decrees, and pass unjust
sentences, and so turn judgment into wormwood,
but there is a time coming in which God will call all
over again, and he will judge righteous judgment, for
there is no unrighteousness in him. (Psa. xcii. 15.)

" He is the just Lord, and he will not do iniquity."
Now here I shall speak to three things,

I. What this justice of God is.

II. Evidence the truth of this attribute, that God is
a just God.

III. Shew you what a fearful thing it is for a sinner
to have to do with the justice of God, and why it is
so.

I. What this justice of God is; justice in God is
either essential or relative: Essential Justice is such
a property of God's nature as that he can do no wrong.
Relative justice is so called with respect to the creature,
and is God's constant will of rendering to man what is
his due, and that will is the rule of righteousness.
Essential justice is in God necessarily. Relative
justice is in God an act of his good pleasure, whence
flow his proceedings with man according to the law of
righteousness, freely constituted between him and them.
Relative justice supposes somewhat due from God to
man in a way of debt, so as if he should not perform it
he would not be just. That which obliges God, if it be
in a way of reward is called merit, and if it be in a way
of punishment is called demerit, though the word
merit is often used for the one and the other; merit is
either absolute or in a way of free covenant, God cannot be a debtor to the creature in a way of absolute
merit, but he hath made himself by way of covenant.
Merit by way of covenant, notes such an obedience in
man, whereunto God by his free promise hath made himself a debtor according to the order of justice. Demerit notes such a disobedience whereunto the punishment of death is due according to the order of justice.
Merit or demerit is a just debt, whether in a way of

reward or punishment. If man had continued in a way of perfect obedience, God could not but have given him life in a way of justice, because of the promise of the covenant. Therefore man having sinned, the demerit of sin being death according to the terms of the covenant, God cannot but inflict death according to his relative justice, which is the rule of his procedure with man. If the elect of God die in their own person, the gospel is void; if man doth not die, the law is void; therefore the elect die in the man Christ Jesus, who satisfied justice as their surety, and unbelieving sinners having no surety to satisfy justice, must die themselves. Though God by his absolute power might have saved man without a surety, yet having fixed the inviolable rule of relative justice, "In the day thou eatest thereof thou shalt die," he could not avoid proceeding by this rule, therefore man must either die in himself or in his surety. The just God will take the demerit of sin. God suffers multitudes of sinners to be pardoned, but not one sin to go unpunished. This relative justice of God is distinguished into two parts. It is either commutative or distributive. Distributive justice is that whereby God renders to every man according to his works; and this justice is either remunerative, whereby God rewards the faithful obedience, and sincere services of believers with glory and blessedness, according to the terms of the covenant of grace, or vindictive justice, whereby he doth reward sin with the punishment due thereunto according to the law. You have them both together set out by the Apostle. (Rom. ii. 7, 8.) "To them who by patient continuance in well doing seek for glory, and honour, and immortality, eternal life;"

there is his remunerative justice, " but to them that do not obey the truth, but obey unrighteousness, to them he will render indignation and wrath," there is his vindictive justice ; and this is that justice we are now to speak to.   Thus you have in short what the justice of God is.

II. Let me clear this, that God is a just God in the sense I have spoken.

1. From the testimony of scripture, which every where declares him to be a just and righteous God. (Deut. xxxii. 4.) " All his ways are judgment, a God of truth and without iniquity, just and right is he." (Psa. xcvii. 2.) "Clouds and darkness are round about him, but righteousness and judgment are the habitation of his throne."   (Isa. xlv. 21.) "There is no God besides me, a just God ;" that of Bildad is very full of emphasis. " Doth God pervert judgment ? or doth the Almighty pervert justice ?"   Man may and often doth pervert judgment and justice, but doth God do so ? The question carries in it the force of a strong negation.   The Almighty doth not pervert justice or judgment.   Nothing can enforce him to it.   There are three things that usually cause men to pervert justice, a fear of greatness, a hope of reward, or affection or nearness of relation.

(1.) A fear of greatness ; the greatness of some sets them out of the reach of justice, as in the case of Zeruiah's sons, "they are too hard for me," saith David; some are so great, men are afraid to deal with them. But no fear can invade the throne of God, for he is Almighty, and the Almighty will not pervert justice.

(2.) Hope of reward.   The prophet speaks of some

rulers that love "give ye." (Hos. iv. 18.) That
is, they are more pleased with receiving rewards,
than in doing right." Such a one was Felix. (Acts
xxiv. 26.) But God is above all gifts. He that
gives to all need not receive from any, therefore
he tells them, (Ezek, vii. 19.) "Their silver and their
gold shall not be able to deliver them in the day of
the wrath of the Lord," and Solomon saith the same,
(Prov. vi. 4.) "Riches profit not in the day of
wrath,"—it may profit in the day of man's wrath, but
not in the day of God's wrath.

(3.) Relation and affection; these often among
men pervert justice, but not with God. "Though he be
as the signet upon my right hand, yet will I pluck him
thence."

2. God commands justice and righteousness
among men in all their actions. It is one part of the
decalogue; all the commands of the second table are to
enjoin righteousness between man and man. "He
hath shewed thee, O man, what is good; and what doth
the Lord require of thee, but to do justly, and to love
mercy, and walk humbly with thy God." (Mic. vi. 8.)
In the acts of commutative justice, see how strict God
is in the common business of buying and selling, (Lev.
xix. 35, 36.) "Ye shall do no unrighteousness in
judgment, in mete-yard, in weight or in measure; just
weights, just balances shall ye have." You that are
traders read these scriptures. (Deut. xxv. 13, 14.)
"Thou shalt not have in thy bag divers weights, a great
and a small, thou shalt not have in thine house divers
measures, a great and a small, but thou shalt have a
perfect and just weight, a perfect and just measure
shalt thou have;" and the Apostle points us to the
same thing. (1 Thess. iv. 6.) "Let no man go beyond

or defraud his brother in any matter, for the Lord is
the avenger of all such." Now he that requires man
to be thus just, shall not he be just? "Shall mortal
man be more just than God?" (Job iv. 17.) It is a
great and undeniable proof of the justice of God, that
he forbids all injustice in men.

3. Another evidence that God is a just God, is,
that justice and righteousness are the very essence of
God. In man justice is a quality or property; though
they are excellent, yet they are but qualities, and
qualities may be separated from the essence. A man
may be a man, and yet neither just nor righteous, but
God cannot be God if he be unjust. It is not a quality
in God, but his very nature and essence. Deny the
justice of God, and you deny his being. Justice can no
more be separated from him, than he can be separated
from himself. If he be not just, he were not God.
All his attributes are one in God, because they are
all one God. They are distinguished for our conceptions, but not divided from his being. Therefore
all his attributes being his essence, must be one,
or else the being of God must be a divided being,
which is blasphemy. Though the attributes of God
are distinguished in regard of their objects and effects,
yet they are all one in themselves. To make it plain
to you by a familiar instance, as when the beams of the
sun shine through a green glass, the beams are green,
when through a red glass the beams seem red, and
yet all the while the sun's beams are the same; so when
the sun shines upon clay it hardens it, and when it
shines upon wax it softens it; or when it shines upon
sweet flowers it draws out the fragrant smell, and
when it shines upon a dunghill it draws out its stench,
and yet the sun's beams are the same still; the difference

is in the objects and effects; so it is in God, when he acts towards the wicked in punishment he is righteous, and when he acts in mercy to his people in saving them he is merciful.

(4.) The very punishing justice of God, is his goodness, the same goodness in God as shewing mercy is. This is evident from that description that he gives of himself, (Exod. xxxiii. 19.) " I will make all my goodness pass before thee, and will proclaim the name of the Lord before thee," and pray what is his name. He tells you, (Exod. xxxiv. 6, 7.) " The Lord, the Lord God, gracious and merciful, long-suffering and abundant in goodness and truth, keeping mercy for thousands, forgiving iniquity, transgression and sin, and that will by no means clear the guilty, visiting the iniquity of the fathers upon the children unto the third and fourth generation," and yet this is his goodness. It is a property of goodness to hate evil, and therefore a property of goodness to punish it; his goodness shines in his very justice, for if he were not just he could not be good. What prince could be good if he did not by the hand of justice cut off those that disturb the state and government? The cutting off of a gangreened member tends to the preservation of all the rest, and therefore it is good. The goodness of every being lies in observing the order that God placed it in. Now sin is a moral distemper, therefore there is a goodness in the very punishing of it. For,

(1.) If it be an act of goodness in God to make laws and enforce those laws with threatenings, it cannot but be goodness to support those laws. The great design of the law and penalty is to promote goodness and virtue, to restrain sin and evil, therefore if there is a goodness in making them, then the executing of them is a branch of the same goodness that made them. The Holy Ghost tells us of the law of God, (and the world is to be governed by that law) that " is holy, just, and good." (Rom. vii. 12.) and needs it must, for the law is an image of the righteousness and holiness of God, and designed to hold the creature in a state of subjection to God and dependence upon him. Now this dependence upon God could not be preserved without a law, nor could the honour of the law be preserved without penalties, nor could penalties signify anything without execution.

(2.) It would argue a great defect in the goodness of God if he should not execute acts of justice against sinners; all his attributes which are part of his goodness do engage him to punish sin; without it, his power would be vilified, his holiness stained, his truth disgraced, his wisdom slighted, his grace scorned. All his attributes engage him to this. Therefore when men turn the grace of God into wantonness, it is but equal that God should turn his mercy into judgment. Justice and judgment are that which supports the throne of God. (Psa. lxxxix. 14.) "Justice and judgment are the habitation of thy throne," the Hebrew word signifies the *basis* or *pillar*, the throne of God stands upon.

(3.) The very threatenings of God, though they carry in them an aspect of severe justice, yet they proceed originally from goodness, and it appears in this, that the punishment is not the primary design of the threatening. God threatens evil to prevent the committing of it, threatens sin that we may not sin, and that God may not execute his wrath upon us

for sin. The intention of God in making the promise
and threatening are very contrary; the intention
of God in making the promise is the fulfilling
of it, but his intention in making the threatening is to prevent the fulfilling it. He promises
that he may be a rewarder, he threatens that he
may not be a revenger. Among men, the supreme
power makes a law, that treason shall be punished
with death; now the first intention of the law is not to
punish the traitor, but to prevent the treason, so that
though justice executes the threatening, yet goodness
makes it, and this confirms that of the prophet, (Ezek.
xxxiii. 11.) "That God hath no pleasure in the death
of a sinner, but that he return from his wicked ways
and live;" the penalty is not put into the law to
punish, but to prevent the breaking of the law. God
threatens damnation to the unbeliever, but the design
of the threatening is not to damn, but to drive men from
unbelief.

4. The justice of God in punishing is a forced
thing, he doth not exercise acts of vindictive justice but
upon cogent [*grounds*;] he hath no mind to punish.
Why doth he forbid sin but to prevent all occasions of
severity against his creatures. God takes all occasions
of mercy, but he [*seeks*] to prevent all occasions of
justice. Christ and the gospel were given for that
end, to bring men to God, that justice might be turned
into mercy; Oh! the goodness of God! mercy is his
darling attribute. The most noble spirits among men
are always the most gentle and merciful. but the
basest minds you will always find are most severe and
cruel. God owns mercy as the genuine offspring of
his own bowels, and therefore he is called the father of
mercy, but where is he called the father of fury and

justice? No, he saith, "fury is not in me." (Isa. xxv.
21.) He calls acts of judgment and wrath "his strange
work." (Lam. iii. 33.) " He doth not afflict willingly
nor grieve the children of men." You find a conflict
(Hosea xi. 8.) between justice and mercy in God.
" How shall I give thee up, Ephraim ? How shall I
deliver thee, Israel ? How shall I make thee as Admah ?
How shall I set thee as Zeboim ?" and mercy gets the
upper hand. " Mine heart is turned within me, my
repentings are kindled together, I will not execute
the fierceness of mine anger, I will not return to
destroy thee, Ephraim." O how God rejoices in the
victory ! Mercy rejoices over judgment.

(5.) There is a goodness in the actual execution of
justice. (Psa. cxix. 39.) " Thy judgments are good."
The present execution of judgment upon the wicked
is of great use,

I. To keep up an awful sense of God in this
world. Man would soon forget God if he did not
sometimes make himself known by the judgments he
executes. (Psa. ix. 16. Ezek. viii. 12.) " They say, the
Lord sees us not, the Lord hath forsaken the earth."
Nay, men would be apt to turn downright Atheists, and
say there is no God, and so religion would utterly
expire in the world. It is good therefore that God
doth sometimes execute justice upon men in this world.

II. He doth it to restrain the many excesses which
impunity would give great occasion to ; such is the
vileness of the heart of man, that were it not for some
fearful awe of God upon him, men would sin themselves into hell. Nothing can make men more daring
in sin than the present forbearance of God. (Psa. l. 21.)
"These things hast thou done, and I kept silence ;" and
what then ? " thou thoughtest I was altogether such

an one as thyself;" and " because sentence against an evil work is not speedily executed, therefore the heart of the sons of men are fully set in them to do evil."

III. God doth it to be a warning to others; he punishes some severely to terrify others by their example, as by our laws notorious villains are hung up in chains, that others may thereby be terrified from doing the like villainy. The judgments of God in one age are to give warning to many ages to come; Lot's wife was turned into a pillar of salt, and that pillar stands in the word of God to this day, to warn us against apostatizing from religion ; " remember Lot's wife." God hath set her up for a pillar to make all the world take heed of sinning against God. The censers of Korah, Dathan, and Abiram, were to be wrought into a plate and made a covering to the altar, there to abide for a memento to others, not to invade the priest's office without a warrant and call from God.

IV. Acts of Divine justice upon sinners are with a design of good to his own people ; the overthrow of Pharaoh and his host, was to complete the deliverance of his people from him ; God often cuts off his enemies to make way for the deliverance of his people.

V. The execution of justice many times proves the occasion of a sinner's conversion. Many are taught the fear of God by the rod of God; " When the judgments of God are abroad in the earth, the inhabitants shall learn righteousness." By this means many times hard hearts have been subdued, and unruly ones have been brought to take up the yoke. So that these things considered, there is goodness even in the punishing justice of God.

III. Let me now bring this to the case in hand to

show you what a terrible thing it is for a sinner to have to do with the justice of God.

1. Justice must be satisfied, for sin hath invaded God's right, violated his law, slighted his authority, broken the order of his government, and hereby the justice of God is provoked, and must have satisfaction; God having constituted his law, which is the rule of relative justice between himself and man, it is impossible that God should dispense with it, so as to give an exemption from punishment in the case of sin. God is the guardian of his own law, and therefore he cannot act the part of a just governor if he suffer it to be broken with impunity.   As he cannot be compassionate if he do not shew mercy to the penitent believer, and as he cannot be true if he should suffer one tittle of his word to fail, so he cannot be holy if he should countenance sin, so he cannot be just unless he should punish sin.   Guilt binds the soul over to wrath, and justice will by no means clear the guilty. If a man die under the guilt of sin, he is as sure to perish as God is just.   If sin be not pardoned to a man here in this world, it will never be pardoned, and if it be not pardoned it must be punished, for it would be unrighteous with God to let sin go unrevenged.

2. If sin must be punished and justice satisfied, then it must be either by the sinner himself, or by some other in his stead, that is capable of that undertaking.   Now the sinner cannot satisfy the justice of God himself, he hath nothing to offer God, nor could either men or angels satisfy for him.

(1.) Not man.   He that cannot redeem himself is less able to redeem another, (Psa. xlix. 7. 8.) "None of them can by any means redeem his brother, nor give to God a ransom for him, for the redemption of the soul is precious, and it ceases for ever." The soul must perish for ever as to anything man can do to redeem it.

(2.) Nor could angels satisfy the justice of God for sinners. The satisfaction must be made to God in the same nature that sinned; but the nature of angels is different from that of the sinner, besides the angels are finite creatures, and what can a finite creature do to satisfy the justice of an infinite God? If one sin sunk so many angels into hell, how can all the angels bear the sins of all the world. Therefore there is one, and there is not another, that is, the Lord Jesus Christ; the Son of God is the only fit person for this undertaking. None but he that was God in the nature of man could satisfy for sinning man. He must be man, because man had sinned, he must be God, because none else could satisfy; the satisfaction could not else be equal to the offence, therefore Christ is God-man. The satisfaction was made in the human nature suffering, and the value of it was from the Divine nature, giving virtue and value to his suffering. Had not he been man he could not have died, and had he not been God, he could not have made satisfaction. He was man to perform it, and God that he might be sufficient for it.

3. No man can have the benefit of this satisfaction made to the justice of God for sin by Christ, but in that way that God hath appointed. It cannot be had but upon God's terms. Though Christ died and laid down his life, and was a sacrifice to justice, and hath fully satisfied the justice of God for sin, yet not one sinner can ever have benefit from the goodness

and mercy of God upon this score, but upon the terms God hath placed our salvation upon; and what are they? The great condition is a penitent believing on the Lord Jesus Christ. "This is the will of him that sent me, saith Christ, that every one that seeth the Son, and believeth on him should not perish, but have everlasting life." By him whosoever believes is justified. So that justification from sin and eternal life are no ways attainable, but by getting an interest in the Lord Christ by a saving faith—Look to it, it is brought to a short issue. "He that believes on the Son hath everlasting life, and he that believes not on the Son shall not see life, but the wrath of God abideth on him." It fell upon him in the first covenant, and by slighting Christ and the grace of the Gospel, it abides on him for ever. So that a sinner in the sense of his lost and undone condition by sin, must go out of himself to Christ, and receive him by faith as the Lord his righteousness, and he must apply this righteousness to himself, or he can never have benefit by all Christ did and suffered. It is not Christ's dying or making himself a sacrifice for sin, which brings the sinner within the reach of pardoning grace and mercy, no; it must be Christ believed on and applied by faith, or thou art as far from mercy, as if Christ had never died to satisfy justice. Here it is, upon this, thousands miscarry for ever, and destroy their own souls, by an ignorant taking shelter in the mercy of God, because Christ hath died: "Oh, say they, Christ hath died for sinners, and I am a sinner, therefore I hope in the mercy of God;" whereas, let me tell you, God never saved a sinner nor ever will, nay he cannot do it, God cannot save a sinner, as such, by the consti-

tution of his own law, by which all sinners are for ever
shut out of heaven. Man breaks God's law, and
none but the righteous and holy can enter into the
kingdom of God, (1 Cor. vi. 9.) "Know ye not, that the
unrighteous shall not inherit the kingdom of God.
Be not deceived." How many deceive themselves.
" I am a sinner, God will have mercy upon me, Christ
hath died, God will have pity upon sinners. God did
not make me to damn me." I tell you an unrighteous
sinner as such can never be saved. He must be
changed, if he be saved, both relatively and really.
—" Except a man be born again, he cannot see the
kingdom of God;" he must be renewed by regene-
rating grace, or he can never be fit for heaven, he
must be pardoned and justified by the righteousness of
Christ, or he can never be freed from wrath and hell,
and have a right to heaven. Now the righteousness
of Christ justifies no man, but as it is imputed to us
by God for righteousness, and God never imputes it
to us till we actually apply it to ourselves, and it can
never be actually applied to us but by a saving faith.
Therefore, no faith no Christ, and no Christ no
righteousness, and no righteousness—no justification
from sin, and consequently no mercy from God.
Therefore, let me tell you, mercy itself, as great
and glorious as it is, cannot save an unbeliever according to the economy of the Gospel.—I speak this
because I would fain take people off from their false
props. They are exceeding apt to fly to mercy. I
say mercy cannot save an unbeliever because he is not
in Christ, and God will not save one soul out of
Christ. This well considered would make Christ of
more esteem with us, than he is. We talk of moral

righteousness which is a good thing among men, but
the misery of this is, men look to be saved by it.   If
a man be saved, it must be in one of these ways ; either
by justice or mercy. If he be saved by justice, it
must be by the first covenant, if he be saved by mercy,
it must be by the second covenant. Now justice
cannot save him by the first covenant, without a
perfect sinless righteousness of his own, and that no
man hath or can have of his own ; then it must be by
mercy ; now mercy cannot save him by the second
covenant, because he will not perform the condition of
it.   The condition of the covenant that God hath
made, is, that he shall accept of Christ, and apply the
righteousness of Christ to the soul.   Therefore mercy
cannot save an unbeliever: for,

(1.) It is not consistent with the *truth* of God.
God hath threatened death for sin, and man hath
sinned ; the truth of God is bound to make good the
threatening either upon the sinner or surety : now the
unbeliever hath no surety, no Christ, no interest in
the Redeemer.   He is under the broken covenant,
and there is no surety to that, he must bear the penalty himself ; God hath said it and he will be true to
his word : nay, God hath sworn it, (Heb. iii. 18.) that
" they which believe not, shall never enter into his
rest ;" Now then, if it be thus that God hath said it, and
sworn it, how can God be a God of truth, and save
an unbeliever ? mercy and truth meet together in
Christ.

(2.) It is no ways consistent with the *wisdom* of
God ; you own him to be the wise God, and Christ is
the wisdom of God. The highest perfection of his
wisdom that ever God discovered to the world, was in

giving Christ and sending him to die. Now if God should save a soul any other way than by faith in Christ, he would defeat the contrivance of the highest wisdom. What need of Christ, if man could be saved by the mercy of God without him? What wisdom was there in sending Christ, if salvation could be had without him?

(3.) How can mercy save where *justice* cannot but punish? Justice would be injustice, if God should spare an unbeliever. As the holiness of God cannot but hate sin, so the justice of God cannot but punish it; indeed God may and doth spare sinners for a time, but that is for the discovery and glorifying of his patience, and in honour to the mediation of Christ, for without this, the curse had taken place the day that sin entered into the world. But to spare an obstinate sinner for ever, would have been an approbation of sin, and God will have all men know he is not an approver of sin. Therefore God having manifested that he will not pardon sin without a satisfaction, and he will have it punished either in the sinner or surety, it is highly reasonable he should be punished himself who rejects Christ, who offered to save him. Mercy can no more save one that remains an object of revenging justice, under the first covenant, than justice can condemn one that lays hold on the blood of Christ in the second covenant. Men have strange notions of the mercy of God. I tell you, all the attributes are equally infinite. His justice is as great as his mercy, and they cannot invade the right of one another; so that it is most plain that mercy cannot save an unbeliever. He hath by his unbelief refused the satisfaction of Christ, and hath wickedly trod under foot the blood

of Christ, and must therefore satisfy the justice of
God himself, and so falls into the hands of the living
God, and this the text tells you is a fearful thing and
this will appear if you consider,

I. How powerful this justice of God is, into whose
hands he falls.   It is not like justice in man that often
hath a short arm and cannot reach.   It is powerful
justice.   It reaches to heaven, for it can save every
believer and therefore will, it reaches to hell and can
damn every unbeliever and therefore will; for God is
just.   What God hath promised shall be performed,
and what he hath threatened shall be executed; he
will not discourage faith in any by not rewarding it,
nor will he encourage unbelief by not punishing it.
" The right hand of the Lord is full of righteousness."
(Psa. xlviii. 10.) His right hand, that is, his power is
infinitely just, and his justice is infinitely powerful.

II. Consider the sureness of a judgment day; it is
as sure as death, (Heb. ix. 27.) nay, it is more sure
than death, for we shall not all die, but we shall all
be changed.   And when this day comes, then this
justice of God shall shew itself, for that is the day of
wrath, and " the revelation of the righteous judgment
of God." (Rom. ii. 5.) Now for the present, God
defers the execution of his justice upon sinners: God
lets them alone; they blaspheme his name, yet he lets
them alone for the present.   Why? not because he
approves of sin, or takes no notice of it, or is not
highly displeased and provoked by it, no, but it is
for two reasons,

1. One is that the sinner may have time to
bethink himself and repent and turn to God, (Rev. ii.
21.) " I gave her space to repent," that is the great

reason why God doth not [*consume*] the sinner, in the very act of sin, that he may give him time to repent ; " therefore the Lord waits to be gracious," (Isa. xxx. 18.) God will have mercy tendered to every sinner before he be executed, and he offers life and salvation by virtue of the blood of Christ, to every soul that will accept it; so that here is an opportunity, a door of hope set open, that the sinner may escape vengeance by fleeing from the wrath to come.

2. Another reason is this, God defers the execution of justice that impenitent stubborn sinners may fill up the measure of their sins. God doth not glorify a believer as soon as he hath closed with Christ, because they have more work to do for God in the world, they have a measure of grace to fill up, that they may be made meet for glory: so neither doth God cast a sinner into hell presently, because they have a measure of sin to fill up, and God gives them time to fill up their measure, and this is the meaning of that saying of Christ to the Jews, (Matt. xxiii. 32.) " Fill ye up the measure of your fathers," and then it follows, " How can ye escape the damnation of hell ?" Justice is deferred till the sinner's measure be full filled, and then the sentence is executed. Know this therefore, you that are yet in your sins, and take boldness in sin because of your impunity, because judgment is not immediately executed—know this, that you shall gain nothing by God's forbearance if it do not lead you to repentance, but a greater vengeance and a hotter hell. The longer you go on in sin, the greater will the vengeance of God be upon thee at last. " By thy hard and impenitent heart thou treasurest up to thyself wrath against the day of wrath and the revela-

tion of the righteous judgment of God:" the longer
you sin the more wrath you treasure up, and the
greater God's vengeance will be at last; as sin increases, so will the wrath of God; the slower justice is
in the progress, the sharper will it be in the issue, and
in the mean time know this, that God will not long
bear with sinners, that are under the gospel call.
The greater your means of grace that you sit under
are, the shorter time will God afford you to improve
them. Where God affords frequent calls to repentance
and turning to God, as they do ripen the believer's
graces, so do they hasten the sinner's judgment.
Therefore, woe to them that sit under the gospel in an
unbelieving state.

III. Consider the rule God judges by, and that will
make his justice terrible; and what is that? it is the
gospel. God will judge both you and me by this
blessed gospel; we shall be tried by and before the
Lord by this gospel, which as it is the best rule to live
by, so it is the worst, the most terrible for a sinner to
be judged by, because the sentence will be the most
terrible that ever God did denounce. Heathens shall
be judged without the law, by moral natural light; they
have none of Moses' law, and therefore shall be
judged by the light of nature: the Jews shall be
judged by the law, but they that live under the
gospel shall be judged by the gospel. (Rom. ii. 16.)
" In the day when God shall judge the secrets of men
by Jesus Christ according to my gospel." (2 Thess.
i. 8.) "He shall come in flaming fire, taking vengeance
on them that know not God, and obey not the gospel of
our Lord Jesus Christ."

This, indeed, is a comfortable truth to all believers,

that they shall be judged by the gospel,—to them that have embraced Christ; for as the gospel hath pronounced pardon and peace to you by Christ, so will Christ himself also in that day; if his gospel acquit you from sin, God will acquit you; "what it binds on earth shall be bound in heaven, and what it looses on earth shall be loosed in heaven." If the sentence of the gospel be for you, and speak peace to you, God will speak peace in the great day, for God will never alter the sentence of the gospel; the sentence of God in the day of judgment shall be upon every soul, according to the sentence the gospel passes on them. He that believes not is condemned already by the sentence of the gospel; therefore, God will condemn him at the last day. This is the fearful case of every unbeliever; the gospel condemns him, and God will judge him by the gospel. Would you know how it shall go with you in the last day of judgment? I tell you: look how you are interested in the grace of the gospel; as your hearts have been wrought upon by the gospel, so will God deal with you. Will you believe what Christ saith? (John xii. 48.) "The word that I have spoken, the same shall judge you at the last day." The word I have spoken, the doctrine I have preached, shall judge you at the last day: God will judge every soul of us by the gospel.

IV. Sinners shall in that day be left to the absolute justice of God. Though man made miserable by sin is the object of mercy, yet man insensible of sin, that slights his remedy, is not an object of mercy but of Justice; therefore the Apostle calls it "judgment without mercy." There is no mercy in the day of judgment for sinners.

V. Consider (but this is one thing more) that that satisfaction which justice will exact of every unbeliever, is such a satisfaction as cannot be made, by reason of the finiteness of the creature; God will have satisfaction, and the sinner cannot give it. The satisfaction is infinite; now this infinite punishment a finite creature cannot bear, and therefore his punishment must be infinite in regard of existing and continuance. Because he cannot satisfy at once (as Christ did,) therefore he must be satisfying for ever; because the sinner cannot bear the wrath of God at once, therefore he must be bearing it for ever. The justice of God shall be always satisfying and yet never satisfied : the debt shall be always paying, yet never paid. " Verily thou shalt not come out till thou hast paid the utmost farthing;" and that is never. He cannot pay it, and therefore must bear the insupportable weight of the wrath of God for ever. Therefore, it is a fearful thing to fall into the hands of the living God; because, as he is the all-knowing and Almighty God, so he is the just and righteous God, and will be so for ever, for he is the living God. It is everlasting righteousness and justice, and this makes it so dreadful. As it is the great comfort of believers to have such a mediator and surety, such an high priest to live for ever to make intercession for them, so this is the great misery of sinners, to fall into the hands of that God, who ever lives to avenge himself upon their unbelief and rebellion; to fall into the hands of a God that knows all their sins, that is so holy, that he must punish them, and so powerful, that he can punish them, and so just, that he will punish all sinners that are impenitent, and that for ever. " Therefore it is a fearful thing to fall into the hands of the living God."

SERMON VII.

―――――

"*It is a fearful thing to fall into the hands of the living God.*" (Heb. x. 31.)

I have opened to you the words, and demonstrated the truth of them, and shewed you to whom it is such a fearful thing; I am now giving you the reasons why it is a fearful thing to fall into the hands of the living God, in the sense in which it hath been explained; I have given you one reason of it.

I. That is, with respect to those attributes of God which make it so dreadful; I told you of three attributes of God which a sinner shall then especially fall under, which will make his case very fearful, and they are,

1. The omniscience of God, whereby he knows all the sins that ever we have done.

2. The power of God, whereby he is able to kill or make alive, and none can deliver out of his hand.

3. The justice of God, which will by no means spare the guilty; I then shewed you why it is such a fearful thing to have to do with God's justice—I spoke to it in three propositions:

(1.) Justice must be satisfied, because sin has invaded his right, violated his laws, slighted his authority, broken the order of his government, and hereby justice is incensed, and must therefore be satisfied.

(2.) If justice receive a satisfaction, it must be either from man himself, or some other in his stead. I shewed you that man cannot do it himself, he hath nothing to do it with, neither can angels satisfy for him, because they are finite creatures, and justice being infinite, cannot be satisfied but by an infinite person in the human nature, and never was any so but Jesus Christ. Therefore, none can satisfy justice but Christ, an infinite person in the nature that sinned.

(3.) I shewed you that none can have any benefit by this satisfaction made to the justice of God by Christ, but upon the terms and conditions God hath fixed the salvation of souls upon, and the great condition is believing on the Lord Christ. Therefore, mercy itself cannot save an unbeliever. I made it out to you by three things.

I. It is not consistent with the truth of God; he hath threatened death for sin, and man having sinned, the truth of God is engaged to make good the threatening, either upon the sinner or the surety. Now the sinner hath no surety, and therefore must bear the penalty himself.

II. It is no ways consistent with the wisdom of God to save an unbeliever. What wisdom was it in God to send Christ to satisfy his justice, if mercy could save without it?

III. How can mercy save where justice cannot but punish? Justice would be injustice, if it should spare an unbeliever. As the holiness of God cannot but hate sin, so the justice of God cannot but punish it. So that it is evident, mercy cannot save an unbeliever. He is an object of justice, for he hath no interest in mercy, he can lay no claim to it; he hath by his unbelief refused the terms of God, the satisfaction of Christ, and trod his blood under foot, and therefore he must satisfy for himself, and thus he falls into the hands of a living God, as he is a God of infinite justice; and what a fearful thing this is, I made to appear by considering five things.

1. If you consider how powerful this justice is.

2. The sureness of a judgment day; and when that day comes, then this justice of God will shew itself.

3. Consider the rule God judges by, and that is the gospel, which as it is the best rule to live by, so for an unbeliever it is the worst to be judged by. It is comfort to a believer that hath laid hold on the grace of the gospel, for the gospel pronounces pardon to them by Christ, and speaks them peace, and so will God in that day; for the sentence of God in that day shall be according to the sentence of the gospel; and wicked men, unbelievers, are sure to be cast, if this be the rule of trial, for the gospel condemns every unbeliever now, and therefore God will condemn him at last; for he judges by this rule, "The word I speak shall judge you at the last day."

4. Sinners will then be left to the absolute justice of God, and that will make it a very dreadful thing; for nothing can be more terrible than for a sinner to have to do with absolute justice.

5. The satisfaction which justice will exact from every unbeliever is such as can never be made; there-

fore it is a fearful thing to fall into the hands of the living God. So I have done with the first reason.

II. That it is a fearful thing to fall into the hands of the living God, will appear, if you consider that all the proceedings of God in the great day of judgment, shall be suited to the ministry of every man's conscience; it shall be such as a man's own conscience shall fall in with, and justify the proceedings of God in. I must speak to this gradually.

1. There is in every man such a thing as conscience. It is essential to the rational nature, therefore essential to all mankind; no man but hath a conscience; the angels, being rational creatures, are not without, either good or bad.

(1.) The good angels in heaven have a conscience, this is plain, for wherever God gives a law of obedience, there must be a principle of conscience; though God hath not in Scripture declared in what way angels are governed, by what laws they are limited, how that law is promulgated; yet the Scriptures tell us this, that all the angels in heaven are God's servants, and do his will, (Psa. ciii. 21), and in 20th. verse, they are said " to do his commandments, hearkening to the voice of his word," (Heb. i. 14,) the angels are called " ministering spirits;" now ministry denotes service from obligation; actual duty from a principle acknowledging subjection to a law, and that law can be nothing but the will of God, for God's will is the supreme law of all creatures, it being the chief rule of righteousness, and the principle that acknowledges subjection to a law is conscience, and if the will of God be the rule, and conscience the principle, of angelical obedience, then the good angels are acted by conscience, and therefore it is that Christ propounds their obedience to us for a pattern. (Matt. vi. 10.) " Thy will be done on earth, as it is in heaven." Now Christ would never have given their obedience to us for a pattern to us, if they had not acted conscience in duty; angels make conscience of obedience to God, so should we; they are above us, and of more noble natures, more like God, and yet this is their glory, that they make conscience of doing the will of God in all things.

(2.) The fallen angels (as bad as they are) those wicked spirits, the devils, have a conscience. Their apostacy hath not extinguished their natural powers. Though their faculties be defiled, yet they are not destroyed; the devils believe and tremble; they cannot think of God without horror. Conscience tells them there is a day of judgment approaching, and the very effect of these reflections is terror and trembling; hence that of the evil spirits to Christ: " Art thou come to torment us before the time ?" (Matt. viii. 29,) conscience told them there was a time a coming of greater torment than what they yet feel, and this is to them matter of trembling, and if there be a conscience in angels and devils, surely then in man. It is most plain in Scripture; you read of conscience above thirty times in the New Testament, though not in the Old the very word conscience, but you find that which signifies the same thing; for the Hebrews have no word which signifies conscience, but it is expressed in other words, sometimes by the heart and spirit; as it is said, " David's heart smote him when he had numbered the people," (2 Sam. xxiv. 10,) that is, his conscience accused him. It is the work of conscience to reflect upon the actions done, and to check for the evil ones.

" Thou knowest all the evil that thy heart was privy to,"
saith Solomon to Shimei; that is, his conscience—there
is therefore in every man a conscience.

2. Conscience is a thing that is inseparably united
to the soul, and is essential to it. In what part of the
soul this conscience is seated, hath caused various
sentiments among the learned; some place it in the
understanding, some in the will, and the like. I think
the proper place of conscience is the whole soul—
what the philosophers say of the soul in reference to
the body, that it is wholly in the whole, and wholly in
every part; that may be truly said of conscience in
reference to the soul, that it is not only a part of the
whole, but wholly in every part. Conscience is in the
understanding and acts there; it is in the will and
checks there; it is in the affections and governs there;
it is in the memory and records there. Conscience
makes the understanding practical, and the will obe-
dient, the affections spiritual, and the memory faithful.
These are all the workhouse of conscience; here it
sits, here it acts, and from hence sends forth its influences into all the actions of a man's life—it extends
itself over the whole man, and is concerned in every
interest, and every motion, from first to last; Conscience ! we may call it an universal spiritual sense, like
feeling in the body, which is not confined to any particular organ, as other senses are; seeing is confined
to the eye, a hearing to the ear, tasting to the mouth;
but this is a sense that runs through all the organs
and members of the body. Every part cannot see and
hear, but every part can feel, and truly such a thing is
conscience, it runs through all our duties and practices : faith looks to the promise, fear to the threaten-

ing, obedience to the command, repentance to sin, but conscience looks to all.

3. The office of conscience is very great: it is the greatest officer under heaven. It is the next and immediate officer under God himself. It rides, as Joseph did, in the second chariot. It hath a very high and awful power. It hath some offices respecting God; some, respecting others; some, ourselves. Some offices to be done in time, and some in eternity; while a man lives, conscience officiates; when he dies, conscience officiates; when he comes to be judged, conscience still officiates; when a man is in his eternal state, conscience officiates then. It is never out of action. As Christ saith in another case, "my Father works hitherto and I work."

(1.) Conscience is God's repository, where the revealed will of God is kept and preserved: God wrote his law on tables of stone, and he writes it also on the fleshly tables of man's heart. This is the book of record. God never discovered more of his will, than he hath written in conscience.—The declaration of his will in the moral law, is no more than what was written upon Adam's conscience; and the declaration of God's will in the covenant of grace is no more than what is written in the believer's conscience. "I will write my Laws in their hearts," (Heb. viii. 10.) There is nothing in the Scripture to be believed or practised, but it is impressed upon the believer's conscience. He can say with David in the person of Christ, "Thy law is within my heart."—Conscience is a system of practical principles, written by the finger of God, for the furtherance and help of the soul in the ways of obedience. Yet how few men make it their work to look into their consciences.—Many can read over great volumes written by other men, and yet never read one leaf in this book of conscience.

(2.) Conscience is to direct and inform us; man hath need of a guide, therefore God hath appointed conscience to lead him. This is the reason of God's writing his law in the conscience, that a man might have a sure guide of his way. Solomon saith, (Prov. xx. 27.) " The spirit of a man is the candle of the Lord," and God lights this candle in us, that all his works may be done in the light. " The way of the wicked is as darkness; they know not at what they stumble ;" and whence is it, but because they have extinguished the light of God in their souls; they have blown out God's candle by their sins ; therefore no wonder if they walk in the dark, and stumble and fall, till at last they lie down in sorrow ; what a happy world would this be, if man would act according to the guidance and directions of conscience. See what David saith, (Psa. xvi. 8.) " I have set the Lord always before me," how so? "My reins instruct me in the night season. I will bless the Lord who hath given me counsel ;" my reins instruct me, and I have set the Lord always before me. Conscience took counsel of God, and David took counsel of conscience, and that let him into the Divine presence. The reason why men live without God in the world is, because they live without conscience in the world; they slight its guidance and leading. It is no wonder that they slight our ministry, when they slight the very ministry of conscience. How can we hope that they should hearken to us, when they will not hearken to the preacher within, the preacher God hath set up in every man.

(3.) Conscience hath an impulsive and coercive power.

I. It hath an impelling power to good. It doth not only inform us what is the will of God, but it instigates to the doing of it; and the more holy and renewed a man's conscience is, the stronger are its instigations, that a man cannot but obey; "We cannot but speak the things that we have heard and seen," (Acts. iv. 20.) As if they should say, God commands us, and conscience forces us, and who shall gainsay us? It is a blessed thing to have a conscience always prompting a man to good, stirring up the grace of God that is in him.

II. Conscience hath a coercive power as to evil. It doth not only inform us about it, shew us what is evil, but cautions against it. It saith to a man, as the angel to John, "See thou do it not." As Solomon to his son, "If sinners entice thee, consent thou not." And wherever grace hath made its entrance into the heart, it willingly comes under the constraint of conscience. This made Joseph give that brave answer to his tempting mistress, "How can I do this great wickedness, and sin against God?" (Gen. xxxix. 9.) as if he should say, it is wickedness, and therefore God forbids it, and conscience restrains me, and therefore how can I do it? Austin tells of a woman, that being solicited by a lewd person to uncleanness, told him, he must then grant her one thing, to hold his hand in the fire one hour for her sake; he refused saying, it was an unreasonable demand, and saith she,

then is it not more unreasonable that, to gratify your
lust, I should burn soul and body in hell for ever?
Oh the power and restraint of conscience where
grace reigns! Even the consciences of wicked men
do many times put forth a restraining force, unless
a man by sin have stifled conscience. Woe to him
that dares sin against the authority of conscience,
for he sins against the sovereignty of God; he that
sins when conscience checks, he sins when God
forbids him, therefore no bounds can hold that sinner
that sins against the restraint of conscience.

4. Conscience takes notice of all a man's ways,
and therefore one calls it, "God's spirit in man's soul."
There is nothing a man doth in the world, but conscience takes notice of it. Every action, word and
thought, is set down in the book of conscience:
wherever a man goes, he carries this with him; when
he is in the dark, in secret, conscience observes him
there; there is no sin any man doth, but it is done in
the sight of two witnesses, and they are, God and
Conscience. We think when we sin in secret, no eye
seeth, but I tell you, God seeth, he makes darkness
light before him; and conscience seeth, and books down
all. God knows the rottenness of an hypocrite, that
his heart is not right in the sight of God; thou that
art a secret adulterer, and thinkest that no eye seeth
thee, doth not conscience look on, and observe all?
Therefore, take heed what you do; do nothing now
that you would not be willing to hear of again at the
day of judgment, for most certainly you shall. It is
said, when father Latimer was examining for his life,
and heard one behind the hangings, writing down
all he said, it made him very cautious what he said.

Conscience writes down all, and this book God will
open at the last day.

5. Conscience is deputed a witness, and this is
the reason why it takes such exact notice of a man's
state and way, it is in order to witness-bearing, that
it may give evidence for or against a man according to
the merit of his cause. Every man hath a witness
within. (1 John v. 10.) "He that believeth on the
Son of God, hath the witness in himself;" conscience
witnesses to the work of grace, to the truth of his faith.
So I may say he that believeth not on the Son of God
hath the witness in himself; conscience witnesses
against him for unbelief, for refusing Christ, for
making God a liar, because he believes not the record
that God hath given of his Son : and this is as a
thousand witnesses ; if conscience witnesses against
us, it will be no comfort whoever applauds us ; and if
conscience clears us, we have matter of rejoicing,
whatever charge may be brought against us. (Job
xxvii. 5, 6.) "Till I die I will not remove my
integrity from me ; my righteousness I will hold fast,
and will not let it go ;" my heart, that is my conscience,
shall not reproach me as long as I live ; men may
reproach me, but my conscience never shall ; I will
behave myself so that my conscience may witness for
me, though all the world witness against me ; this is
one of the great offices of conscience, and one great
end why God placed it in man, to be a witness hereafter ; and indeed there is none so fit to be a witness
between God and us in the great day, as a man's own
conscience, and this will appear if you consider three
things.

(1.) It is a witness of God's own appointing, and

God hath ordained it, and set it up to give evidence, both to saints and sinners, and it is a faithful witness that will not lie.

(2.) Conscience stands indifferent between God and man, and therefore the fitter to be a witness. Interest leads to partiality, but he that is indifferent, is the liker to be for the equity of the case. Conscience is a thing between both parties—it is not so of God, but it hath something of man; nor so of man, but it hath something of God in it, and therefore the fittest to give evidence.

(3.) None can know so much of a man, as his own conscience doth; the devil knows much of us, he knows every overt act of sin that ever we did, but yet there is very much he doth not know of a man; I may say, there are many secret sins, inward sins, latent sins, sins of thought and affection, which Satan is no ways privy to, nor can he be while they are hid there, and therefore he can give no evidence concerning them. Many sins a man is guilty of in the secrets of his soul, that the devil knows nothing of, till they come into act; but now conscience within knows all; the spirit of man is the candle of the Lord searching all the inward parts. (1 Cor. ii. 11.) "What man knows the things of a man save the spirit of a man that is in him?" this is his conscience. So that you see there is no witness so proper and fit as conscience to give evidence for or against a man in the great day; therefore, God hath told us in his Word that he will proceed in judgment with every man in the great day, according to the testimony of his own conscience. Saints and sinners, believers and unbelievers, shall all stand or fall by the evidences of

their own consciences ; the process of that day will be
according to what is charged and proved—God is a
righteous judge, and the judgment of that day will
be a righteous judgment : it is called the day of
the righteous judgment of God, because then he will
judge upon clear evidence, and will manifest his righteousness. Now, there can be no clearer evidence
than the witness of a man's own conscience ; thus shall
it be in the great day; and this, I think, is made plainly
out, (Rev. xx. 12.) where it is said, speaking of the
great judgment day, "The dead stood before God,
and the books were opened, and the dead were judged
out of those things which were written in the books,
according to their works." What books are those out
of which men shall be judged ? The book of God's
Omniscience, and the book of a man's own Conscience.

God will have one book and man another, and both
shall agree to a tittle ; and whereas it is said the books
were opened, it is to be understood of a divine irradiation, whereby God doth enlighten conscience to do its
office in that day ; sin now hath blinded the sinner's
conscience, so that he seeth not the hell of sin that
is in his heart and nature. He makes a mock of sin,
laughs at it, and knows no evil in it. But in that day
the case will be altered ; God will then so wonderfully
enlighten conscience, that all his past sins shall come
into his view, and shall be plain and open before him.
Now if every sin be written in the book of conscience,
and if that book must be opened, and God will set
every sin before a man, it is a dreadful consideration.
(Psalm l. 21.) "These things hast thou done,
(speaking of their adultery and other wickedness,) and
I kept silence, and thou thoughtest I was altogether

such an one as thyself, (as if I approved and liked
sin, as if I had no enmity to sin, because I did not
presently punish it;) but (saith God) I will reprove
thee, and set them in order before thine eyes;" not
a sin done but God will bring it into remembrance,
and the sinner shall have a full view of it. (1 Cor. iv.
5.) "Judge nothing before the time, until the Lord
come, who will bring to light the hidden things of
darkness, and will make manifest the counsels of the
heart;" secret heart sins, God will bring all to light and
make them manifest; and this is that which men are
to understand by opening the books. When God
shall open conscience in that day, by letting in light,
then the sinner shall see every sin, every lust, and
every vile affection there: the books shall be opened,
and then it follows, the dead were judged out of those
things which were written in the books, according to
their works; that is, they shall be judged by God's
Omniscience, and according to the witness of Conscience; so that every man at the great day shall stand
and fall before God, by the evidence of his own conscience. So then by this a man might know, if he would
but look inward, and keep intelligence and hold a
communion with his own conscience, he might know
how it is like to go with him in the judgment of God.
If our hearts condemn us not, saith the Apostle, that
is our own consciences, if upon due search they acquit
us from hypocrisy and reigning sin, then have we confidence towards God, we have liberty of access now,
and boldness in the day of judgment hereafter. A man
may go to the bar of God with comfort, if his conscience speaks him peace, if that condemns him not.
Again, saith he, if our consciences condemn us, God

is greater than our hearts and knows all things. If conscience condemns, God is greater and knows more, and then it follows he will condemn us much more. The Apostle in this scripture, doth plainly intimate thus much to us, that the voice of conscience is the very voice of God. "What it binds on earth is bound in heaven, and what it looses on earth is loosed in heaven." It acquits or condemns us in the name of God, therefore God will acquit or condemn. If conscience speaks us peace in the blood of Jesus applied by faith, God will speak us peace; but if conscience condemns us, God will ratify the sentence of conscience; therefore (I say) as the consolations of conscience are most sweet, so its condemnations are very terrible and dreadful.

6. Conscience is an inseparable companion. It is with us whatever we do, and goes with us wherever we go; it can no more be separated from a man than the shadow can from the body. It accompanies us whilst we live, and when we die. Conscience is then with us, and is more active and vigorous than ever; and after death when the soul and body part, the soul and conscience do not part; wherever the soul goes, that goes; if to judgment, conscience goes with it; if to heaven or hell conscience goes with it. It will be every man's companion in the other world for ever. Oh how glad would the damned be, if they might but leave their consciences behind them, when they leave this world, and go into eternity! But it cannot be, for,

7. Conscience is the seat and centre of the wrath of God in all the damned; for look, as the toad leaves a filth and slime behind it, so all the corruptions and

filth of sins settle upon the conscience; "their mind and conscience is defiled." (Tit. i. 15.) This is the great privilege of all believers; that their consciences are purged from the guilt and filth of sin by Christ's blood. (Heb. ix. 14.) Hereby they are so purified that they become the region of light and peace, but all the guilt of an unbeliever's whole life fixes and settles upon the conscience; conscience is not only engaged to God as a judge, but is a principal guide and direction of the soul in its whole course. It is the bridle of the soul to restrain it from sin, the eye of the soul to direct its way, and therefore it is principally chargeable with all the evils of the life, and if it be so, what a treasure of guilt must be heaped up on the unbeliever's conscience! (Rom. ii. 5.) He speaks of "sinners treasuring up wrath against the day of wrath;" that is, by increasing and adding more guilt, for guilt and wrath are treasured up together; for as guilt increases, so wrath increases, till the measure be full, and then God calls for an account.

8. The sinner carries all the guilt that is upon his conscience to the bar of God; for as conscience follows the sinner wherever he goes, so doth guilt follow the conscience, yea to the very grave, and to judgment. "His bones are full of the sins of his youth." (Job. xx. 11.) That is, his conscience is as full of sin, as his bones are of marrow; and in the next words it follows, they shall lie down with him in the dust; the meaning is, that sin shall never leave the wicked man alive or dead; neither in this world nor in the next; the sins of believers die before them, and that is comfortable, but the sins of unbelievers go to the grave with them, and that is dreadful. Believe

this, unless a man dies to sin while he lives, his sin shall live with him when he is dead; they go down into the grave with him, and to judgment, and to hell with him, he and they shall never part. As the graces of a believer, so the sins of unbelievers follow the soul wherever it goes: therefore as the Holy Ghost saith, (Rev. xiv. 13.) " Blessed are the dead that die in the Lord, for they rest from their labours, and their works follow them," follow them to judgment, to heaven, and eternal glory; so I may say, cursed are the dead that die not in the Lord, for their sins follow them, and needs they must, for nothing but pardoning grace can remove guilt, and without faith in the Lord Christ, there can be no pardoning grace, therefore their guilt remains ; as Christ saith, " Because ye believe not, ye shall die in your sins." (John viii. 23.) Oh how glad would sinners be, if they might go to the grave, and sin not go with them ; but ye shall die in your sins, saith Christ, that is, they shall never leave you, but shall follow you to judgment, and shall lie upon your conscience to eternity ; for though acts of sin pass, yet the guilt of it abides.

9. Conscience will be the sinner's tormentor in the next world. Guilt followed with wrath is tormenting ; and conscience, which now is the centre of guilt, shall then be the centre of wrath, and being filled with the wrath of God, oh how will it torment the sinner ; therefore it is called " a worm, a never-dying worm," (Mark ix. 44.) to set out the greatness, and inwardness, and everlastingness of its gnawing torments ; it is one of the greatest miseries in hell. The torments that a man bears in hell from the

charges of his own conscience, are the greatest misery
of hell. By this raging of conscience in this world, we
may give a little guess at it. In the midst of all our sins
and pleasures, it is a very hell upon earth, as you see
by the woeful example of Cain and Judas, and Spira
and child; and if it be so, that conscience is such a
dreadful thing, when it rages in a man here, what will
it be when it shall be filled up with the wrath of God.
Pangs of conscience here are but as the first-fruits of
hell. It will then be very dreadful, especially in four
things.

(1.) By reflecting and looking back on what is past;
this will heighten the punishment of loss. When thus
the sinner considers the heaven, the glory and happiness he is for ever deprived of, and that by his own
folly; when he shall consider, upon what fair terms
salvation by the blood of Christ, was offered to him,
how much time he had to work out his own salvation;
what opportunities God put into his hands; what
variety of means God afforded him; for what trifling
matters he lost his immortal soul; and again, besides
this punishment of loss, he shall find by sad experience
what before he would not believe, what a dreadful
place hell is, what a fearful thing it is to fall into the
hands of the living God, how often he was warned to
flee from the wrath to come, what tenders were made
to him in the name of Christ, yet none would prevail.
Again, when he shall consider that he himself was the
cause of his own ruin, that he hath destroyed himself
by his own hands; when he is lashed by cords of his
own twisting, tormented by a fire of his own kindling;
and when to all he shall add this, that this hell, and
wrath, and misery, was through his own choice; God

and his ministers set before him life and death, heaven
and hell, and he refused heaven and eternal life for
the sake of his base lusts—who can forethink what
the terrors of such a reflection as this will be ?

(2.) All the charges and reflections of conscience
shall then be so positive, and self-evident, as shall
leave the sinner destitute of all manner of excuse; for
when conscience convinces and condemns, there is
no standing before it. Every sinner is now a self-
destroyer, and in that day he shall be a self-con-
demner. When God condemns, conscience will condemn too, and so it will justify the righteous judgment of God; every mouth shall then be stopped, as
the man that had not the wedding garment was
speechless : he was convinced of the righteous judg
ment of God, and of his own sin.

(3.) Conscience will be always upbraiding the sinner
in hell, with his own wilfulness and obstinacy against
Christ, and his madness in sinning, as the cause of
all, and this will be like a continual rubbing of a green
wound with salt and vinegar. The upbraidings of
conscience will make it a worm indeed.

(4.) Lastly, add to all this, that conscience shall be
still looking forward to all that is to come ; and the
dreadful expectation of wrath without end makes it a
never-dying worm. The guilt of past sins, and the
sense of present torments, and the dread of their everlasting continuance, which will then fill the soul, will
make it a most insufferable tormentor; so that the
sinner shall in that day be his own executioner; as
God inflicts punishment so shall conscience; he shall
be tormented by conscience, as by a worm that never
dies; and this makes it evident, that it is a fearful

thing to fall into the hands of the living God, because the proceedings of God in the day of judgment with sinners, shall be suited to the ministry of a man's own conscience, such as his own conscience shall fall in with, and justify all the proceedings of God.

SERMON VIII.

"*It is a fearful thing to fall into the hands of the living God.*" (Heb. x. 31.)

I am giving you the reasons of the truth, why it is such a fearful thing to fall into the hands of the living God.

I. The first reason was with respect to those attributes of God that make it so, especially his Omniscience, his Power, and his Justice.

II. I gave you the second reason the last time; and that was because all the proceedings of God in that day will be suited to the ministry of a man's conscience, and such as that shall fall in with. I spake to this gradually in nine conclusions, and shall not look back, but proceed to the third reason.

III. It is a fearful thing to fall into the hands of the living God, because all that do so are in a covenant wherein the great design of God is to glorify his justice; there is no room for mercy there; either perfect duty or absolute misery are the unchangeable terms of that covenant. Do well and live, or sin and die, is the only voice you shall hear, so long as you hold by that tenure, and are under that covenant. God asked

Adam when he fell, what hast thou done? He did not ask him if he had repented. (Ezek. xviii. 20.) " The soul that sinneth shall die ;" the least breach of that covenant is fatal, and the penalty of it is intolerable ; foregoing sins cannot be expiated by subsequent duties, paying new debts will no way quit the old score. All the dispensations of God to man in that covenant are judicial, but the worst is to come, and that is, that it puts the sinner into the hands of God : when he deals with his people, it is in and by a media-tor, but he deals with sinners alone, and therefore his dealing with the one is all in mercy, and with the other in judgment. It is an unspeakable misery (though the natural man does not consider it) to be under the covenant of works. There is a vulgar mistake abroad, which supposes that the first covenant was disannulled and repealed upon the fall, and that God now deals with us upon new terms, as if the covenant of grace did wholly exclude and shut out the former contract, wherein they think Adam only was concerned ; but the consideration of Adam's being a public person would sufficiently shew the grossness of that mistake, for that covenant was not made with Adam personally, but representatively, as the head of all mankind, and therefore not only with him, but with his seed ; and every natural man, whilst natural, and a son of Adam, is obliged to the tenure of Adam's cove-nant, as much as Adam was. The form of the law runs in universal terms, " Cursed is every one that continueth not in all things written in the book of the law to do them." (Gal. iii. 10.) And this rule brooks no exception, but that of free grace, through an interest in Christ, and therefore all natural men are described by this term, that they are " under the law." (Gal. iv. 5,) that is, under the bond and curse of the covenant of works. If this law had been repealed and laid aside presently upon Adam's fall, then Christ had not come under the bond and curse of it, as our substitute and surety, for he was to take our debt upon him, and to submit to the duties and penalties of our engagements ; therefore it is said in the place aforementioned, that " he was made under the law, to redeem them that are under the law." And again, (Gal. iii. 13.) " Christ hath redeemed us from the curse of the law, being made a curse for us."

Again, the law is not repealed, because it is an unchangeable rule, according to which God proceeds ; " not one jot or tittle of the law shall pass, till all be fulfilled," (Matt. v. 18.) that is, till all be fulfilled by the creature, or upon the creature, or by and upon his surety for him. It is the covenant of works that condemns all the sons of Adam. The vigour of it brought Christ from heaven to fulfil it for all believers. Either we must have Christ to fulfil it for us, or we must for the breach of it necessarily perish for ever; therefore the Apostle James says, that at the day of judgment, God proceeds with all men according to one of the two covenants, (James ii. 12, 13.) that of works, or that of grace ; some are judged by the law of liberty, that is the covenant of grace, some have judgment without mercy, that is, by the law of the first covenant. The two covenants have two principal confederating parties, that have contracted for them and their heirs, (viz.) Adam and Christ, therefore so long as thou art Adam's heir, thou hast Adam's engagements upon thee : the covenant of works was made with Adam, and his seed

who are [*all*] natural men; the covenant of grace
was made with Christ and his seed who are all believers. Now God will own no interest in them that
claim by Adam. As Abraham was to reckon his seed
by Isaac, and not by Ishmael, (in Isaac shall thy seed
be called) so all God's children are reckoned by
Christ, and in covenant with God in Christ, they are
the seed: and that is the covenant wherein the great
design of God from first to last is to glorify his grace;
but the design of God in the covenant of works is
to glorify his justice, and therefore you read of no
grace, no pity, no mercy, in that covenant from first to
last. God reveals himself there to be a just God,
rewarding good and punishing evil; there is nothing
in that covenant, but strict justice. In the covenant
of grace, God makes another representation of himself; he shews himself gracious and merciful; " I will
be merciful to your iniquities," (Jer. xxxi. 34.) but there
is nothing in the covenant of works but strict justice,
and therefore, there is no such thing there as the forgiveness of sin. The voice of pardoning mercy was
never heard in that covenant. Nothing the creature
can do, can attain one dram of it, God does not look
at any man's repenting or returning from sin there,
but only considers whether he hath sinned or not. As
in a court of justice, when matters of a capital nature,
and such as relate to life and death are tried, the inquiry
is into the nature of the fact, and not into the quality
of the person, there is no regard had whether the person be penitent, but whether the fact was committed
or not, and if he be found guilty, the law condemns
him, and no repentance can avail him. So it is in
God's court of justice under that covenant; for as he

sits on a throne of grace in the one covenant, so he sits on a throne of justice in the other, and where he sits on this seat, every thing is managed according to the rules of strict justice; justice indicts; justice examines; justice pronounces sentence; justice executes the sentence. So that whoever hath sinned receiveth according to all the evil that he hath done. Hence is it (as I said before) that when Adam had sinned, the inquiry is not, " hast thou repented of thy folly?" but " what hast thou done ?" and God proceeds upon that. Oh ! how great is the difference between the two covenants, that of works in Adam, and that of grace in Christ. The voice of the one is, "the soul that sins shall die." The voice of the other is, "As I live, I desire not the death of a sinner;" in the one covenant, God condemns both sin and the sinner, but in the other he condemns the sin, and spares the sinner, and the reason is, because the one covenant hath a mediator, and the other hath none; in the covenant of grace sin is laid upon the surety, and the sinner goes free, but in the other, sin and the sinner are condemned together, for in that covenant there is no mediator, no surety; nor did there need any, for when the covenant was first made, man being in a holy and righteous state, with an heart and mind fitted to answer the heart and mind of God, there was a full agreement. " Now a mediator is not a mediator of one," (Gal. iii. 20.) that is, of parties that are agreed, and between whom there is no difference—therefore the first covenant was an immediate covenant wherein man had to do with God without any Christ, and all the transactions in that covenant between God and man were managed in an immediate way. It was a covenant without a mediator, and so it is still, for though the nature of man be altered, the nature of the covenant is the same still. Sin hath broken the covenant, but it hath not altered it; it is the same for ever, and therefore as it was without a mediator before the fall, so it is still; and if it be so, then every soul that is in that covenant is in a Christless condition; so long as man lives under it, he lives without Christ, and if he dies under it, he dies in a Christless condition, and without Christ, and therefore must necessarily fall into the hands of strict justice; for the design of God in that covenant is to glorify his justice, and therefore the subjects of it shall have judgment without mercy, wrath without mixture, not one drop of mercy mingled to moderate the fierceness of God's indignation, and "who can abide the fierceness of his wrath!" (Nah. i. 6.) When God sets himself to glorify his justice, he doth ever join vengeance to it; therefore he is still " a judge and an avenger." (Rev. vi. 10.) There is a great deal of difference between a judge and an avenger, and between justice and vengeance; a judge commonly does acts of justice in the behalf of others, but an avenger is one that does justice on his own behalf; and therefore of old, the next of kin seeking the life of the murderer was called an avenger of blood, and God speaks after the same manner of himself. " I will avenge me of my adversaries." (Isaiah i. 24.) Abused patience provokes justice, and that is mixed with vengeance. And when God will put forth his vengeance for the glorifying of his justice,—Oh! how sad must the case of that miserable sinner be upon whom it falls. He comes to render " vengeance on them that know not God, and that obey not the Gospel," (2 Thes.

i. 8.)   And what the issue of that will be, the next verse tells you, "who shall be punished with everlasting destruction;" and this is the reason why the apostle says here, in the text, "It is a fearful thing to fall into the hands of the living God," because he is a God of vengeance; do but see the verse preceding the text, "vengeance belongeth to me, and I will repay it, saith the Lord;" therefore it follows, "It is a fearful thing to fall into the hands of the living God.   Vengeance is the actual execution of judgment upon sinners, according to their desert, without any mixture of mercy, and therefore vengeance is appropriated to God alone; "to me vengeance belongeth," and it doth so, upon a two-fold account.

1. As being that which no creature hath any interest in.   This is intended in that of David, (Psalm xciv. 1.)   "Oh! God to whom vengeance belongs," and he repeats it, "to whom vengeance belongs, shew thyself;" the repetition of it implies that it belongs to God, and none else, and therefore it is forbid to others. (Rom. xii. 19.) "Dearly beloved, avenge not yourselves, but rather give place to wrath," and why? "for it is written, vengeance is mine," none have to do with vengeance but God, and the reason is, because it respects only sin in its own formal nature, and so it is sin against God, and therefore—

(1.) Though men may inflict punishment upon sin, they do it principally upon other accounts; whatever of vengeance is in punishment is merely an emanation from the divine constitution.

(2.) No creature can take the just measures of the desert of sin, so as to give it a just recompense, and therefore they have nothing to do with vengeance.

(3.) The power of the creature cannot extend to the just execution of vengeance, because sin deserves eternal punishment.

(4.) Pure vengeance (as such) is not to be trusted to man, nor would he know how to manage it, but would run into one excess or another to the ruin of his own soul.

For such reasons as these, God hath reserved all vengeance to himself, and though he hath allowed the punishment of offenders to the magistrates and men in authority, in order to the peace and good government of the world; yet vengeance (as it denotes giving satisfaction to ourselves in the punishment of others,) is forbidden to all persons both public and private.

2. In this appropriating vengeance to God, there is this included, that in due time God will execute it. " I will repay it, saith the Lord;" God oftentimes exercises great patience and forbearance, and doth not suddenly avenge himself, for he is God and not man, and this makes wicked men secure, and despise the threatenings of God for sin,—" Let the Holy One of Israel come, that we may see;" (Isaiah v. 19.) because vengeance is not speedily executed, therefore the hearts of the sons of men are set in them to do evil, but God hath his set time for execution, and then he will not spare ; hence he calls it the day of his righteous judgment, "the year of recompence, and the day of vengeance," (Isa. xxxiv. 8.) and from this consideration of the vengeance of God against sinners, the apostle brings in the text by way of inference : as if he had said, seeing he is a just God, and justice is mixed with vengeance, and this vengeance belongs to God alone, and the day is coming

wherein he will repay it, therefore, it is a fearful thing
to fall into the hands of the living God. That is the
third reason.

IV. It is a fearful thing to fall into the hands of the
living God. Because of the impartiality of the sentence that, in that day, shall be passed by God upon
the sinner; and that it will be impartial, appears in
three things.

1. There will be no distinction of persons.

2. The sentence will be suited to the nature of the
cause.

3. No sin shall escape the sentence.

This shews God's justice to be very impartial, and
that makes it dreadful.

1. There shall be no distinction of persons, it
shall not be then as it too often happens now; judges
corrupted or bribed, may favour one more than another, sometimes they aggravate a matter, and amplify
an evidence, beyond the merits of the cause, on purpose to cover the injustice of the sentence: and
sometimes they smother and lessen the evidence, to
diminish the guilt, and so make way for a favourable
sentence, according as they are biassed towards the
person before them. But the righteous God cannot
be inclined, either to favour or severity, upon any such
terms. God will not favour the guilty to shew his
respect, nor condemn the innocent, to the reproach of
his righteousness. The Scripture tells you, there is
" no respect of persons with God, nor taking of gifts,"
(2. Chron. xix. 7.) implying, that it is many times
gifts and bribes that cause respect of persons. God
respects none, not the meanest for pity, nor the highest for fear of their greatness; what is it to accept, but

only to shew more respect to the man, than to the matter, to be more swayed by the circumstances of the person than by the merits of the cause; now " God accepts no man's person," nor does he regard the rich more than the poor, no man shall fare the better in that day, because of his riches, for " riches profit not in the day of wrath," (Prov. xi. 4.) nor shall the poor man fare the worse for his meanness, and mark the reason ; "for all are the work of his hands," and that in a double respect, viz. in regard of their natural, and their civil state.

(1.) In regard of their natural state; God hath made them both alike, with a body of the same parts, and a soul of the same powers ; the rich man's body hath not one member, nor his soul one faculty, more than the poor man's hath.

(2.) In regard to their civil state ; they are both the works of his hands in this sense too, that is, he makes one man rich and the other poor, as himself pleaseth ; and therefore, though man may regard the one more than the other, yet God will not. He is " without respect of persons judging according to every man's works." (1 Pet. i. 17.) No degree of greatness will give a man the least advantage in that day. " I saw the dead, small and great stand before God." (Rev. xx. 12.) Kings then leave their crowns and sceptres behind them, and are denuded of all their robes of state, and shall carry nothing with them to the bar of God, but their works. And as no outward greatness, so no spiritual privileges, will avail a man in that day, without real holiness. It is very natural for men to presume upon these ; they are members of the reformed church, and of the strictest sect in religion, and in this, value themselves. But this proves them no more Christians than being of a company of merchants, proves a man a rich citizen. " Many shall say to me in that day, Lord, Lord, have we not prophesied in thy name, and in thy name cast out devils, and in thy name done many wonderful works; then will I profess unto them, I never knew you, depart from me, ye workers of iniquity." (Matt. vii. 22, 23.) As all men are equally subject to his laws, so shall they be equally accountable for all their actions.

2. Though there be no distinction of persons, yet there shall be a distinction of causes. For if the sentence be different, (go ye cursed, and come ye blessed) then the causes must needs be different. The justice of the sentence stands in its suitableness to the nature of the case, and God says, every man shall be judged according to his works. The Apostle tells us, (Gal. vi. 7, 8.) " Whatsoever a man sows, that shall he also reap. He that sows to the flesh, (in sin, lust, and wickedness) shall of the flesh, reap corruption ; but he that sows to the Spirit, (in faith, love, and holiness) shall of the Spirit reap life ever-lasting ;" here is a sowing and a reaping, and as a man sows, so shall he reap. Beloved now is our sowing time, you and I are sowing for eternity, and when is the harvest ? Why, that is in the next world, in the great day of God, and what we sow here, we shall be sure to reap the fruit of there. The seed that is now sown, will come up, and ripen in eternity. Be it good seed (such as faith, repentance, obedience, and holiness,) or bad seed (such as unbelief, indulging sin, and lusts, and love of the world,) the harvest will be according as the seed is, for God hath said—every

man shall reap the fruits of his own doings. (Jer. xxi. 12.) So that this (by the way) may confute that ignorant mischievous notion, that many silly souls have sucked in, and which has too much fomented the Atheism of this generation, viz: " If I am elected I shall be saved, and if I am not elected, I shall be damned, when I have done all I can :" and upon this, men cast away all care of God, and duty, and an immortal soul, that they may perish in their lusts with quietness. Let me tell you this is a very ignorant, and abominable gross mistake; for eternal election gives no man a right to heaven ; it is his believing in Christ, and applying the merits of Christ to his soul, that gives him his right to heaven. God ordains a man to eternal life, but it is faith that entitles him to it, and therefore it is said, " as many as were ordained to eternal life believed." (Acts. xiii. 48.) An elected person is not saved merely because he is elected, but because he complies with the conditions of salvation, and comes up to those terms of life which God hath established in the gospel. Besides there is no such thing as an election which separates between the end and the means, therefore to say, " If I am elected, I shall be saved, live as I will ;" is foolish nonsense. The same act of God's will which decreed our salvation, hath decreed our believing, and sanctification also ; the Apostle is express in it, (2 Thess. ii. 13.) "God hath from the beginning chosen you to salvation, through sanctification of the Spirit, and belief of the truth," that is, through faith and holiness. God hath as much elected me to believe, as to be saved, and therefore, " without holiness no man shall see God." (Heb. xii. 14,) so (1 Pet. i. 2.) " Elect according to

the foreknowledge of God the Father, through sanctification and obedience." He that is chosen of God,
is "chosen in Christ," that he may be conformed
to Christ. (Eph. i. 4.) "Whom he did foreknow, he
did predestinate to be conformed to the image of his
Son." (Rom. viii. 29,) that is, he decreed they should
be like Christ, first in grace and holiness, and then in
glory. We are elected to glory by grace, for there can
be no salvation without a disposition of the subject
thereunto, and that disposition lies in a work of saving
grace wrought in the heart, and therefore it is an everlasting truth, no grace, no glory; no conversion, no
salvation; no obedience, no inheritance; "for Christ is
the author of eternal life to them that obey him,"
and to them only. (Heb. v. 9.) Therefore I say, this
is a foolish suggestion, "if I am elected, I shall be
saved, &c." The question is, dost thou believe? Art
thou holy? for if God hath elected you, he hath elected
you to these. The same thing may be said (on the other
hand) concerning reprobation, no man ever perished
merely because he was a reprobate, but because he was
an unbeliever and disobedient; God's secret will is not
that which we are to guide ourselves by, but his
revealed will; his secret will is a rule to himself, but
it is no rule to us. (Deut. xxix. 29.) "Secret things
belong to God, but those things that are revealed
belong to us, and to our children." Look to the
word of God, to what he hath there discovered, and
directed to, with respect to our salvation. We are
not first to look to God's purposes concerning us, but
to his precepts given to us; not to what God hath
done before time, but to what he would have us do in
time. The great law of God concerning you and me

is, that we should believe in Christ, and this hath
salvation infallibly annexed to it, without exception
of any one soul, and this I say, that whatsoever the
secret decree of God is, yet, as there is no man can
be saved, but by believing, so there shall no man be
damned, but for sin ; God will not reckon with men
for what his secret decrees are, but for what their
works are, and by them they shall stand or fall.
When God deals with believers, he brings their works
to the rule, and judges them by their works; the
reward is dispensed according as the rule is, and as
their works agree with that ; " the words that I have
spoken, they shall judge you." (John xii. 48.) They
to whom the gospel of God promiseth eternal life,
shall infallibly obtain it, and none shall obtain it that
are excluded by the Gospel; those, who being sensible
of sin, do cordially [*mourn*] for it, and entirely depend
on the grace of God as revealed in Christ, shall
certainly be saved and glorified ; and as one believer
hath excelled another in obedience and service here, so
shall he have a more excellent reward than another
believer hereafter, God will crown his own graces
according as the saints have improved them.   He that
employs and trades but with two talents, with his
utmost skill and diligence, shall have a greater
reward than he that had ten talents, and was less
careful to employ them to his master's advantage.
God will not swerve from his established rule ; " he
that sows sparingly shall reap sparingly, and he that
sows liberally, shall reap bountifully." (2 Cor. ix. 6.)
And if God will be thus impartial in his retributions
to the saints, then he will be so much more, in his
punishing sinners; for the reward of the saints, is the

reward of their duty, and that is the effect of rich grace
and favour; but the recompense of sinners is their due,
and deserved by justice; therefore the severity of the
sentence will be in proportion to the number and nature
of their sins.   So that, look, as the saints are all alike
saved, but not all alike glorified, so sinners shall be all
alike damned, but not all alike tormented.   Sins of ignorance will find a hot hell, but sins against light and knowledge will find a much hotter. (Luke xii. 47.) " He that
did not know his Lord's will, and did things worthy of
stripes, shall be beaten with few stripes; but he that
knew his Lord's will and did it not, shall be beaten
with many stripes."   Therefore the case of the poor
blind heathens will be much more tolerable than that
of the Jews, because they had not such means of
knowledge, and the case of the Jews will be much
more tolerable than that of us Christians who have
such a Gospel, and such means of grace as the Jews
never had.

The clearer the light, the stricter the precept,
the holier the examples, the louder the calls, and
the richer the promises that are set before us,
the more severe and intolerable shall be the judgment of every soul, that sets light by them.   There
is no light so clear as the light of the Gospel.
It is said on its first breaking forth, "the people
that sat in darkness saw great light;" no precepts
so strict as those of the Gospel, no example so
holy as the example of Christ set before us, there
is no call so loud as that call of the Gospel, no
promises so rich and great as the promises of the
Gospel; therefore no judgment so heavy as the
judgment of them that perish under the Gospel;

for as their guilt is, so shall their judgment be. God will proportion the sentence according to the sin, and the punishment shall be exactly suited to the nature of the crime.

3. There is no sin shall escape the sentence of that day. This Scripture is very full to this purpose, (Eccles. xii. 14.) " God will bring every work into judgment, with every secret thing, whether it be good or evil." So saith the Apostle, (2 Cor. v. 10.) " We must all appear before the judgment seat of Christ, that every one may receive according to the things done in the body, according to that he hath done, whether it be good or bad." Those sins that have been acted in the close hiding place, and concealed from all manner of notice, shall then be made manifest, our Lord tells you, (Mark iv. 22.) " There is nothing hid which shall not be manifested ; neither is there any thing kept secret, which shall not come abroad ;" all the sins of commission shall then be brought to the bar, whether they be sins of youth, or sins of riper years, sins of lesser or greater guilt, of a crimson or of a common dye, none shall escape ; no, not one ; how can evil works escape when an idle word shall not ? (Matt. xii. 36.) " I say unto you, that every idle word that men shall speak, they shall give an account thereof in the day of judgment :" and if for every idle word, how much more for all unclean, impure, and filthy words, all corrupt communications, lying, swearing, all wicked profane blasphemous words? Oh, what an account must be given for these ! Lord, how many have been sunk into hell by the weight of their own tongues, and perished by the sword of their own mouths. Solomon hath an excellent proverb to

this purpose, (Prov. xiii. 3.) " He that keepeth his
mouth, keepeth his life, but he that openeth his lips
wide shall have destruction." That of Christ is
the same. " By thy words thou shalt be justified,
(if they be good) and by thy words, thou shalt
be condemned, (if they be idle and evil)." (Matt.
xii. 37.) It would grieve one to hear what language
fills the streets ; what cursing, swearing, and filthy
discourse is abroad, such as stains the ears of a
Christian. Remember this, light words weigh heavy
in God's balance: one saith of this Scripture, if
there were no other text in the Bible to prove
our need of another righteousness than our own,
in which to stand before God, this were enough.
Oh ! what need have you and I to be much in
the use of David's prayer. " Set a watch, O
Lord, before my mouth, keep the door of my lips."
(Psa. cxli. 3.) All our sins of omission shall then
be brought to light, not only what you have
practised, but all the good you have neglected ;
not only what you have done, but what you have
not done. These are great sins, " to him that knows
to do good, and doth it not, to him it is sin ;" (James
iv. 17.) that is, it is a great sin ; and needs it
must, for while we own God in our understandings,
we do hereby deny him in our conversation ; while
we acknowledge religion, in the truth of it, we deny
it in the power of it. Oh how many are our omissions ! from carelessness, from perverseness, from
delays, from slothfulness; aye, and God knows how
many, from a contempt, and slight of duty ! But
Christ tells us, the guilt of these neglects shall
be charged in that day. Do not you remember

that text? "I was an hungry, and ye gave me no meat, (go ye cursed)." I tell you, the neglect of improving seasons of grace, and those blessed opportunities God hath put into our hands of doing and receiving good, will make your account very dreadful; yea, if you had not one open sin of comsion to answer for. All the sins that ever the sinner hath been guilty of in the whole course of his life, from first to last, shall be judged by God. These three things then do clear the impartiality of the sentence of God, in that day when sinners fall into his hands. There shall be no distinction of persons. The sentence shall be suited to the nature of the cause, and no sin shall escape the sentence, which is another reason why " it is *such* a fearful thing to fall into the hands of the living God." And we must be the greatest sots in the world, if we do not consider it.

How should such a doctrine as this awaken every soul of us to consider our case; to reflect upon our state, to enquire how it is with us ? Am I converted ? or am I not ? If not, how should we seek, pray, and labour, to get an interest in Christ, without any more delays ! How should we strive to repent of all our sins, words, actions, omissions, and commissions, secret, or open sins, sins of heart, sins of life, and to labour for grace and holiness ; this is the use the Apostle makes of the same doctrine, (2 Peter iii. 11.) " Seeing that all these things shall be dissolved, what manner of persons ought we to be in all holy conversation, and godliness :"

and again, verse 14. " Seeing ye look for such things, be diligent, that ye may be found of him in peace, without spot, and blameless." The Lord grant that you, and I, may make such a use of this doctrine.

SERMON IX.

" It is a fearful thing to fall into the hands of the living God."—(Heb. x. 31.)

That which I am upon, is to give you the reasons of this truth, why it is such a fearful thing. The

I. Is with respect to those attributes of God which make it so.

II. Is this, because all the proceedings of God in that day shall be suited to the ministry of a man's own conscience, and shall be such as conscience shall fall in with.

III. Is, because all that fall into his hands in the sense explained in the text, have to do with God in such a covenant, where the great design of God is to glorify his justice.

IV. It is a fearful thing, because of the impartiality of the sentence that shall then be passed, which I made evident by three things.

1. There shall be no distinction of persons.

2. The sentence shall be suited to the nature and merit of the cause.

3. No manner of sin shall escape the sentence.

V. Is this, "It is a fearful thing to fall into the hands of the living God," because there is no way of being delivered out of his hand. It was a proud saying of Nebuchadnezzar, (Dan. iii. 15.) "Who is that God that shall deliver out of my hand?" There was a God he knew not, that could, and did deliver out of his hand. "If he cut off, and shut up, who can hinder him?" (Job xi. 10.) Who can turn God from his purpose, or make him change his course, or alter his mind, or revoke his sentence? There are but five ways that I can think on of being delivered out of the hands of God's wrath in that day; either by way of justification, or supplication, or opposition, or appeal, or redemption, but none of these can avail a sinner in that day.

1. It cannot be by justification, for the most righteous person breathing, cannot dare to justify himself before God. It is true every believer shall be justified, he hath one to plead his cause, who will justify his person, but he dare not justify himself. "If I justify myself, (saith Job,) my own mouth shall condemn me," (Job. ix. 12.) that is, my very plea shall be turned into sin, this will appear two ways.

(1.) From the insufficiency of any man for such an undertaking. How can he that is unrighteous, justify himself before God, that is infinite in righteousness and holiness? therefore, if a man attempts this, his words will prove him guilty, when he pleads not guilty.

(2.) He that justifies himself before God, must do it by the merit of his own doings, he must bring forth all his duties, and performances, and all his good works; but this will not do, because the evil he hath done is more than his good; if he mentions his duties, he must mention his sins too, and then his own mouth will condemn him, for his sins are more than his duties ; therefore Job totally declines this plea of personal righteousness, and so doth Paul, (1 Cor. iv. 4.) " I know nothing by myself," (saith he) I have no evil to charge upon my conscience yet, (saith he) " I am not hereby justified ;" therefore, he tells you what his great care was, (Phil. iii. 9.) "that I may be found in Christ, not having mine own righteousness, which is of the law, but that which is through the faith of Christ ;" now if the most righteous man that breathes cannot justify himself before God, how can a carnal unsanctified sinner do it, that is destitute of all righteousness ? what hath he to plead with God ? the believer who is under the power of renewing grace, hath much righteousness of his own to *act*, but none to *plead ;* he hath a righteousness to sanctify him, though it cannot justify him. But the sinner hath none to act, and can therefore have none to plead, and therefore he can never hope to be delivered out of his hands this way.

2. It cannot be by way of supplication, for God will in that day be inexorable. Though now he hath an ear to hear, tender bowels to regard, answers the prayers of the destitute, saith, " ask and ye shall have ;" yet in that day, he will be inexorable. Now he is wrought upon (if I may phrase it so) by supplication, prayer hath a mighty prevalency with God in the present day, Jacob " wept and made supplication," (Hos. xii. 4.) and by this, (it is said) he had power with God, and prevailed." Therefore Job resolves upon this course, (Job ix. 15.) " I will make supplication to my judge ;" that is, I will throw myself down at the foot of God, I will deprecate judgment

and sue for mercy. Prayer overcomes when nothing
else can, and why? Not as it is an act of ours, but as
it is an institution of God, he hath ordained it, as a
means to that end, and therefore it is a prevailing
means with God; but it is but during the present state
that it is so, no supplications can prevail with God,
when once sinners are fallen into his hands, because it
ceases to be an ordinance of God; then it hath none of
the stamp of his institution upon it, and therefore can
have no prevalency in it; we are taught thus much, by
the parable of the rich man, (Luke xvi. 24.) that "being
in torment, he cried and said, Father Abraham, have
mercy upon me, and send Lazarus to dip his finger in
water to cool my tongue, for I am tormented in this
flame?" But what is the answer? "Between us and you,
there is a gulph fixed." The meaning is to shew that
their state in that day is eternally determined, there is
a gulph fixed. "If a man sin against the Lord, who
shall intreat for him?" he must be left to the righteous
judgment of God.

3. Nor can opposition or resistance prevail. If
God will not withdraw his anger, (as in that day he
never will,) the proud [*and haughty*] shall stoop under
him, men may slight his word now, but they cannot resist his power then, can the spider withstand the
besom, and the arm that sweeps with it? No more
can the sinner withstand God, when he comes to sweep
them down with the besom of destruction; rebels may
be too hard for an earthly prince, but the Almighty
cannot be hindered by weakness from exercising power;
he overcomes when he judges, that is by executing the
sentence. Though men resist his laws now, and will
not submit to his rule, they cannot resist the sentence

of his punishment then; as they must bow to his
sovereignty, so they must fall under the power of his
wrath. A prisoner in this world may possibly make
his escape, and avoid his sentence, but none can from
God, he hath the keys of hell and death, and none can
deliver out of his hand; neither bribes nor power can
avail to rescue them, therefore the Prophet saith, " consider this ye that forget God, lest I tear you in pieces
and there be none to deliver :" none can deliver out of
his hand. The strength of God is an invincible thing,
therefore his throne is represented, (Dan. vii. 9.) " as a
fiery flame; fire is a masterless element, burns all before it. No man can resist the meanest creature, when
it comes against him armed with a power from God ;
Pharoah as great as he was, could not withstand an
army of lice, nor keep the frogs out of his bedchamber;
a few worms armed with a commission from God devour
a proud Herod: God can make the sea overflow and
swallow up the earth, as he did in the flood; if he
speaks to the earth, it shall open, and swallow up rebellious sinners, as it did Korah and his company.
What force can repel the Almightiness of God which
overturns the mountains, which shakes the earth out
of its place, and makes the pillars of it tremble?
Hence that good man cries out, "the Lord is wise in
heart, and mighty in strength." " Who shall say to God
what dost thou !" His Almightiness is as much beyond
our strength, as his infiniteness is beyond our understanding; therefore, there is no being delivered out of
his hand, by opposition or resistance.

4. Nor is it possible to escape the sentence of that
day by any appeal. It is some relief to a man's mind,
that when he is cast in one court, he may appeal unto

o

another, he may be cast in one court, and acquitted in
another, but there is no appealing from the righteous
bar of God, nor reversing the sentence he passes.
Shall a man appeal to the law? Alas! that justifies
the judgment, and condemns every sinner; Shall he
appeal to the gospel? It is the slighting and despising
of that out of which the sentence arises, the sentence
of God upon sinners at the last, only ratifies the sentence which the gospel now passes upon them here—
Shall he appeal to the mercy of God and his goodness?
I know many flatter themselves with the thoughts of
this; 'God is full of mercy, I hope he will shew me
mercy;' But alas! this is that, which they have abused
all their lives long, and for which the sentence is pronounced.   "Thou despisest the riches of his goodness
and forbearance, and long suffering, and treasurest up
to thyself wrath against the day of wrath;" therefore
thinkest thou this, O man, that hast hopes of mercy,
and restest upon his goodness in thy sins and disobedience, thinkest thou this, O man, that thou shalt
escape the judgment of God? Shall men despise the
goodness of God now, and yet think to escape by
appealing to it then? Shall they slight mercy now,
when it may be had, and yet think to appeal to mercy,
when the date of it is out? O what folly is this!
Were you never told of seasons of grace, and that the
offers of mercy had their limited times? Hath not the
word of God told you, "now is the accepted time, now
is the day of salvation." Now God offers mercy to
sinners, and there is no mercy for them in the other
world, who have refused the offers and tenders of it in
this.   There can be no appeal from God to any other
in that day; he being above all can be accountable to

none, and therefore there is no escaping by way of appeal.

5. There is no escaping this sentence by way of redemption. None can redeem a sinner, when once he is fallen into the hands of God. There is a redemption provided for lost man, a sufficient one, a glorious one, a blessed one, that is able to redeem the vilest sinner that repents, and that is the Lord Jesus Christ, our blessed Redeemer: he is the plank of mercy, upon which we may escape the hazard of an eternal shipwreck. The loss of sinners by the fall had been as irrecoverable, as the loss of the fallen angels, had not God contrived a method of redeeming, above the reach of all human wisdom; this is the wonder of angels, "the great mystery of godliness." (1 Tim. iii. 16.) It is the matter of the saint's triumphant song in heaven. (Rev. i. 6.) And well it may, when we consider that a nobler kind of creatures are finally lost, and no Redeemer appointed for them. How strange is it, that God should have more regard to sinning man, than to sinning angels! to take up the nature of man rather than that of angels, and be a Redeemer to man and not to angels; to save an earthen pitcher, and let a vessel of gold be lost! O how should every sinner value a Redeemer! The very name of Christ (saith Bernard) is, *Mel in ore, melodia in aure, et in corde Jubile;* Honey in the mouth, melody in the ear, and a Jubilee in the heart. The Apostle saith, "To you that believe, he is precious." (1 Pet. ii. 7.) There is a twofold preciousness in Christ. One in respect of his essential excellency, as he is "the only begotten Son of God, the brightness of his Father's glory, and the express

image of his person :" the other in respect of what he
is to us; he is precious in respect of his relative use-
fulness, and suitableness to all the sinner's wants;
all this is implied in his being a Redeemer; he redeems from all evil; he redeems to all good; he is a
Redeemer from hell, and wrath, and a Redeemer to
heaven and glory; he hath wrought out eternal redemption for us.   None can express the preciousness
of Christ, but those that have had a sense of guilt and
wrath, and have fled for refuge to the hope set before
them, and to such, Christ is precious indeed; they
that understand the worth of an immortal soul, and
the dreadfulness of the wrath of God, and how sufficient the blood of Christ is to ransom from it, these
will take him for their Redeemer; and to such he
will be so, by pardoning sin, removing wrath, and
giving peace with God, and making the soul free
indeed, and " delivering him for ever from his Judge."
(Job xxiii. 7.)   But though the benefit of this blessed
redemption be so great, yet it is not to be had hereafter, if an interest in it be not secured by the soul
here; and therefore the counsel of the Holy Ghost
is, " kiss the Son, lest he be angry."   (Psa. ii. 12.)
Kiss the Son, that is, the Lord Christ : this kissing
the Son, is by shewing submission to Christ, by faith
and obedience : to kiss the Son, is to receive and embrace Christ, as our King, our Priest, and Prophet;
to receive him in the whole of his mediatorship; and
this is the way, and the only way, to escape the wrath
of God; without this, it is utterly impossible to avert
it : " For he that believes not, the wrath of God
abides on him."   It shall abide upon him for ever,
and there can be no removing of it; no ransom

can then deliver from it. (Job xxxvi. 18.) "Because there is wrath, beware lest God take thee away with his stroke, then a great ransom cannot deliver thee." A ransom is a price paid for the delivering of captives out of bondage ; and thus Christ gave himself a ransom for sinners ; but here is a case where no ransom will be taken, though it be never so great. If God once takes thee away with his stroke, then a great ransom cannot deliver thee. If once a sinner falls into the hands of the justice of the living God, it will be a vain thing to think of getting off by a ransom, though never so great. You read of a two-fold ransom for the children of God in Scripture.

(1.) The destruction of the wicked is sometimes made the ransom and price of their deliverance : so it is said, (Prov. xxi. 18.) " The wicked shall be a ransom for the righteous, and the transgressor for the upright." How is the wicked a ransom for the righteous ? Will the wicked man give himself a ransom for the good man ? Will he lay down his life for such as he hates to the death ? It cannot be. But the meaning of it is this, that God will save and deliver the righteous by the destruction of the wicked; rather than the righteous shall perish, the wicked shall be destroyed to save them. Thus God speaks by the prophet, (Isaiah xxxiii. 3.) " I gave Egypt for thy ransom ;" for Israel : that is, God destroyed Pharoah and the Egyptians in the Red Sea, to preserve his own people; thus, the righteous are delivered out of trouble, by putting the wicked in his stead.

(2.) There is another ransom for the people of God, and that is the precious blood of the Son of God. " We are bought with a price !" (1 Cor. vi. 20.) " He

gave himself a ransom for many," (Matt. xx. 28.)
for all that lay hold on him by faith. This is a great
ransom, and yet there are some cases, wherein this
ransom, the blood of the Son of God, will not deliver.
Though the blood of Christ hath in itself an infinite
and intrinsic virtue to redeem, and deliver any sinner,
let the sin be never so great ; yet there are some cases
the blood of Christ will not afford any relief under ;
such as these,—

   1st. Such as are impenitent and obstinate in sin ;
that resolvedly go on in their lusts, against the calls
of God, and the means of grace ; the blood of Christ
is no ransom for such.   Christ came to save us from
our sins, but not to save us in our sins.

   2nd. Such as are unbelievers ; though they cease
from the outward practice of sin, if they do not close
with Christ by faith, his blood is no ransom for them.
As Christ will not save presumptuous sinners, who
believe without repentance ; neither will he save in-
credulous sinners, who repent without believing.

   3rd. Such as are apostates and turn from God ; the
blood of Christ is no ransom for such.   (Heb. x. 26.)
" If we sin wilfully after we have received the knowledge
of the truth, there remains no more sacrifice for sin."

   4th. There is another sort of sinners that shall
have no benefit by this ransom of the blood of Christ ;
and they are such as are actually fallen into the
hands of the living God in the other world : the virtue
of Christ's blood doth not operate there ; it was never
designed to that end.   Christ is a Redeemer upon
earth, but not in hell ; his blood is ransoming blood
now in the day of grace, but it will not be so then in
the day of justice.   You hope in Christ when you are

past hope, and trust him when it is too late. I tell you, his blood operates only during the seasons that God hath appointed for the tenders of it; and that is, the season of grace. Now is the time of tendering Christ's blood; now is the time a sinner may have benefit by this ransom. Now it operates, and effects a blessed redemption for all that receive and apply it; but there is no tender of this after this life, and therefore no soul can have benefit by it then; for if he be not redeemed here, he is lost for ever; if ever it be done, it must be done here; redemption is not a thing to be done hereafter; if ever you are saved by Christ, you must be saved now. Now is the day of grace. Redemption, it is true, is not completed till the final judgment, which is, therefore, called the day of redemption; but your redemption is begun here, if ever you are saved hereafter: all that shall be saved in that world, must be redeemed in this. Oh, how should all of us look betimes after redeeming grace, while we may have it! " Seek the Lord while he may be found, call upon him while he is nigh." Now is the time of applying Christ's blood, while it is operative and effectual, for though it may be in its own nature powerful, yet it is not operative and effectual, but during the appointment of God; and that is, while the day of grace lasts, and no longer; and, therefore, do not deceive yourselves, though it be ransoming blood now, it will not be so when you are fallen into the hands of God, for from thence, there is no redemption. Christ is said to deliver us from the wrath to come: the wrath to come is hereafter, but the deliverance from it is here. We must be redeemed now, if at all, for then we cannot;

the redemption of the soul ceases for ever. When God once " takes thee away with his stroke, then a great ransom cannot deliver thee;" the blood of Christ himself cannot, and the reason is, because the state of sinners, when they are in the hand of God, is unalterable; they are in an eternal state. Here the condition of a man is uncertain and mutable; here a man is a child of wrath to-day, and by the power of grace made an heir of God to-morrow; born, and then new born: here he goes under many changes; relative changes and real changes; from a state of guilt to a state of justification; from a state of bondage to a state of adoption; from a state of darkness to a state of light; from a state of sin to a state of grace: many changes here; and blessed are they that know this change, but in the other world, there are no changes of state; the state he then enters into, he abides in for ever. Both saints and sinners, all that go hence enter into a new, but never-ending condition: whether they go to heaven or hell, whether they rise to the resurrection of life or damnation, they are equally put into an everlasting condition. (Matt. xxv. last verse.) " These shall go away into everlasting punishment, and the righteous into life eternal." Which way soever the miseries of the wicked are expressed in Scripture, they are still said to be of an everlasting duration. Hell is darkness; this is a darkness that shall never be day; it is everlasting darkness; as it is said of the glory of heaven, " There is no night there;" so, of the darkness of hell, there is no day there. (Jude xiii.) " For whom is reserved the blackness of darkness for ever." It is darkness, because there is no light of God's countenance shining in that place; it is blackness of darkness, to express the extremity of the misery; and it is blackness of darkness for ever, to set out the duration of it. Again, is hell called a prison ? (1 Pet. iii. 19.) It is said of the spirits of the old world, that they are in prison, that is, in hell; this is such a prison as that they who are cast in, shall never come out of. If it be out of the reach of Christ's blood to fetch the soul from hell, it must needs be out of the reach of the saint's prayers; for the efficacy of all prayers is in the blood of Jesus. The prisoners in this state are not prisoners of hope ; no, these are prisoners of despair, for they that are once cast in there, are for ever locked up by him that hath the keys of hell and death. (Job xii. 14.) " He shutteth up a man, and there can be no opening." Those whom God's power shuts in, no key can let out. The chains that God puts upon a sinner can never file off. Again, Is this state called "the wrath of God ?" (Eph. v. 6. Rev. xiv. 10.) This wrath is such as abides upon the soul for ever. Therefore, it is said in the text, " It is a fearful thing to fall into the hands of the living God," because, he being the living God, his wrath must needs be a living, a lasting wrath, and, therefore, it is a fearful thing. Sometimes it is called a worm, as conscience in that day will be a fearful corroding thing, and that is a worm that shall not die. (Mark ix. 44.) " Where the worm dies not." The living God makes the sinner's conscience a never dying worm. Again, sometimes it is called fire, which is a fit metaphor to express God's wrath by ; for as fire is the most dreadful element, so is God's wrath the most dreadful wrath. There is no fire like this, for it burns,—

Internally; visible fire burns only visible matter, but this burns invisibly and inwardly. It burns that which no other fire can touch, and that is the soul of man. God is a spirit, and his wrath is a fire that can reach the spirit. But that which makes this fire terrible indeed is, it burns *Eternally,* everlastingly, therefore called a fire that shall never go out, that shall never be quenched, "everlasting fire." (Matt. xxv. 41.) Great fires here, though they be dreadful, yet they go out one time or other, these fires consume themselves by devouring that which feeds and maintains them; but this fire is kindled and preserved by the everlasting wrath of God, (Isa. xxx. 33.) "Tophet is ordained of old, the pile thereof is fire, and much wood; the breath of the Lord, like a stream of brimstone, doth kindle it," so that, look, how long the life and breath of God remains, so long this fire must burn. " Our God is a consuming fire," (Heb. xii. 29.) It is not called so because the fire of his wrath consumes, but because he consumes sinners by the fire of his wrath ; but yet this fire doth not consume one sinner as to his being, but only as to his well being—it doth not annihilate his person, but his hope. The great dread of common fire is, that it destroys and consumes what it burns, but the greatest dread of this fire is, that it burns, but will not consume ; it is a consuming fire, but doth not consume the body, for the body as well as the soul of the sinner shall remain in this fire for ever, and never be consumed. Oh ! the folly of men to kindle the fire of God's wrath, and by unbelief, to throw themselves into it ? Will any man in his right wits cast himself into the fire ? Indeed you read, in Matth. xvii. 15. of one " that fell often into the fire," but he was a very luna-

tic; but none so mad as obstinate sinners, who fall into
the fire of God's wrath willingly, and so shall perish for
ever. Oh that God by this, would awaken every sinner
out of his security, that he might flee from the wrath
to come; because it is a wrath that none can deliver
thee out of, no deliverance out of God's hands; no
deliverance by justification, or supplication, or opposition, or appeal, or redemption itself; therefore it is a
" fearful thing to fall into the hands of the living God,"
and that is the *fifth* reason.

VI. It is a fearful thing to fall into the hands of the
living God, because it is the last of God's dispensations to man, and the last is the most terrible. The
glorifying of the elect, and the destruction of the
wicked, are the last works of God; when this world
shall be folded up as a garment, and a final conclusion
be put to all the dispensations of God that are now
on foot—he comes then to save the godly, and to
throw sinners into their everlasting state of destruction.

The sinner is reserved to the day of destruction, and
he shall be brought forth to the day of God's wrath,
when many wraths shall be wrapt up in one, for then
shall the sinner be the object of all God's wrath.
The wicked is reserved to the day of wrath—as Pharoah was preserved in the ten plagues, to be drowned
and destroyed in the sea, so are many sinners kept
from lesser plagues in this world, to perish in the sea
of God's wrath—God preserves the wicked, till the
lesser plagues are over, and then the sinner and
his sin shall be brought forth together into judgment, they shall be brought forth to the day of wrath.
All the evil days which the wicked escape here, it is

but reserving them to the evil day, from which there is no escaping—God's last works in the world are his saving believers, and destroying sinners, and he will so manage these, as that he will therein shew himself to be God indeed. The believer shall know what a God he is for grace and mercy, and the sinner shall know what a God he is for justice and wrath.

It is a certain rule, that God's latter works exceed the former! I could shew this by a variety of dispensations in the world. The making of heaven and earth was a glorious work, but there is another creation to come, which far exceeds that, new heavens and new earth; the giving out the covenant of grace, how darkly was it dispensed to Adam; (Gen. iii. 15.) it was more explicitly made known to Noah; to Abraham, yet more plain and full; David had it more clear and full than all the former; but this covenant was never so gloriously revealed, as by Christ in the Gospel; that is the last dispensation of the covenant, and therefore the greatest and best, and therefore called " the better covenant." The worship of God, how much more carnal was it of old under the Jewish state, than now it is under the Gospel; then it was in sacrifices, and divers washings, and the like, but now his worship is more spiritual, more raised and noble, (John iv. 23.) "the hour is coming, and now is, when the true worshippers shall worship the Father in spirit and in truth." Gospel worship is a better worship, and therefore called the time of renovation, (Jer. iii. 5.) " In those days, saith the Lord, (that is, in the days of Messiah) they shall no more say, the ark of the covenant of the Lord, neither shall it come to mind, neither shall they remember it, neither shall that be done any more"—

you must know there is a Synecdoche in the words; the ark is put for all the legal ceremonies, whereof the ark was a chief part, and the meaning is, that the whole ark with all its ceremonies should utterly cease when Christ was come, for he answers all the uses of the ark. In the ark was laid up the pot of manna, Aaron's rod, the tables of the law. Now Christ is all this, Christ is the hidden manna, the bread of life, Christ is the rod of government, in him is the whole law fulfilled; and now Christ reigns in his church by his word and Spirit, therefore all the former things shall cease, therefore it shall no more be said. " The ark of the covenant of the Lord."

The great blessing of the Spirit, how sparingly was that given out at first, to a very few in number, and that in a small measure, in so much that it is said comparatively, the spirit was not given; it was not given, that is, in comparison of what was to be, when Christ had ascended; for the fullest enjoyment of the extraordinary gifts, and saving graces of the Spirit was reserved till Christ's ascension, as the fruit of his exaltation and triumph; so that the Spirit is said to be " poured out" in that day; (Joel ii. 28.) therefore there is a greater measure of the Spirit enjoyed under the Gospel than ever was before, and let me tell you there is yet behind, another pouring out of the Spirit promised, that shall be greater than any ever yet was. Thus you see by these hints, that still the last works of God are the greatest in a way of mercy, and truly it is the same in a way of judgment! still the last judgments are the greatest; therefore you read of these threatenings, (Lev. xxvi. 18.) He threatens to make an addition of seven times greater judgments, if they would not hearken to him, and so he goes on with yet seven times more, four times over, to shew us that there is a gradation in wrath, and the farther God goes on in a way of wrath with any people, the greater still it is. You read of little wrath, greater wrath, and wrath to the utmost—" God is first as a moth," (Hos. v. 12.) that is a little creature and consumes gradually, but then in the ver. 14. " God is said to be a lion, and that imports great wrath, and then it follows, I will take away and none shall rescue ;" there is first a kindling of wrath, and then there is a flame of wrath, and at last unquenchable fire ; so that God's last works are his greatest, whether it be in a way of mercy to his people, or in a way of judgment to the wicked world, and God will observe the same method to the last. It shall be thus in the last day ; God's last works to believers shall be the greatest, God will do more for believers, than ever he hath done. First, he gives grace, then more grace, then a perfect man in Christ Jesus, and so a meetness for glory—grace is in the beginning, little, but in the end, it is glorious. God gives the tokens of his love by degrees. First, we see through a glass darkly, and then face to face ; love first breaks forth to the soul in union to Christ, then it shews itself more in our communion, till at last it is perfected in the full enjoyment of God : so it is in the dispensations of God's wrath to sinners, his last works are his greatest works ; in the next world, they shall have all his wrath, and how terrible must it be, when the angry God, the sin-revenging God will pour out all his wrath upon the sinner. As the salvation of the righteous will be a great and glorious salvation, wherein eternal love shall be perfected upon the saints, so the destruction of the wicked shall be a great and dreadful destruction, in which eternal vengeance shall be for ever perfected upon the sinner, therefore it must needs be a " fearful thing to fall into the hands of the living God."—O that God would awaken your hearts, that these things may make impressions upon you, and sink down into your hearts; they are the words of God; if we do not know what the wrath of God is, and the dreadful effects of it, how shall we be awakened to fly from it by a timely repentance, and diligent laying hold on Christ, and improving the means of grace, which God hath appointed to this end, that we may be delivered from wrath, and partake of eternal glory, by Jesus Christ.

SERMON X.

" It is a fearful thing to fall into the hands of the living God."—Heb. x. 31.

That which I am upon, is giving you the reasons of this truth, why it is such a fearful thing.

I. With respect to those attributes of God which make it so.

II. Because all the proceedings of God in that day shall be suited to the ministry of a man's own conscience.

III. Because all that fall into his hands have to do with God, in a covenant where the great design of God is, to glorify his justice.

IV. It is a fearful thing, because of the impartiality of that sentence that shall then be past, which appears in three things.

1. There shall be no distinction of persons.

2. The sentence shall be suited to the nature of the cause, and,

3. No sin shall escape the sentence.

V. There is no way of being delivered out of his hands.

VI. Because it is the last of God's dispensations to man ; the glorifying believers, and the destruction of sinners, are the last of God's works in this world.

There are yet two reasons more to insist on now ; and therefore,

VII. It is a fearful thing to fall into the hands of the living God, because we shall then have to do with God immediately; so much the phrase of the text doth in ordinary speech import : to fall into a man's hands is to have to do with him, not by proxy, but by himself. And reason and justice requires that the punishment of sinners in that day should be immediate, that God should punish them with his own hands ; for,

1. How else can the punishment carry in it, any tolerable satisfaction to justice ? for justice requires an exact proportion, as far as the case can admit, between the demerit of the sin, and the punishment of it, as far as the subject is capable of ; now the punishment can never carry a due proportion to the sin, unless it be from God's immediate hand, for let the demerit of sin be considered, and wherein doth it chiefly consist, but in this, that it is immediate against God ? Though it is true that the nature of sin is an inordinate lusting after undue objects, seeking satisfaction in creatures ; yet the great foundation evil of sin lies in the turning away from God, for therein there is an immediate slight put upon God. It is a contempt cast upon the good-ness and blessedness, that is to be had in him. If it could be supposed that sin was nothing else, but the gross and [sensual] part that lies in the enjoyment of creatures, then a punishment by creatures might have suited it, but it being an immediate reflection upon God himself, as all sin is, none can fill up a proportion

of a full and meet punishment of such an evil, but
God himself. Though all sin be not done immediately
against God, yet all sin is an immediate reflection upon
God. It casts a contempt upon his Sovereignty and
Holiness, and it is highly reasonable that such an indignity should be vindicated by God himself. Let me
allude to that of Eli, (1 Sam. ii. 25.) " If one man sin
against another, the judge shall judge him, but if a
man sin against the Lord, who shall intreat for him ?"
and by the like reason, I infer, if one creature rob
another, a creature of the same kind can recompense
it ; if a man shed the blood of a man, as far as it is a
wrong merely to the creature, man may recompense it,
" by man shall his blood be shed." But if a man sin
against God, who shall recompense it; but God in that
day, wherein he will be glorified ? Therefore it is but
just and equal that the punishment of sinners in that
day should be from the immediate hand of God.

2. It is according to equity and justice, that, that
which hath been the chiefest in sinning, should be the
chiefest in suffering. This is a rule among men, and
it is according to the justice of God, that the principal
in sinning, shall be the principal in suffering. Now
the principal in sinning, is known to be the soul of man,
that is the sink of sin, the forge where all sin is first
formed. The body doth but serve the designs of the
soul in sinning, therefore the members are called
instruments of unrighteousness—It is the soul plots
and contrives sin, the body acts it ; yea, in some and
the greatest sins, the soul hath an immediate hand—It
is chief in sin, and therefore should be the chief in suffering. Now the soul cannot suffer, unless it be immediately from God; this is plain from that saying of our

Lord, "fear not them which can kill the body, but cannot kill the soul." Who or what can reach the soul but God himself? It is out of the reach of all creatures. Neither angels, nor devils, are able to terrify the conscience, till it hath first been made tender and raw by God. God only can fill it with wrath; it is a great mistake among divines to say, the devils are the great tormentors of man in hell—I would know who it is torments the devils themselves, certainly none but God? and the same God with whom those spirits have to do, will have to do with the soul of man.

3. It is highly reasonable that the punishment of sinners, in that day should be immediate, for else the soul would be out of the reach of suffering itself, for all mediate punishments executed by creatures are short and deficient, too weak to reach the soul and conscience; therefore if justice will have its perfect work, it is requisite that God himself put his own hand to the execution, for it may be said of all punishments, what the Apostle said of those legal ordinances, that they could not make the service perfect, as pertaining to the conscience." So all outward torments, take them, without God's wrath mixed with them, cannot make a perfect or complete punishment, as pertaining to the conscience.

4. No creature can convey the whole of God's wrath into a lost soul, nor discover it, in the full power of it; who knows the power of thine anger? and yet, if God doth but give us up into the hands of a mere creature to torment us, these very creatures assisted by the common concurrence of God's power are very dreadful; suppose a man was thrown into a furnace of fire, and this fire always burning, and his body held

continually in the torment without consuming, it would be very terrible; but suppose that God should not only use the ministry of creatures against a man, but should arm them with his wrath, so that they should deal with the sinner above their own strength, so as it should appear that the hand of God was in it, it would be still more terrible than the former; but alas! what is this to God's immediate wrath, as it is inflicted from his own hand. Whatever it is that comes most immediately from God, is most affecting, whether in a way of mercy or judgment. The love of God conveyed in ordinances is a sweet enjoyment, but it is a far lower dispensation than immediate communications from Himself in heaven; so wrath expressed by a creature, is not like wrath inflicted by the hand of God, this fills the soul brim full of terror, this cuts off the soul; "thy fierce wrath goeth over me, thy terrors cut me off," saith Heman: the strokes of God were so heavy and sharp, that they did not only cut into his soul, but [*penetrated*] so as to cut it off, and this puts him into the condition of a man in hell, in his own sense; "I am free among the dead," saith he. They are not the strokes of a creature that I feel, or anger expressed by creatures, but such as they that are in hell do feel, that are cut off by thy hand.

God's power, though never so great, yet, in working by instruments, is abated and lessened in working. The weight of God's little finger is heavier than the loins of the whole creation of God.

5. All other dealings and ministry of God have been slighted by sinners in this world, therefore God in the great day will deal out punishments to them with his own hand. Favour and methods of mercy

will not do. " Let favour be shown to the wicked yet will he not learn righteousness," (Isa. xxvi. 10.) " Though I redeemed them, saith the Lord, yet have they spoken lies against me." (Hos. vii. 13.) The great design of the patience and goodness of God is, to lead men to repentance, and to forewarn them to flee from the wrath to come, but such is the wickedness of their hearts, that they thereby treasure up to themselves wrath, against the day of wrath. Do we not sometimes see a man cast upon a bed of sickness, brought to the very brink of death and hell, and by God's wonderful patience snatched like a brand out of the fire, and yet they return again to sin more than ever ; instead of performing their sick-bed promises, and making good their feigned resolutions of a new life, by which in their sickness they flattered God, and deceived themselves, they break forth into more vileness than ever, as if they would fetch back the lost time in sinning ; so that methods of mercy in this world will not do ; "because judgment is not speedily executed, therefore their heart is fully set in them to do evil;" nor will judgments do, either in the threatening or execution ; " Lord when thy hand is lifted up they will not see." (Isa. xxvi. 11.) They belie the Lord, and say it is not he ; nay, let judgment be executed upon them and the decree bring forth, yet will it make no lasting impression upon them to cure them of their lusts. It is said of Israel, (Psa. lxxviii. 31.) " The wrath of God came upon them, yet they sinned still." It is the nature of clay to grow harder by the fire. Metal melted in the furnace, will when taken out, return to its wonted solidity. When Pharoah saw that the plagues were gone, he sinned yet more, and hardened his heart. How many judgments doth God

successivelly send upon Israel, one upon the neck of
another, and what is the effect of them? "Yet have
they not returned unto me, saith the Lord." (Amos iv.
6.) "I have given you cleanness of teeth, and want of
bread in all your cities, yet have you not returned unto
me, saith the Lord," and in seventh verse.—"Also I
have withholden rain from you, and caused it to rain
upon one city, and not upon another, yet have ye
not returned to me, saith the Lord; I have smitten
you with blasting, and mildew, when your gardens and
your vineyards, and your figtrees increased, the palmer
worm devoured them, yet have you not returned unto
me, saith the Lord,"—"I have overthrown some of
you, as God overthrew Sodom and Gomorrah, and ye
were as a fair plant plucked out of the burning: yet
have ye not returned unto me saith the Lord." Here
is judgment upon judgment, stroke upon stroke, and
yet no returning to the Lord. No judgments will do
upon an impenitent people, therefore it is just with
God to take wicked men into his own hand, when all
other means and ministry are slighted, and made of no
effect. It is a righteous thing for God to interpose
then, in a more immediate way, and magnify the glory
of his own power in the just destruction of incorrigible
sinners.

VIII. It is a fearful thing to fall into the hands of
the living God, because God in the next world shall
be all in all. (1 Cor. xv. 28.) "That God may be
all in all." But you may say the same of Christ.
(Col. iii. 11.) "That Christ is all in all;" there is
no contradiction in the words, nor disagreement, for
the one is spoken in the present tense, the other in
the future, Christ is all in all, that is now; God shall
be all in all, that is hereafter; so that these two ex-

pressions are to be understood of the difference of time; in the time of this world, Christ is all in all: in eternity, God is all in all. Christ is all in all in the present state, but, God shall be all in all, in a future state of glory; Christ is all in all in point of administration, all in a way of fullness, all in a way of merit and purchase, all in a way of conveyance, for all the good we enjoy in this world is through Christ; Christ is all in point of light and life. " In him was life, and the life was the light of men;" he is all in all duties; all in all privileges; all in all the providences and ordinances; his righteousness is all in the business of justification; his death is all in the benefit of satisfaction; his spirit is all in point of sanctification; his intercession is all in the matter of our acceptation; his peace is all in the benefit of our consolation. Thus Christ is all in this world in point of administration : but God shall be all in all in the next world, in respect of immediate dispensation. Christ is all in all, in the designation of the mediatorial kingdom by the Father to the Son; God shall be all in all, in the resignation of the same kingdom from the Son to the Father. (1 Cor. 15—28.) " Christ shall deliver up the kingdom to God the Father, and then shall the Son himself be subject to him that put all things under him, that God may be all in all." Now in what sense must this be understood, to shew you where the force of the reason lies ? In what sense is God said to be all in all, in the other world?

1. Not in opposition to Christ, as if Christ were of no use in the other world, though the mediatorial office of Christ shall cease as to administration; yet he shall be for ever head of that spiritual union. We are

members of Christ's body when we are in heaven, and as grace here is derived from Christ our head to us, so hereafter we shall enjoy God in Christ to eternity.

2. God's being all in all in that day, is not to be understood in respect of essence and being; as if at last all things should be resolved to God, as some have dreamed. As God " is above all, and in all, and through all," as it is said, (Eph. iv. 6.) so he shall be all in all: but it is no where said, that God is all things, or that all things are God himself, or that all things shall at last be resolved into God. This is blasphemous nonsense. Creatures in the eternal world shall be creatures still, they shall abide as creatures then; the angels shall be angels for ever; the saints shall be saints for ever; though their natures be glorified, yet they shall not be deified. How then must this be understood, that God is all in all in the next world? Why thus; both as it refers to saints in a state of glory, and sinners in the state of misery; God shall be all in all in heaven, in a way of blessedness, and he shall be all in all in hell, in a way of vengeance. In that state as he shall be all in all to saints, so he shall be as really so, to all sinners. Now because the one will greatly illustrate the other, therefore I shall speak to it in both senses, that by the sweetness of his being all in all to saints, in a way of reward, you may have a fuller view of his being all in all to sinners, in a way of punishment. Therefore,

1. In the state of glory, he shall be all in all.

(1.) In opposition to all creatures.

(2.) In the room of all ordinances.

(3.) In distinction to those graces which are necessary for our enjoyment of him in this state.

(1.) In opposition to all the creatures; God is all in all to us in the creatures, but then he shall be all in all to us without them; whatever good we enjoy in the creature, it is from God. What is that which is the true comfort of every enjoyment, but only that of God that is enjoyed in it? The good of personal comforts, as life, estate, health, gifts, parts, is all from God; the good of relative comforts, father, mother, brother, sister, yoke-fellows, or friends, all is from God in them. There is no sweetness, nor pleasure, nor true comfort, in any or all of them, but what God puts into them; you call them your blessings, but it is not from the nature of the things themselves, but from that of God which is enjoyed in them; time was when there was nothing but God, and then all good was in him only, and as the creature's essence, and existence is from God alone, so must all its goodness be. As he gave being to the creatures for man's sake, so he puts goodness into them for man's use and comfort, therefore all that is sweet, or any ways refreshing in the creature, is from God; all is nothing, if God be left out. I remember a saying of some of the Rabbies of the names in the Hebrew for *husband and wife,* (אִישׁ אִישָׁה יָהּ אֵשׁ) that the name of God is contained in them, as a symbol of God's gracious presence, if they live according to God's commands, but if they depart from him, and God departs from them, taking away the word signifying God, there remains a word that signifies fire, to intimate that there is nothing but fire and wrath, where God is left out. I wish you did well consider this, and believe it, it would make us more thankful in the enjoyment of mercies, and outward comforts, and content in the

want of them.   No creature hath any real sweetness
in it, further than we enjoy God in it; if God be left
out, they are but a line of cyphers, with never a figure.
But though God be all in all now in all the creatures,
yet in the other world, God shall be all without them.
God will in that day, wholly stop and dry up the
current of all creature channels, and will of himself
immediately supply the want of all second causes whatever.   This is plainly proved by that saying of Christ
to the captious Pharisees. (Luke xx. 34.) " The children of this world marry and are given in marriage, but
they which shall be accounted worthy to obtain that
world, and the resurrection of the dead, neither marry,
nor are given in marriage;" intimating that the creatures
shall no more hanker after any finite thing, but shall
be possessed by God.   The soul now is much solaced
with earthly enjoyments, but then it shall be filled
with God wholly, and wrapt up in God, and satisfied
with God everlastingly.   The creature is now most in
the affection of most Saints, but then it shall be
nothing in any, for God shall be all in all.

(2.) As he will be all in all in opposition to the
creature, so he will be all in all in the room of all ordinances.   It is a great privilege here to have the ordinances of God, because God is enjoyed in them, but
it will be a greater privilege then, not to have the
ordinances, because God is enjoyed without them;
while you are here, your Father knows you have need
of these things, you have need of the word to instruct
you, and the sacraments to nourish you, but these can
be of no such use in heaven; the use of means necessarily implies the absence of the end.   When we are
got to the haven, we quit the ship, and have done with

sailing; we have done with the way, when we are at the journey's end. All motion naturally terminates at the centre, and all means cease when we have the end; therefore saith the Apostle, " Tongues shall cease," prayers shall cease, then the believer shall never pray more, for where God is all, the soul can need nothing, and where there is nothing needed, there is nothing to be asked; when we have done with sinning, we have done with sorrowing; the ministry shall then cease, for there can be no need of labourers, when God hath gathered his harvest in. Ministers are called stars, we now walk by starlight, but where there is no night, there the brightest star is useless. The word of God shall then be out of date, for there can be no need of the guidance of the word of God, when we shall be swallowed up in the life of God; the glass through which we now behold this glory shall be broken, for the shadows shall flee away in that day of brightness.

(3.) God shall be all then, in distinction to those graces, which are necessary for our enjoyment of him in this state. Our highest communion with God in this state is carried on by believing, but in the other world, God shall be all, and faith shall be nothing ; no not so much as an instrument or condition of enjoying God. " Faith (as the Apostle defines it,) is the evidence of things not seen," but it can be no evidence of things not seen there; " For there we shall see him as he is." Heaven will be full of believers, when the body of Christ is complete, and yet there shall not be one believer there, for then all good is in present fruition. As the sinner lives by sense here, so the glorified saint shall live by sense hereafter. Here, in this world the worst state cannot set us below believing, because some good may be enjoyed, and the best state cannot set us above believing, because some good is still to be received; but where all good is enjoyed, there faith ends, and that is in heaven. I might instance in other graces, as hope, desire, and the like, but I come to the

2. Thing, and that is this. As God is all in all to saints in heaven, so he is all in all to the sinners in hell: as he shall be all in all to the saints, to make their happiness perfect, so he shall be all in all to sinners, to make their misery complete.

(1.) He shall be all in all to sinners, in opposition to all they have made their all in this world. Pray what hath been the sinner's all in this world? Not God, for they say to God, "depart from us;" not Christ, no, for they make light of him: "we will not have this man to rule over us," they say to Christ, as the devils did—"what have we to do with thee?" God is nothing to sinners in this world; Christ is nothing in their esteem; he prevails nothing, signifies nothing to them; his ways, his love, his blood, his grace, are esteemed as nothing. The sinner's all, is in the creatures, in the things of this world, the "lust of the flesh, the lust of the eye, and the pride of life:" there lies the sinner's all, and where it is thus, there God is nothing: the creature is his chief good, and that which is his chief good is his god, and that which is his god, is his all. Where a man's God is, there his heart and love, there his pleasure and comfort is, there his whole business is, there his desire and delight is: the Apostle speaks of some " whose god is their belly; that mind earthly things." (Phil. iii. 19.) They savour and relish nothing but what suits sensual lusts, and earthly affections. Now will a time come, when all the creatures shall cease, and be no more. That man, whose god is his belly, his god must perish, and then there will be nothing left but God himself; and then the sinner will have to do with God only. So it was with the rich man. " Thou, in thy life time, receivedst thy good things, but now thou art tormented." He was stripped of his good things, and now there was nothing left but wrath in the room of them. And how dreadful must it be for a man to be stript of his portion, and all the comforts of his life, and have nothing to possess, but the wrath of God in the room of them. The sinner must have to do with that God in that state, whom he would neither love, fear, seek, or serve, and what a fearful thing will it be to have to do with such a God !

(2.) God shall be all in that world, in the accomplishment of all the threatenings of his word. How many are the threatenings of this word of God, and how dreadful are they against impenitent sinners ! Some threatenings respect the power of God, some the justice of God, some the holiness of God, and some the sovereignty of God, and all of them are filled up with the wrath of God. Therefore it must needs be a miserable state that lays a man under God's threatenings. God hath spread out the expansum of his word over the rational world, and he rules all by it, and will judge all according to it. It is the decree of God that he will judge all by his word, and the decree shall bring forth either in mercy or in wrath; and as the promises shall be delivered of all the blessings that are in them, so shall the threatenings be delivered of all the plagues that are in them ;

therefore it is a dreadful thing for a man to lie under
the threatening of God; but yet sinners are so hardened in sin, that they slight the threatening of God,
make a mock of it like those, (Isa. v. 19.) " Let
him make speed and hasten his work, that we may
see it, and let the counsel of the Holy One of Israel
draw nigh, that we may know it." Like that, (Jer.
xvii. 15.) " Behold, say they unto me, where is the
word of the Lord, let it come now;" as if they should
say, let God do the worst he hath threatened to do;
but what saith the prophet Amos to this? (Amos v.
18.) " Woe unto you that desire the day of the
Lord, to what end is it for you ? the day of the Lord
is darkness, and not light." It is a day when all the
threatenings of God shall be executed upon sinners,
and that is wrath to the utmost : a day wherein all
the attributes of God shall set themselves in array
against them, and that will make them miserable
indeed. As it is the fulfilling of the promises that
perfects the believer's blessedness, " he hath given us
exceeding great and precious promises," but yet all the
blessed promises of this book of God can never make
a man completely happy, though he believes them,
and rests upon them, and rejoices in the hopes of the
fulfilling of them, without they are fulfilled; it is the
accomplishment of the promises that makes the soul
completely happy ; for when the promise is fulfilled,
then the creature is put into the fruition of the chief
good ; when God shall be all that the promise hath
made over, then the believer's happiness is perfect—
so the threatenings of God can never make a sinner
completely miserable, though they are full of wrath
and vengeance without the fulfilling of them ; but

when God shall be all to the sinner that the threatening mentions, when he shall be all in a way of wrath
and vengeance, how miserable then must the soul
be ! As all that is in the promises of God is in a way
of grace and love ; so all that is in the threatenings of
God, is in a way of wrath and judgment. It is the
wrath of God that is the sinner's hell; that is the
darkness, the fire, that shall torment the sinner for
ever. I know it hath been much agitated among the
schoolmen, whether the fire of hell, which God hath
prepared to torment the devil and wicked men, be
material fire, or metaphorical. Some would have it
to be material fire, because it shall torment the bodies
of men; others deny it to be so, because it cannot
then work upon spirits, as the devils, and the souls of
men are; and, therefore, Durandus and others have
invented a way, that the power of God can elevate and
make use of corporeal agents, to work upon spiritual
substances ; but these are but niceties, and inventions
of men ignorant of the Scriptures, and of the terrors of
God. Let me tell you, as there is no tormentor there,
but God's power, so neither is there any fire there but
God's wrath ;. it is commonly preached, but I think
unwarily, that the devils shall be the tormentors of
the soul in that day; but where have they learned
this ? Or how is it possible that it should be so ? If
you consider,

That no creature whatsoever can be an instrument of God's wrath ; the soul of man is such a kind of
a vessel as will hold more than all the creatures in the
world can put into it, it is capable of more torment
than all the creatures in heaven and earth can inflict,
and therefore when God pours out his wrath at the

last he doeth it by no creature, no, he doth it immediately.   The greatest acts of God are those that are
done by himself, without means or instruments; as
when God lets out his love into the soul in lesser
measures, then he uses the ministry of the creatures,
he doth it by the word and ordinances; but when God
pours out his love into the soul, to the utmost, pray,
what creature can convey the love of God to the soul?
No creature can convey all the love of God to the soul,
but he himself doth it by himself immediately; therefore the blessedness of the soul in the other world
is made to lie in the immediate enjoyment of God. So
now in lesser judgments, and lower dispensations of
wrath, God doth it by the creatures, Aye, but when
he comes to pour out his wrath upon sinners to the
utmost, no creature can be employed therein.—God
doth it immediately by himself, therefore he works not
by devils.

2. How can the devils be the tormentors of others,
who shall be deepest in the torments themselves?
they have been the first and greatest in sinning, and
therefore shall be the deepest in suffering, for hell is
chiefly prepared for the devil and his angels.   Now
pray, who shall torment the devils, who can have
power over them, but God himself?   It is done immediately by God's own hand, they fall into the hands of
the living God, therefore it was that they dreaded
Christ when he was in the flesh; "art thou come to
torment us before the time?"   And sinners are appointed to partake with the devils in the same
torments, and therefore the God that torments the
damned spirits, that God will be the tormentor of
every sinner, for they are in the same "fire that is pre-

pared for the devil and his angels." It is the same fire, and torment, and wrath, that they all lie under. Therefore look, whatever that is that torments the devil in that state, and that must be the torment of them that, in a way of sinning, have given themselves up to the devil; as they have been companions in sinning, so they shall be in suffering: so that all the miseries and sufferings of hell are from one and the same hand, the power and spirit of God inflicts them immediately upon one and the other; for as the Eternal Spirit shall in heaven, be a spirit of adoption, and glory to the saints for ever, so in hell he shall be a spirit of bondage and wrath to wicked men for ever; and this is the breath of the Lord, that kindles the fire that torments them.

3. There is not (that I know,) one word in all the Scriptures that gives countenance to this doctrine, of making the devils the ministers of God's vengeance in that world. God doth not think it unworthy of his greatness to be the executioner of his own vengeance, therefore it is said, " vengeance is mine, and I will repay saith the Lord," and in that dreadful place. (2 Thess. i. 7, 8.) " Christ comes in flaming fire, taking vengeance upon them that know not God, who shall be punished with everlasting destruction." How? " from the presence of the Lord, and the glory of his power." There shall be as real a presence of God in hell, as in heaven; Satan hath no such office as to be God's executioner in the eternal world. Indeed now he is in office, and acts as a tempter to draw us to sin; therefore he is called " Abaddon," a destroyer, a murderer, and in the day of judgment, he shall act as an accuser, but he shall not be the executioner of God's eternal vengeance.

4. Satan's power and kingdom and dominion shall end before Christ's, and that is in this world. The devil's ministry cannot be said to last longer than the ministry of good angels, and that is but during this life; they come to gather the elect to the last judgment, and at [*that*] judgment their ministry ends, and saints and angels shall then go to heaven together, and enjoy God together; so shall the devil and sinners go to hell, and lie under the weight of God's wrath for ever. The good angels shall be principalities and powers no more, and satan shall be prince of this world no more: for all rule and authority shall be put down, whether good or evil; for the Scripture tells us, "Christ must reign till he hath put down all rule and authority," therefore whatever the power is that satan hath over wicked men in this world, yet he shall have none in the next. As the good angels shall minister no more in love to the elect; so the devils shall ministry no more in wrath to the reprobate; but God shall be all in all. And what is said of the tormentors in hell, the same may be said of the torments themselves. The darkness, the flame, the devouring fire, the everlasting burning, these are nothing else but the immediate infinite wrath of "God who is a consuming fire." (Heb. xii. 29.) God is all in all to sinners in a way of wrath and misery, the punishment both of loss, and sense, lies in this:—Divines tell you the misery of hell consists in two things, the punishment of loss, and the punishment of sense, and it is so: the punishment of loss is, in losing the favour and comforting presence of God, and the punishment of sense, is in lying under the immediate wrath and vengeance of God, and that is another sort of misery, than to be left to be tormented

by devils or any creatures: what is the wrath of all
men and devils, to one frown of God? If God
be all in all in point of comfort, and blessedness,
to saints in heaven, then he is all in all in point
of vengeance, to sinners in hell. In heaven there
is no need of any ministry of creatures, to convey the love of God to the soul; there all those pipes
are cut off, they are only for our present state of dis-
tance, but there God is all; so in hell, God hath no
more need of ministry of creatures there to convey his
wrath, than he hath of the ministry of angels in heaven
to express his love. This then is the reason, why it is
so dreadful a " thing to fall into the hands of the living
God," because you will fall into the hands of God immediately, and have to do with the wrath of God
indeed.

By way of use, then, from so awful a truth, so
tremendous a doctrine as this is, shall I ask you one
question? Have you secured this God to be your all
in the next world, in a way of grace and love? Pray
answer it. I tell you, and I am sure you will say so too,
it is a thing of the greatest importance under the
heavens of God, the securing an interest in God to be
our all in a way of grace, for let me tell you,

1. God will be our all in that world, whether you
have secured him or not. Christ gives up the kingdom,
and God takes the management of all, and all the administration is then in the hand of God; God will be
your all in that world, whether you have secured him
or not; if he be not so in a way of mercy, then he will
be so in a way of wrath.

2. If any thing short of God be your all now, he
will bring that all to nothing; God never engages

against what a man loves, till a man loves something besides God, for then he makes that to be his god, and degrades God; whatever a man loves most, either it is God, or something set in the place of God, and that is his idol, and God hath said, he will destroy our idols; he will not bear that we make any thing an Idol, for he is a jealous God, and will not give his glory to Idols.

3. There is a day coming when you will need God, do you not believe this? now you think you do not need him; you have the creatures, and pleasures, and pastimes, and comforts, and enjoyments, and trades, and relations, to please the heart withal. And you can do, you think, without God, as God knows many do, they place other objects in God's stead; but there is a time coming when all the channels of creature enjoyments shall be dried up; the creature shall be no more, and then how dreadful will it be to have our affections left in height, and heat, and have nothing to place them upon. It is one of the miseries of hell: if thou hast no portion in God, thou art undone for ever. Look, what a man makes God to be to him here, that, God will be to him for ever. Is God your portion? Have you chosen God? Have you taken him for your chief good? I tell you, then he will be so for ever, for every man is eternally happy, or miserable by his own choice. Every man shall have that in the next world, which he chooses in this, either happiness or misery. If we have chosen God, he will be our God for ever, but if in this world, God be nothing to you in a way of faith, and love, and duty, and service, and obedience, and holiness, he will be nothing to you in the next world in a way of grace,

but all in a way of wrath and torment; therefore, how doth it concern you and me, whether we have secured God, to be our all in the next world, and this you may know if you consider,

(1.) Have you taken Christ for your all? Have you in a sense of your lost estate by nature, and your undone condition by the fall, have you sought after Christ, and closed with him as your all here? do you see all in him? do you fetch all from him? Is he all to you in point of righteousness, all in regard of interest and reliance? if thus you have made Christ your all here, then you have secured God, to be your God for ever.

(2.) Have you made God your chiefest good, your highest Lord, and your last end? if so, you have secured him to be your God for ever. This one thing will infallibly determine the case of your soul, for if God be your chief good, then you love him above all; if he be your highest Lord, then you will serve him before all; and if he be your last end, then you will make him the centre of all [*your duties,*] and make every duty to observe this end. But what will be the case of sinners, that have set light by Christ here, that have neglected God, broken his commands, slighted his call, refused his counsel, and turned their backs upon all the tenders of grace? What shall become of them? God will be all in all to them in the next world; not in a way of mercy and grace, but in a way of wrath and vengeance; for he is the living God that you have slighted, and know "that it is a fearful thing to fall into the hands of the living God."

SERMON XI.

" It is a fearful thing to fall into the hands of the living God." (Heb. x. 31.)

I have explained the terms and demonstrated the truth. I have given you the reasons, why it is such a fearful thing to fall into the hands of the living God.

I. With respect to those attributes of God which make it so.

II. Because all the proceedings of God in that day, shall be suited to the ministry of a man's own conscience.

III. Because all that fall into his hands, in the sense of the text, have to do with God in such a covenant, wherein the great design of God is to glorify his justice.

IV. It is a fearful thing, because of the impartiality of the sentence that shall then be passed, wherein there shall be no distinction of persons, and the sentence shall be suited to the nature of the cause, and no sin shall escape the sentence. Again,

V. Because there is no way of being delivered out of his hand.

VI. Because it is the last of God's dispensations to men: the glorifying believers, and the destruction of the wicked, are the last of all the works of God. and,

VII. Because we have then to do with God immediately.

VIII. Because in that eternal state, God shall be all in all.

These are the reasons why it is such a fearful thing to fall into the hands of the living God.

I come now to answer some objections, which may seem to diminish the awfulness of this serious truth. The

I. Objection is this. How can it be such a fearful thing to fall into the hands of the living God; when it hath been the choice of many; many have done it, and done it in pursuance of their eternal advantage. So did David, (Psa. xxxi. v.) "Into thy hands I commit my spirit;" so did Stephen, (Acts vii. 59.) Therefore how can it be such a fearful thing to fall into his hands, seeing believers do so freely commit themselves into his hands.

Now in answer to this you must know,

1. That the hands of God have a very different sense, admit of various acceptations in Scripture. There is the hand of his care, the hand of his power, and the hand of his vengeance.

(1.) The hand of his care; care in Scripture is expressed by the hand. (Num. xxxiii. 1.) "Israel went out of Egypt under the hand of Moses and Aaron," that is, by their care, "thou leddest thy people like a flock, by the hand of Moses and Aaron," (Psa. lxxvii. 20.) that is, by their care and conduct; so here the hand of God imports the care of God. The Lord Christ hath by office, this care of the souls of all the elect: God the Father hath given them to him to redeem, and believers commit them to him to save; the souls of believers at death, are to pass into heaven through an enemies' country, through the devils kingdom, for he is the prince of the air, and would be apt enough to waylay them, if Christ did not concern himself particularly for them; this believers know, and therefore commit themselves to his hand.

(2.) There is the hand of his power, for in scripture, power is often expressed by the hand, (Deut. xxxii. 36.) " The Lord shall repent himself, for his servants, when he seeth their power is gone;" that their hand is gone, so the Hebrew; (Dan. vi. 27.) "he hath delivered Daniel from the power of the lions," from the hand of the lions; so here, the hand of God is put for the power of God, the hand of Christ is put for the power of Christ. He hath power to kill, and to make alive, to pardon sin, to bind Satan, to change, convert, and save souls, and all that by faith commit their souls to him, shall experience his power in their salvation; " I will give unto them eternal life, neither shall any pluck them out of my hand." (John x. 29.) " The Father which gave them me is greater than all, and none shall pluck them out of my Father's hand;" therefore saith David, " into thy hands I commit my spirit."

(3.) There is the hand of his wrath and vengeance, and this is the hand in the text. It is a fearful thing to fall into the hands of God's wrath, and this is the hand that all impenitent sinners fall into at last, and these are the hands that all the people of God dread and tremble at, and therefore commit themselves into the former, that they may thereby escape the latter.

2. We must distinguish committing our souls into his hand, and falling into his hand; there is a great difference between them, as much as is between faith, and unbelief, for the one is an act of faith, the other the fruit of unbelief. A man commits his soul into God's hands, because he would secure it, but he falls into his hands because he cannot avoid it; it is great wisdom to commit our soul to Christ. Satan would destroy it, and we ourselves cannot preserve it, therefore it is our wisdom to commit it to him, that is able to keep it. (2 Tim. i. 12.) " I know in whom I have trusted, and am persuaded he is able to keep that which I have committed to him;" the depositum that he commits to the care of Christ, is his soul. Faith is a grace of great confidence and trust; when once it hath brought the soul to a true union to Christ, there is no condition it can be in, but it will trust itself upon him; faith practises a continual trust in the care and power of Christ, and that in these three cases more especially.

I. In the time of conversion.

II. In the time of distraction.

III. In the time of dissolution.

I. At the time of conversion, when faith is first wrought in the soul, it is busy in multiplying acts of trust, and now the soul is brought into a new condition, full of sweetness and comfort, and therefore comes out of the wilderness, leaning upon her beloved.

II. In the time of great trouble and distraction; these drive the soul to Christ; so it did David in the instance given, for the 31st Psalm was penned at the time when he was persecuted and pursued by Saul; that he was in very great straits appears from the second verse, "deliver me speedily;" danger (it seems) was at his heels, and in the fourth verse "pull me out of the net they have laid privily for me." Now in these great fears, you have David acting his faith, "Into thy hands I commit my spirit."

III. The time of dissolution is a peculiar season of strong reliance. There is in the believer, a principle of faith which teaches him to do what God would have him, and to die when God would have him; he is not only to live by faith, but to die in the faith. "These all died in faith." (Heb. xi. 13.) This is called a "dying unto the Lord," a way of dying we little understand. (Rom. xiv. 8.) Now such a committing the soul into his hands is far from falling into his hands, for it hath a threefold end in it, which secures from falling into his hands; an absolute perfection, an immediate fruition, and an after re-union.

1. It trusts Christ for conferring upon it an absolute perfection, which it could not attain here, and therefore seeks it where it is to be had, in the divine presence. A state of grace is, at best, a state of imperfection; under the highest attainments, some darkness is mixed with our light; we know but in part, our love to God hath much coldness in it. No believer is thoroughly sanctified, though sanctified

throughout. The best edition of a Christian in this life is full of erratas; he will never be free from them, till he be stamped with an impression of real glory. Heaven is the proper place of " the spirits of just men made perfect," therefore doth the believer put himself into the hands of Christ, that the work of God begun in him here, may be perfected hereafter. A Christian is not satisfied with such an imperfect conformity to God, and low attainments in grace, he longs for the perfection of his state, and puts himself into Christ's hand for the end.

2. It commits the soul to him in order to an immediate fruition, for the full sight of God is not in ordinances but in the light of glory. This is the blessedness of heaven, this is the blessedness of angels, to live in the views of the face of God; this is the blessedness of the human nature of Christ, to live in the enjoyment of God, and the blessedness of God, to live in the eternal enjoyment of himself, as being the chiefest good. Now this blessedness is attainable by the believer only in heaven. All enjoyment of God in that state is by virtue of its union, and eternal membership with Christ, and by virtue of this union it is that the soul sees God.

3. The believer trusts Christ for an after re-union at last, for the believer goes to heaven by halves; the soul enjoys him, but the body lies in the dust; the soul hath a great love to the body, and would not willingly be divorced from it. It is content to quit the flesh in the present state, for a better life, but not to part with it always; for the glory of the soul in the presence of God in heaven is not fully complete without the body share in it, therefore the state of the case

lies thus. If we lived in a house which was our own, and the walls were ready to fall, and the roof to drop in, we would be willing to go from it, for a while, but not to lose the ground and materials, but have it built in a better form and fashion, and so return again. The flesh, the soul's house, grows out of repair, and is ready to drop, and therefore the soul is willing to leave it for the present, but not for ever; therefore the believer commits his soul into the hands of Christ, as for the perfecting of grace, and for the full fruition of God, so for a re-union with the body, which Christ will come again, and change, and "make it like to his glorious body;" that as the body and soul have served God together here on earth, so they may together enjoy God for ever in heaven; and when the soul leaves the body it parts with it, looking for it again; for,

(1.) A man cannot be completely happy, no not in heaven, till the body be raised again, the soul alone doth not constitute the human nature without the body, therefore, though the soul be a spirit, and can live apart, yet it was not made to live apart for ever, and therefore it remains, as it were in a state of widowhood, when it is without its old companion, and is destitute of one half of itself, till the body be raised again, and re-united to it.

(2.) It is agreeable to the justice and goodness of God, that the body that had a share in duty and obedience, should also have a share in the recompence; shall the body be partner with the soul in the work of God, and shall the soul go away with all the reward? This is not equal—it is the body that undergoes all the hardship; what wearinesss, and straits, and tireings in obedience doth the body undergo, which the soul feels nothing of ; have the bodies of believers been yielded up to God, " as instruments of righteousness," (as the Apostle calls them) (Rom. vi. 13.) and shall they have no part in the inheritance ? Hath the body been mortified, and crucified, and kept under, for the sake of Christ, and shall it have no share in the glory of Christ ? The body of Christ is glorified in heaven, therefore so shall the body of every believer; therefore I say, the body of every believer shall be raised to share with the soul in its eternal state; the wicked are but in part punished by what they feel under the wrath of God, and the godly are but in part rewarded, till the body be re-united to the spirit, and made to share with it in all.

(3.) The Lord Christ in all his mediatorial under-takings, had a respect to the body as well as the soul, (1 Cor. vi. 20.) " Ye are brought with a price, there-fore glorify God in your bodies, and in your spirits, which are God's." And is not the body in covenant union to Christ as well as the soul ? " Know ye not that your bodies are the members of Christ ?" (1 Cor. vi. 15.) And the spirit of Christ sanctifies the body as well as the soul; " I pray God (saith the apostle) you may be sanctified throughout, in body, soul, and spirit." (1 Thess. v. 23.) and is not " your body the temple of the Holy Ghost ?" (1 Cor. vi. 19.) he dwells in it, and why doth he dwell in it, but to make it meet for glory?

(4.) We read of some saints that shall be found alive at Christ's coming, and shall not die at all ; shall never quit the body, but shall be changed, (1 Cor. xv. 51.) " Behold, I shew you a mystery, we shall not all sleep, but we shall all be changed," that is of mortal, be made immortal; such saints as shall be found in the flesh when the Lord Christ shall come shall never die at all, but their natural body shall be made spiritual for ever. So it is said, (1 Thess. iv. 16, 17.) " For the Lord himself shall descend from heaven, with a shout, with the voice of the archangel, and the dead in Christ shall rise first; then we which are alive and remain shall be caught up together with them in the clouds, and so shall we ever be with the Lord." So that the bodies of saints in that day shall not be dissolved, but changed and perfected; their substance shall remain, only endued with new and glorious qualities. Now, how unequal would it be for some saints to have glorified bodies, and others not!

(5.) To what end doth the spirit of God maintain an union with the very bodies of the saints while they lie in the grave? It is a great truth, that the spirit of God doth maintain an union with the very flesh of a believer, even when it lies rotting in the dust, (Rom. viii. 11.) " If the spirit of him that raised up Jesus from the dead dwell in you, he that raised up Christ from the dead shall also quicken your mortal bodies by his spirit who dwells in you;" here we may see how the body of a believer rises; it is by the virtue of the spirit of God dwelling in him; if ever the spirit dwells in the body of saints, it dwells in them for ever, and this will appear, if you consider,

1. The relation of God to believers is unchange-able and indissoluble; now the union of God to believ-ers is to the person, not to the parts but to the whole. both soul and body; the relation cannot be broken between God and the body, any more than it can

between God and the soul, therefore the apostle saith, " When we die, we are the Lord's:" that which dies, dies in union to God, for can you imagine that when the bodies of believers rot in the dust, they are no more in union with God, for if so when the body drops into the grave, it drops out of covenant, but this cannot be, for believers are said " to die in the Lord," (Rev. xiv. 13.) What is that which dies? not the soul, but the body. It dies in the Lord, in union to God, therefore it is said "to sleep in Jesus." It is the body that sleeps, and it sleeps in union to Christ, and the Spirit, and in covenant with God.

2. The analogy of the personal union, and the mystical, makes this necessary; there is a personal and a hypostatical union between the Godhead, and the manhood of Christ, and when they were once united, they were never divided again ; When the body of Christ was in the grave, was his body then in a firm union to the Godhead ? So the bodies of saints when they are in the grave, and the soul in heaven, yet even then, the body remains in union to Christ; Christ will not lose any of his mystical body, (John vi. 39.) " This is the will of him that sent me, that of all which he hath given me I should lose nothing, but should raise it up again at the last day;" he speaks here of the body that must be raised again, or else something would be lost of the gift of God, and his own purchase. Believers shall be raised by the power of the spirit, for to what [end] can it be supposed that the spirit of God should maintain his union to the body of a dead believer, but to raise it to glory at last.

And if any should object that, by this argument, the bodies of the wicked should be glorified at last, because they shall be raised, I answer, It is true they shall be raised, but not to glory ; for they are raised from a different cause, and to a different end.

1. From a different cause ; saints rise by the power of the spirit, the power of Christ as mediator ; the wicked are raised by the power of Christ as Lord ; the godly rise by virtue of their union to Christ as their head, the wicked by virtue of the power of Christ as their judge ; the one rise to have a sentence of condemnation executed upon them, the other by virtue of Christ's life and resurrection shall enter into a state of blessedness, in the enjoyment of God and Christ for ever ; therefore they rise,

2. To a different end, one rises to receive the reward of grace, the other of sin, "for God will reward every man according to his work," (Matth. xvi. 27.) Believers rise that they may be glorified for ever, the wicked rise to be tormented for ever ; as it was with Pharaoh's butler and baker, both are lifted up out of the dungeon, the one in a way of exaltation, the other to execution ; so that in the resurrection, both saints and sinners are in the hands of God, the saints are in the hands of a reconciled and loving God, who will for ever glorify them, but the other fall into the hands of the living God, who will for ever avenge himself upon them.

II. Objection is this. How can it be such a fearful thing to fall into the hands of the living God, when that to some, we find, even in this world, it hath been an eligible thing ? David chose rather to fall into the hands of God than man, therefore how can it be such a fearful thing ? To answer this you must consider,

1. The relation David stood in to God ; for God

deals with every man according to the relation wherein
he stands to God; now David was in the nearest
relation to God, he was one whom God had made a
covenant with, as he tells you in the fifth verse of the
foregoing chapter, "God hath made with me an everlasting covenant." That which put David upon making
this election of falling into the hands of God rather
than man, was the sense of his covenant interest, he
knew he could never miscarry in an everlasting covenant, he was safe in the main, the covenant secures
good to us out of every dispensation of God;
"all things shall work together for good," therefore
Jacob, from the sense of his covenant interest, urges
God with this plea, when he was in STRAITS, (Gen.
xxxii. 12.) "Thou saidst, I will surely do thee good;"
he infers this from his covenant interest, for in cove-
nanting to be our God, he hath engaged to do us good.
David was one of God's children, and therefore seeing
he must be scourged, he chooses rather to be under a
rod of his father's making than man's: to be scourged
by a tender father is better than to be scourged by a
bloody enemy, that hath neither mercy nor pity.

2. You must distinguish between the anger of
God, and the hatred of God; there is the hand of his
chastening anger in this world, and the hand of his
heavy wrath in the next; now anger is highly consistent with love; God may be, and often is, angry with
his own children, and makes them to know it to their
cost, but in the [*midst*] of all, his heart is still upon
them, and his love to them: (Psa. lxxxix. 32.) "I will
visit their transgressions with a rod, and their iniquity
with stripes," there is his anger; but there is love in
the next words, "my loving kindness will I not

Q

take from them;" but the hatred of God is no ways consistent with love, it is co ntrary to it. Now David speaks of falling into the hands of God's chastening anger, for that endures but a moment, and not of falling into the hands of his avenging wrath, for that hath no end.

3. We must distinguish of "falling into the hands of God." There is a falling into his hands by final impenitency and obduration; thus, all that live and die in sin fall into the hands of the living God, and this is that which is intended by the expression in the text, which is such a fearful thing. But then there is a falling into his hands by putting ourselves into his hands, by a humble resignation to the will of God. Thus David did in the case of Absalom's conspiracy against him. "If I shall find favour in the eyes of the Lord, he will bring me back again, but if he thus say, behold I have no delight in thee, here I am, let him do as seems good unto him." It was by this Shimei saved his life, by putting himself into David's hands, (2 Sam. xix. 16—23.) "Shimei hasted to meet David, and fell down before him, and said, let not my Lord impute iniquity to me;" he puts himself into his hands, and by this submission he is overcome, "therefore the king said to Shimei, thou shalt not die;" and so Benhadad's servants hearing that the kings of Israel were merciful kings, came to the king with sackcloth upon their loins, submitting to his mercy.

Thus by putting ourselves into the hands of God we may prevail with him, and obtain mercy from him.

4. You must distinguish of state. There is a state where mercy acts chiefly, and a state where mercy acts no more. Upon the stage of this world, mercy acts its part and shews itself in more objects, and

in more instances, than the judgment of God doth; that must have its course and triumph in the next world; here all sinners share, more or less, in the mercy of God. " The Lord is good to all," (Psa. cxlv. 9.) " He makes his rain to fall, and his sun to shine upon the just and the unjust." (Matth. v. 45.) and this mercy David had an eye to ; the sense of the faithfulness and mercy of God directed his choice, when the three judgments were tendered to his choice, the famine, the sword, or pestilence. He chooses the last, because herein he had to do with God only, in the others there was the hand of man too; in the sword there is the bloodiness and cruelty of man, much barbarity but little mercy, and therefore he chooses the plague, for therein he had to do with God only, who is a God of great mercy. It is better for any man, not only for a good man, as David here, but even for sinners to fall into the hands of God in this world, than man's, because this world is a stage of mercy : but in the next world the case is altered ; mercy hath done its work, there is no more mercy for sinners; God will put up all pity and tenderness, and betake himself to acts of justice and vengeance.

5. You must consider the duration of falling into the hands of God. It may be for a season or for ever ; in this world for a time, or in the next world for eternity. David chooses to fall into the hands of God, but not to lay there for ever; it was but for a little time, but three days pestilence, and what is this to everlasting wrath and vengeance. This objection therefore is of no force to take off the edge of this truth, for though to fall for a few days under his

chastening anger may be tolerable, yet, to fall for ever into the hands of his avenging justice is intolerable.

III. Objection is this. How can it be consistent with the justice and righteousness of God, to punish temporal sinning with everlasting suffering, to inflict eternal vengeance for momentary offences, to throw a sinner into misery that shall never end, for committing a few sins here that quickly have an end? This hath made some conclude against the eternity of hells' torments, as if God were so merciful, that he would not let them lie under his wrath for ever; but I answer this, with the Apostle, "Is God unrighteous that taketh vengeance? God forbid." (Rom. iii. 5, 6.) God is holy, just, and righteous, when he doth punish momentary offences with everlasting torments. And this will appear, by considering,

1. It is meet for the governing of the world, that the penalty should be thus stated, for the preserving the authority of God's law in its full force and vigour, and to render it more solemn and awful. The design of God is, to have the punishment overpoise all the temptation a man can have to sin; there is in man since the fall, such a propensity to sensual things, that without this fear of hell, nothing is able to keep it down; fleshly lusts are so pleasing to corrupt nature that they need to be checked with the severest remedies, therefore God hath told us before hand, that if we live after the flesh, we shall die; God wisely balances the sinner's delights with awakening fears, that by setting eternal pains against momentary pleasures, we may the better escape temptation. The pleasures of sin, which are but for a season, entail upon us torments that are eternal. God hath so wisely

proportioned the dispensation of pleasure and pain, that it is left to our own choice whether we will have it here or hereafter; whether we will enjoy that pleasure which is the fruit of sin, or that which comes hereafter, as a reward of grace. Things at hand will far more prevail than things to come, if they be not considerably greater; here the pain is short, and so is the pleasure, and in the other world they are both eternal; and this becomes the wisdom of God, that, as they which work out their salvation with fear and trembling here, should have pleasures at the right hand of God for evermore; so they that will have their pleasures here, should have everlasting misery in the other world.

2. No law observes this, that the continuance of the punishment should be no longer than the continuance of the offence. Punishments inflicted by human laws are of a far longer continuance than the doing of the crime. Shame, banishment, imprisonment, all these may be inflicted for life, for a fact done in one hour; it is ordained by the wisest states, that many crimes which may be done in a few minutes, shall be punished with the death of the offender; and is it not most just then, that offences done against God should be punished with everlasting death?

3. Common reason allows, that there ought to be a proportion between the nature of the offence, and the quality of the punishment; now sin against God, is such an immense thing, that nothing less than an everlasting punishment can be equivalent to it.

This will be plain, if you consider two things.

(1.) The greatness of the majesty against which sin is committed. Every sin is a base depreciating of God, and this is enough to make the guilt of it infinite,

because it is done against an infinite God, and therefore it deserves an infinite punishment; now a finite
creature cannot bear an infinite punishment, therefore
God makes it infinite in regard of continuance. The
creature cannot pay the whole debt at once, therefore
he must be paying it for ever.

(2.) There is an eternity in sin, not only an objective
eternity, as being committed against an eternal God,
and as deserving eternal punishment, but a further
eternity in sin, and that is with respect to the disposition and will of the sinner, which is so fixed in sin,
that if the sinner should live for ever, he would sin for
ever; he is never weary of sin, and he desires to live
here always, that he may always enjoy his lusts, and
though he lives ever so long, yet he never thinks it
time to return to God. The men of the old world,
what a great age did they live to, eight or nine hundred years, and yet they made no other use of it than
to indulge their lusts. A sinner would certainly go
on in sin to the world's end, if death did not hinder
him; his will is to sin everlastingly. By the same
reason that he loves his sin, and would act it for a day
or a month; by the same reason he would act it for
ever. As in the case of duty, so in the case of sin,
God looks more at the will than the deed. What
hinders a sinner from being a sinner still, who leaves
not sin, till sin leaves him. He that would sin, and
cannot, he sins in willing, and is it not just, that they
should never cease suffering, who if they had lived for
ever, would never have left sinning? and is it not just
that their eternal obstinacy should be punished with
an everlasting punishment? Again there is an actual
eternity in man's sin, for though death puts an end to
their lives, it doth not put an end to their sins, for

hell is as full of sin, as suffering; though schoolmen
say, that after this life, they are not capable of merit or
demerit, yet they grant that they sin even in hell:
though when the creature is under the actual condemnation of the law, it ceases to be any further [*ame-
nable to its enactments;*] so that, though the demerit
of the law ceases, yet the nature of sin remains.   The
law of God is of moral equity, and binds the creature
for ever, both in heaven and hell, and therefore the
nature of sin still remains; and therefore it is just with
God that there should be an everlasting continuance of
the punishment, and hence it is that the misery of the
damned is without redemption, or hope, or alloy, for
ever.

(4.) It is just with God that the sinner should
be punished with everlasting misery, because he
chooses it, by refusing an everlasting felicity.   The
purchase our Lord made by his death, is an everlasting blessedness, and God by his infallible promise
assures us, that all who sincerely believe and obey him,
shall be rewarded with heaven for ever ; for all the
rewards of God in the last day, whether of love to the
saints, or punishment to the wicked, are all everlasting
and run into eternity; now if the tender and promises
of everlasting glory be despised, there is nothing left
to be the sinner's portion, but everlasting misery ; it is
the fruit of his own choice, for it is certain God will
give to every man in the next world, that which he
chooses in this.   I have set before you everlasting life,
therefore choose life, that you may live; he that
chooses life shall have it, and he that chooses not life,
but willingly cleaves to his lusts, he doth in the event
choose death and hell, and he shall have it; he that

chooses sin, chooses it with all its attendants, misery and wrath, for they cannot be separated from it, therefore if he chooses it for himself, it is just that he should inherit his own choice; he that chooses God for his portion, shall for ever enjoy him, and is it not then just that he that chooses misery, should for ever lie under it? Is it not just that God should say to such, "Depart from me into everlasting fire," that say to God here, "depart from us; we desire not the knowledge of thy ways?" There can be no complaint in hell against God, where the punishment, how great soever it be, is nothing else but the fruit of a man's own choice, for he that chooses sin as his way, doth by consequence choose the end, which is hell and misery, therefore if he falls into the hands of the living God, he can blame none but himself, it is the fruit of his own choice.

All the use I would for the present make of this, is to shew the folly of sinners; what greater folly can any be guilty of, than to indulge sin, and gratify lust, and neglect God, and Christ, and all the means of grace? Is it not folly for a man to make himself eternally wretched and miserable by his own choice? This shall be the woe of the damned, that they chose it; but you will say, did ever any man choose to be miserable? Ay, thousands, and ten thousands. Every man that knows there is a God, and that he hath an immortal soul, and must give an account to God of all he doth in the flesh; that knows that sin will end in eternal death, and yet indulges sin and lust, chooses to perish and to be miserable for ever; he loves hell and death. (Prov. viii. 36.) "All they that hate me, love death," they do not love death in the event, but they love

death in the cause, they love their sins and lusts and
pleasures, that God hath entailed death upon, and
therefore are said to love death. Is it not folly to
do that in respect to your souls, which your discre-
tion abhors with respect to your bodies? You will
not drink poison, though never so sweet and pleasant,
because there is death in it, yet how doth the sweetness of sin draw us to commit it, though there be
hell and damnation wrapt up in it? Is it not folly
to run the hazard of hell and death, for the
satisfaction of a lust? Is it not the greatest folly
for any man out of a fond desire of present satisfaction, to run the hazard of eternal torments? As he
that parted with a crown, for a draught of water in
his distress cried out, " For what a short pleasure
have I lost a kingdom?" So this will be the cry of
the sinner, " for what a short pleasure in sin have I
lost eternal happiness." Therefore, to cure the folly
of these mischiefs, it is good to counterbalance our
desires with frequent thoughts of what is to come.
I am not to live always. I may be in another world,
before another Lord's day come. I must appear
before the eternal God, to give an account of all I
have done in the flesh, and can I dwell with everlasting burnings? And can I endure the endless
wrath of incensed justice? Think of this, when
thou art about to please the flesh and gratify thy
lusts. Can I bear the wrath of God for ever? Oh
what will a man do, in that everlasting night of
darkness? We are apt to think a Sabbath, a sermon
long, and wish they were ended; but how long will
the miseries and torments of hell be! When once
they begin they shall never end, for there, conscience

shall be a worm that never dies, and the wrath of
God, a fire that never goes out.   Oh ! then, that you
would endeavour to cure your present prevailing lusts,
with the frequent forethoughts of the heat of the
everlasting wrath of God, "for it is a fearful thing to
fall into the hands of the living God."

SERMON XII.

" It is a fearful thing to fall into the hands of the living God." (Heb. x. 31.)

I HAVE shewed you in what sense God is the living God, and opened the notion of falling into his hands; made it out that it is such a fearful thing, to whom it is so, and the reason why it is so. That which now remains is to make some improvement of this by application, and the

I. Use shall be for information in several inferences.

1. If so be, it be such a fearful thing to fall into the hands of the living God, then I infer, how great is the evil and mischief of sin ! What a cursed nature is it of! There is nothing more discovers it than this, that it is against the living God ; an eternal being is affronted and provoked by it : the greater the object the viler the injury that is done against it : the dignity of the object aggravates the offence. The fame of common persons bears but a common [*aspersion,*] but to defame a sovereign is treason; how horrid a thing then must it be to defame the living God ! Now sin dishonours and degrades him. Many things set out

the evil of sin, as the mischief it doth ourselves, our neighbours, and families, and the nation : our bodies, and our souls : but nothing discovers the monstrous evil and ugliness of it like this, it is against the living God.

(1.) It is a violation of his law. " Whosoever sins transgresses the law." (1 John iii. 4.) And whose law is it, but the law of the living God? Sin contemns his authority, slights his dominion, and denies his Sovereignty. " Who is the Lord that I should obey him ?" said Pharaoh : so saith every sinner ; " Let us break his bands asunder, and cast his cords from us." We hold it to be a great evil to break the laws of a dying man; what is it then to break the laws of the living God ?

(2.) It is a dishonouring his name. " Through breaking the law dishonourest thou God ?" (Rom. ii. 25.) This lays his glory in the dust, puts a contempt upon every attribute, and degrades him in all his excellencies ; therefore the Holy Ghost gives such names to sin, calls it unrighteousness, because it dishonours God's righteousness and justice ; it is called folly, because it despises the wisdom of God; it is called unthankfulness, because it puts a slight upon his grace and love ; it is called a lie, because it affronts the truth of God ; it is called filthiness, because it is a disparagement to his holiness.

(3.) It is an invading of the life of God, as far as the nature of a finite act can reach. Not that God can die. The reason that any thing decays, is either its own native weakness, or a superior power in something contrary to it; now there is no weakness in the nature of God, that can introduce any corruption, nor can he be overpowered by any thing else : a weaker cannot hurt him, and a stronger cannot be. Therefore sin cannot effectually and really invade the life of God, but it hath that in the nature of it which would do it. There is a tendency in every sin to [*invade*] the being of God, and deprive him of his immortality; therefore it is, as Aquinas saith, "All sin strikes at the very being and life of God." What a cursed thing is sin ! Fools make a mock at it, as if it were nothing, but if ever the Lord open our eyes to see the opposition and injuriousness of it to the living God, it will make our souls tremble at it.

2. I infer hence, how dreadful is the sinner's case, that dies in sin, without repentance and an interest in Christ ! the dread of his case appears in this, that he falls into the hands of the living God; for pray do but consider a few things that will make it appear to be so.

(1.) This living God is privy to all the sins that ever thou hast committed, great or little, open or secret, sins of thought, word, and deed, in the light or in the dark : the living God is privy to all thy unbelief, thy pride and worldliness, thy drunkenness, adultery, swearing, lying, envying, unjust dealing, atheism and blasphemy, thy unprofitableness under the means of grace, and incorrigibleness under the rod, sins of omission and commission, personal and relative sins, they are all open to the eyes of God: "there is no darkness or shadow of death where the workers of iniquity can hide themselves." O how many sins are there that we are ashamed to commit before a dying man, and yet are not ashamed of them before the living God !

(2.) This living God will call thee to account for all thy sins, for every sin: he that now lives to make intercession for sinners in a day of grace, lives to make inquisition for sin in a day of judgment. True is the language of the Apostle, (2 Cor. v. 10.) " We must all appear before the judgment seat of Christ, that every one may receive the things done in the body, whether it be good or evil."

(3.) As soon as ever you leave this world, you fall immediately into the hands of this living God: there is no sleeping of the soul in the grave; it is turned naked out of this world, stript of all its comforts here, and so goes naked into the presence of this living God, and hath to do with him in a way of wrath and vengeance.

(4.) This living God is able to punish sin for ever, and in that he lives for ever, the sinner's hell must be for ever. It is the living God that kindles that flame in the sinner's soul, that must never die; there is great reason why the sinner's hell should be eternal, because every sin is against the life of God, which is an eternal life; therefore there is an eternal guilt in sin, which he must suffer under to eternity: as long as God lives, the sinner shall live to be miserable. It is a fearful thing to fall into the hands of a just God, who can as well cease to be God as to be just; his justice obliges him to avenge every sin done against him, Again, it is a fearful thing to fall into the hands of an angry God, whose wrath burns to the lowest hell; but of all, it is most fearful to fall into the hands of the living God. As it is the believer's happiness that they have one that ever lives, to make intercession for them, so this is the sinner's misery that God lives for ever to avenge himself upon them : his life runs through all his attributes; his power, his wrath, his justice, are so dreadful, because it is the wrath of the living God, therefore it must be a fearful thing; nothing aggravates the terror of judgment like it.

3. I infer hence, the sinner's misery is eternal. After we have spent a few days here, we must go into an eternal condition, that shall never change nor end : the body for the present goes to the grave, but the soul returns to God, that is, to be put into its everlasting state, either of happiness or misery, for the sinner's hell is as eternal as the believer's heaven, so that there is no end of the sinner's suffering under the wrath of God. It is a death that never dies, and an end that never shall have an end.

4. The soul of man is immortal, and shall abide for ever ; it hath not an immortality in its own nature absolutely so : " God only hath immortality." (1 Tim. vi. 16.) but a derived dependant immortality from the pleasure of God, how else could it be fitted for an everlasting state ? God hath made promises that travail with everlasting mercy, to be the believers' God for ever, to bestow an endless blessing upon them, to give them eternal life and the like; now if the things promised are everlasting, then the soul must live everlastingly, or else the promises of God are vain and delusive; for how shall they be fulfilled unless the soul abide for ever, on whom they are for ever settled ? How can God be my God for ever unless I live for ever to enjoy him ? and, on the other hand, there are in the Scriptures many threatenings of eternal misery after this life against sinners; such as

that, (Mark ix. 44. 2 Thess. i. 8, 9.) where you read of "everlasting destruction." Now how can the sinner feel an everlasting destruction if he hath not an everlasting duration? Or how can it be said their worm never dies, if the soul dies? If the being of the soul hath an end, then the punishment must have an end; therefore the soul must be immortal. It falls into the hands of the living God; and so long as God lives the soul shall not die, and therefore there is no end of their sufferings.

5. I infer hence, it is no ground for security that God at present delays and defers the execution of his vengeance: God hath great reasons for this, to glorify his patience. All God's attributes shall be glorified. In the other world, patience is an attribute that receives no glory; there is no room for the exercise of God's patience in the eternal state, therefore God will glorify it here. And now sinners abuse it by security and presumption, therefore sinners slight his threatenings and despise his judgments, and so harden themselves in sin; "because sentence is not speedily executed, therefore the hearts of the sons of men, are fully set in them to do evil." The great execution of wrath is reserved for another state, for the other world; therefore it is called "wrath to come." The great manifestation of his mercy and justice is reserved for that time; then he shall shew the riches of his mercy in the vessels of mercy prepared for glory, and the greatness of his wrath in the vessels of wrath fitted for destruction.

6. Again, I infer hence, why should any murmur or repine at the prosperity of wicked men here, as if the proceedings of God were unequal? and yet this

is too common. (Mal. iii. 14, 15.) " Ye have said it
is vain to serve God, and what profit is it that we
have kept his ordinance, and that we have walked
mournfully before the Lord of hosts? and now we call
the proud happy; yea, they that work wickedness are
set up; yea, they that tempt God are even delivered."
This was David's stumbling-block, (Psa. lxxiii. 3.)
" I was envious at the foolish when I saw the prosperity of the wicked." This is to [*judge*] the wicked
man before he hath done his work. Every thing is
beautiful in its season. What though the corn in the
field hang down the head, and the weeds overtop it,
stay but till the harvest, and then you will quickly
see, which is for the garner, and which for the fire;
go into the sanctuary, and there you will see the ways
of the Lord are right, though transgressors stumble
and are offended at them.

7. Lastly, how should the ministers of the
Gospel put forth all diligence and faithfulness for the
saving of sinners, seeing " it is such a fearful thing to
fall into the hands of the living God." How did the
sense of this awaken the blessed Paul in his work!
" Knowing (saith he) the terrors of the Lord, we persuade men;" and the same he presseth upon Timothy,
(2 Tim. iv. 1.) " I charge thee before God, and the
Lord Jesus Christ, who shall judge the quick
and the dead at his appearing and kingdom;
preach the word, be instant in season, out of
season; reprove, rebuke, exhort with all long-
suffering and doctrine."—Why with all long-suffering? Because, they that deal most plainly and faithfully with souls, usually make themselves most envied; but it is better to provoke their wrath, than

to be guilty of their blood; there is no guilt like the guilt of the blood of souls. We should not think much of the expense of our breath, for that for which Christ was at the expense of his blood. Shall Christ spend his life to redeem souls, and shall not we spend our pains to save them? Surely it is a sad judgment to a people when such ministers are set over them, that neither understand the worth of their own souls nor of those that hear them.

II. Use is by way of terror, for this text must needs be matter of terror to all impenitent sinners; how dreadful will it be, when this living God takes up the controversy between him and them into his own hand; you hold ministers severe, and rigid, and censorious now in preaching such terrible things, though it is your mercy that God speaks to you by man; what then will you do when God shall deal with you immediately by himself? Oh how dreadful will every sinner's case be in that day! Nothing makes a man's case so miserable as when he must have to do with an everlasting God in a way of wrath; his justice is everlasting justice, and will not let thee go till thou hast paid all; his power is everlasting power, and there is none can deliver out of his hand. And is it not a fearful thing, especially if you consider there shall be wrath without pity, misery without mercy; therefore to fall into the hands of the living God is the greatest of all judgments. The schoolmen say, that an annihilation is a worse evil than the greatest suffering and torments; but (as Christ saith in another case,) "They err not knowing the Scriptures, nor the power of God." You read of them that "called to the rocks and mountains to fall upon them, and hide them from the wrath of the Lamb;" and of them that "seek for death, and cannot find it;" then there is something worse than annihilation. What a favour would the damned account it to be for ever annihilated! What our Lord saith of the son of perdition, we may say of all such, "it had been good for them they had never been born." For a man to be made a rational creature, and as such the subject of God's vengeance and wrath for ever, surely as Solomon saith, "an untimely birth is better than he." This text is like the hand-writing upon the wall, that may well make every impenitent soul to tremble; there is such a day coming when God will say to the sinner, Stand forth and answer to thy charge, what canst thou say for thy pride, thy drunkenness, uncleanness, and the like? these sins thou hast been warned of, but thou didst persist in thy wickedness, with a brow of brass, and an heart of stone; thou hast refused the offers of salvation; what canst thou say that sentence should not pass upon thee? Will not every sinner be found speechless in that day? Oh that knowing the terrors of the Lord you would be persuaded to fly from the wrath to come. As the Lord hath seconded his word by a promise, with an oath, that they might have strong consolation who fly for refuge to lay hold on the hope set before them: so he hath confirmed the word of his threatening with an oath; therefore he hath lifted up his hand to heaven and sworn, "As I live I will reward vengeance to mine enemies;" and again, "the Lord hath sworn by the excellency of Jacob, surely I will never forget any of their works." (Amos viii. 7.) Oh how great is the stupidity of man, that will not believe the word of God, nor tremble at the oath of God; it is this sottish stupidity that improves the atheism in the heart into this sad presumption, that "the Lord will not do good, neither will he do evil;" to such I would say, with the prophet, (Isaiah xxviii. 22.) " Be ye not mockers, lest your bands be made strong;" or with the Apostle, (2 Pet. ii. 3.) " Though they sleep, yet their damnation slumbereth not." You may mock, but " God will not be mocked at, for what a man sows that also shall he reap."

III. We may make use of it by way of trial; I have shewed you formerly, that though it be a fearful thing to fall into the hands of the living God, yet it is not so to all. It is a desirable thing to them that believe in Christ to fall into the hands of God, for they fall into the hands of mercy. What made Balaam wish that he might die the death of the righteous, but that there is a great deal of difference between the death of a righteous, and the death of a wicked man ; all die in the same manner, but they do not all die in the same state. Believers die in the Lord, they die in faith, and that makes death a blessedness ; but unbelievers die in their sins, so saith Christ, " if you believe not you shall die in your sins," and that makes death accursed. The truth is, we are in an age wherein men are so hardened in sin that no voice is loud enough to awaken them; however I will do my duty, and if nothing will awaken, then, as Christ saith, sleep on : give me leave to ask you,

1. How do you entertain this truth? Do you believe this word? the more clear and distinct the assent is, the more it conduces to a practical improvement; do you believe that there is a day coming wherein you will have to do with God, and be

judged by him to your eternal state? If you do, then,

2. Do you seriously consider it and suffer your thoughts to dwell upon it? This is of great use to make truths practised. Many have escaped hell and wrath by entertaining awakening thoughts about it; what is not in our thoughts cannot be the object of our hopes or fear; that is the reason why so many are surprised by death and judgment; that the day of the Lord comes upon them as a thief in the night, is for want of due consideration. He that considers a good is stirred up to seek for it, and he that considers an evil is moved with fear to avoid it; so " Noah being moved with fear prepared an ark;" this is a moral means which God hath often blessed to spiritual purposes; this awakened Job, " what shall I do when God rises up? when he visits, what shall I answer him?" If you did but seriously consider of a day of judgment, and the strict account we must give to our impartial judge, oh how would this quicken us to the use of means to prepare for that dreadful day.

3. Do you often call yourselves to account? What condition am I in? How stands the state of my soul? The day of judgment will be as a man's state is, terrible or comfortable as his state is good or bad. Therefore I would now deal with every person here present, as a fallen, lost sinner, for such we are all by nature, born children of wrath, (Eph. ii. 3.) " We are by nature children of wrath, even as others." And I have this to say further from the authority of this truth, that every soul of you, whom God, when he comes, finds in that state, is undone eternally; mercy itself cannot help you. Therefore let me ask you,

what is your state? Do you find a saving change
wrought in you or not! Can you make it out that you
are pardoned and justified? What sense have you of
sin? Did you ever see the evil of it? If not, you are
undone, for can you think that God who hath made
every sinner feel sin in this world, will not make you
feel it in the next? if you have felt sin, did you ever
fly to Christ for refuge? and if you did, how did you
it? Was it only to Christ as a deliverer from the wrath
to come, or to Christ with true faith, to give up yourselves to him and subject your hearts to him? If you
have taken Christ for your Lord, as well as your
Saviour, by taking up his yoke and giving up yourselves to obedience to his will, then your pardon is
sure and your state safe.

IV. But I come now to an use of exhortation. If
it be such a fearful thing to fall into the hands of the
living God, then,

1. Labour to get an affecting sense of this awful
truth, that every unconverted sinner must fall into the
hands of the living God. Oh that this Scripture were
but seriously believed! most men's faith is but pre-
tence because it hath so little effect, cold speculation,
an empty opinion rather than a sound belief; and this
proves it, because it produces so little fruit: O did we
believe this truth, what manner of persons should we
be! How cautious are we in other cases where there is
danger! If a man did suspect his house falling, he
would not stay in it; but we know that, [to abide] in a
natural estate is the way to be undone, and yet we
continue in it. There is none of us but do know that
sin is the most hurtful thing in the world to the soul,
that the wages of it is death, and yet we will venture
upon it to our ruin.

There are two things which, to a considering mind, are matter of wonder; one is, that any man should reject the Christian religion, it is so reasonable; and the other is, that any man that doth embrace it, should live so contrary to it; Oh labour therefore to get an affecting sense of this awful truth.

2. If it be such a fearful thing to fall into the hands of the living God, let us then be wise and labour to prevent it while we may; this is my end, to stir you up, to prevent this evil; it must be prevented, or it will certainly be the lot of every sinner, and if it be done, it must be done quickly. If we close not with Christ now, to-morrow God may withdraw and we may never have a season of grace again; consider,

(1.) Is not your life continued for this end? Have you the power of your own lives, to lengthen them as you please? Can you live as long as you will? You cannot think so, and if you own yourselves to live, and move, and have your being in God, then you should consider, what God continues your life for; is it to eat and drink and sleep? No, the great end of living is to retrieve the misery of a lost estate, and to close with Christ, and so to live for ever.

(2.) What are the Scriptures given out for, why hath God revealed his will in his word? but to acquaint you with the state of your case Godward, and to shew you what need you have of a Redeemer, and how sufficient a Saviour he hath provided, and how you are to close with him, and to submit to his precepts. This is the great end why God hath given us his word.

(3.) Consider that thy day is a day of grace, for wherever the Gospel comes, it brings a day of grace with it, that is, not only overtures of grace and pardon made by it, but the working and striving of the Spirit of God goes along with it. Now should not this be attended to, especially when it is designed of God in mercy to prevent the loss of an immortal soul? Dost thou not know that God will not wait always, and thy day of grace may be ended before thy life ends, and the Spirit of God may never strive with thee more? Oh how should this awaken us!

(4.) Consider this, what is like to be the event of dying unreconciled to God? Thou art by nature in an utter enmity against him, and he hath made thee tenders of peace and they have been slighted; therefore, where will it end? It must end either in repentance and turning to God, or in eternal misery.

(5.) Consider what you are to do for your souls. Are you to sit still in a state of enmity and perish there? The patience of God waits, and wilt not thou be thoughtful about thy soul? It is a great point gained, when a man's thoughts are concerned about his soul, how he may avoid eternal vengeance.

Therefore in order to the redressing of matters, and preventing the evil in the text, of falling into the hands of the living God, take these four rules.

1st. Seek and sue for reconciliation with God, and there is no way to obtain it but by Jesus Christ. The arms of Christ are the only hiding place from the wrath of God. If you would not fall into the hands of the living God, you must fly into the arms of a dying Christ. There is no way to escape eternal misery but by flying to Christ. How did Noah escape the flood but by preparing an ark? and this is the ark we must be shut up in, if ever we escape the deluge of God's wrath.

2nd. Labour to be deeply humbled under the sense

of sin; that is the way to find mercy; God hath told us, 'fury is not in him;' but that though when briers and thorns set themselves in battle against him, he will go through them and burn them, yet if any man will take hold of his strength to make peace with him, he shall make peace."

3rd. You must see that your close with Christ be right and according to the rule; it must be such a close as includes a covenant, a taking and giving; there must be acceptation and resignation. As you must receive Christ for yours, so you must be resigned to Christ to be his, and this must be done, not merely as an effect of the fear of future vengeance, but a changed heart, and a renewed mind. Your whole transaction in this matter must proceed from a renewed nature, and a vital principle of grace, or else what you do in this thing will neither be sincere or lasting.

4th. Plead earnestly with God for his Holy Spirit, for there can be no effectual work in the heart, where the Spirit of God is not the worker; no firm union between Christ and the soul, if the Spirit of God be not the firm uniting bond.

3. Take this living God for thy portion and chief good; consider here,

(1.) What is offered to thee : This living God tenders himself to be thy portion. This is the greatest good; more than heaven and earth is worth; he that is the great, the eternal Being, this eternal God, is offered to be thy portion; there is no portion like this, none so full; there needs no more to make thy happiness perfect; he is the Lord of life, the Lord of grace and of glory; the universal good; there is no portion so durable as this; it is an everlasting portion;

now what else can you call so? Can riches, relations, crowns, or kingdoms, be called so? No; these will all fade and wither; therefore choose God now, that you may enjoy him for ever: if you do not, what will you do in a dying hour? to whom will you fly for comfort then? You think you can live without him, but can you die without him? It is he must judge you to an unchangeable state of life or death; he will pass the sentence which will make you happy or miserable for ever.

(2.) Consider upon what conditions it may be had. It may be, you may think so great a good cannot be had without dear rates: I tell you the terms are so good, as nothing can be cheaper; it is impossible that any thing should be cheaper than only acceptance; God requires nothing of you but that you will heartily receive him. O how free is the grace of God! How bounteous and real are his tenders! He doth not say, If thou wilt remove mountains, divide the sea, create a world, I will be thy God; or if thou wilt satisfy my justice, do what the law requires, and merit my love; I will be thy God; no, no, all this is done to our hands; all that God desires, is, that he may be accepted and owned; and canst thou deny so reasonable a service as this is? If God had bid you do the greatest things imaginable, wouldst not thou have done it, if it was in thy power? How much more when he saith only, Look to me and be saved, turn to me and live, believe in me and thou shalt never die, take me for thy God and I will be thy God for ever.

(3.) Consider God's end in all this. Why would he be thy portion and thy God? Hath God any need of thee? Is it any happiness to him? No; for God can be no more perfect than he is. It is thy eternal good that God designs in all this. It is thy good and eternal advantage that God aims at, that thou may'st escape hell and wrath, and secure blessedness, and happiness for ever.

V. I come now to a word of comfort; and it is to all such as have this living God to be their God. Every man is happy or miserable, as this God is to him. They that have idols for their Gods are miserable, because they do not live; those that serve the belly and have it for their God, are miserable, because God will destroy both it, and them; those that love and choose this world for their God are miserable, because the fashion of this world passeth away. Of all people under heaven, you are the happy people who have the living God for your God. Your propriety in him, is that which administers good to you and comfort, under all conditions in the world. Though relations, husband, wife, or children should die, yet God lives. So David, (Psa. xviii. 46.) In the midst of all his fears he doth rejoice in this; " the Lord lives, and blessed be my rock, and let the God of my salvation be exalted." Again, It is comfort under all deadness in walking with God; this is the daily complaint of a believer; of a dead heart, dead affections, dead frames of spirit; the living God is able to quicken you; it is he that made thee to live at first, and he can increase that life. Again, it is comfort in the midst of temptation. Oh how busy is Satan to destroy this life, the spiritual life, by force and fraud, by sin or suffering, by himself or by his instruments. Oh the methods, the tools he uses to this end, and yet nothing can do

it, because the life of every believer is secured by God.
" Our life is hid with Christ in God." (Col. iii. 3.)
He must extinguish the life of the living God before
he can destroy the life of one saint of God. Again, it
is comfort in death and dissolution; the living God
lives for ever, and so shall you. The body and soul
must part, but they shall meet again; but it is impossible that the believer and God should ever part; it
is from the consideration of the everlastingness of the
years of God, that Habakkuk doth infer the eternity
of believers. (Hab. i. 12.) " Art thou not from everlasting, O Lord, my God, my holy one?" and what
then ? "We shall not die but live." As God shall live
for ever to be enjoyed, so the believer shall live for
ever to enjoy him. O what comfort is this to you,
that your God is a living God! This is the great
thing that every believer hath to glory in, now and
for ever, that God hath made him so wise, as to
choose that God for his portion that lives for ever.
Whatever it is that makes God an object of comfort to the soul, is, because he is the living God.
For,

1. If God be the living God, then his covenant is
a lasting covenant, for the duration of it is equal to
the life of God; it is founded upon his eternity, or
else it could never be made good. If the life of God
were not eternal, he could never fulfil the promises
that are eternal. (Rev. iv. 3.) You read of "a rainbow round about the throne like an emerald;" the
rainbow is an emblem of the covenant, and this rainbow is not like other rainbows; the rainbow hath
many colours, but this hath but one, and that is
like an emerald; a stone most green. Now the co-

venant of God is set forth by this, to note its eternal
duration; therefore David calls it "an everlasting covenant." Oh, what a comfort is this to be in an everlasting covenant with the living God!

2. If God be the living God, then he being our God
is a durable good, an everlasting possession; "this
God is our God for ever and ever;" for ever in this
world, and for ever in the next; how many comfort
themselves in their great enjoyments, their yearly in-
comes, which last but a little while. Oh what a comfort is it then to have a living God for a possession,
whose years never fail; he lives for ever; while God
is eternal, and always the same, it is not possible that
they who partake of this spiritual life should not also
partake of eternal. And this enjoyment of God shall
be ever the same, as high and sweet after millions of
ages, as it was the first day. Then will be fulness
of joy always present, without a thought of being past,
or to come, but always present. It is sweet and pleasant in its delights, and eternal in its duration.

3. It is a matter of comfort in the sense of the mutability of our present state; this use David makes of
it in (Psa. cii, 11, 12.) "My days are like a shadow
that declineth, and I am withered like grass; but
thou, O Lord, shalt endure for ever;" this was the
comfort of his soul in his fading condition, to think of
an enduring life in God; this is my comfort, that
though my present state is fading, yet God, with
whom I shall live for ever, is eternal; "my heart and
my flesh may fail me, but God is the strength of my
heart and my portion for ever." You that have the
life of Christ in you, have in you the beginnings of
eternal life; and though the old building be pulled

down, yet you have " a building of God, a house not made with hands, eternal in the heavens." Oh the comfort of having a propriety in this God, that is a living God; the thought of it should be refreshing to you, while this text shall be a terror to the wicked; for "it is a fearful thing to fall into the hands of the living God."

FAREWELL SERMON;

BY M. MEAD.

———

*Grace be unto you, and peace from God our Father,
and from the Lord Jesus Christ.*—(1 Cor. i. 3.)

You will wonder possibly that I should pitch on the
Apostle's salutation for my valediction, and make that
the conclusion of my preaching, which he made the
beginning of his writing, and therefore I have made
a double plea for it: I find that this was a form of
blessing peculiar to this Apostle, both in the beginning
and end of this epistle; for as there is scarcely one
epistle but begins with it, so many end with it likewise. As in (Gal. vi. 18.) " The grace of our Lord
Jesus Christ be with your spirit." So in the 2nd of
the Thessalonians, the last verse of the last chapter,
" The grace of our Lord Jesus Christ be with you all."
So that, finding the Apostle to use it frequently at the
beginning and end of his writing, I thought, as I
made it the matter of my prayer for you in the beginning, so I might make it my farewell to you in the
ending, and therefore, " Grace be unto you, and

peace from God our Father, and from our Lord Jesus Christ."

Besides this, as Isaac said to his Jacob, concerning his venison, when his father asked him, "how he found it so quickly?" he answered, "Because the Lord thy God brought it to me," the same I may say of this Scripture; for, considering of what subject I should speak in my last labours here among you, this Scripture came to my thoughts, and opening the book, came immediately to my sight, and therefore I may say God brought it to me, which I no sooner looked upon, but methinks I saw the Apostle on Mount Gerizim, and his mouth filled with blessing, for what greater blessing can a man wish, than that which comprehends all blessings, and that is grace and peace. Being therefore now to part, I thought to go to the top of the mount, and leave with you, "Grace and peace from God our Father, and from our Lord Jesus Christ." In which words there are two generals:

I. A double blessing desired.

II. A double spring discovered.

I. A double blessing desired; and that is grace and peace. Grace is of all blessings the richest; peace is of all comforts the sweetest: both these the Apostle begs for the Corinthians, and so do I for you, beloved. "Grace be unto you, and peace from God our Father, and from our Lord Jesus Christ."

II. Here is a double fountain discovered, and that is the Father and the Son: God and Christ. The Father is called the God of grace, the Son is called the Prince of Peace: not that grace is from the Father, without peace, nor peace from the Son without grace, but both grace and peace are from God the Father, through the Lord Christ.

The order of the words is worth noting: " Grace be to you, and peace ;" first grace, then peace ; for there can be no peace without grace, nor grace, but there will be peace ; but there can be no true peace but from God ; nor from God, but as he is a Father ; nor from God as a Father, but as our Father ; and he cannot be said to be our Father, but through our Lord Jesus Christ ; and therefore he saith, " Grace be unto you and peace, from God our Father, through our Lord Jesus Christ ;" both are manifested as a golden chain linked together ; not grace without peace, nor peace without grace ; but both conjoined together to cram the believer's soul with grace and peace. Now from the order of the words, we might raise several observations :

I. That peace is the fruit of grace.

II. That grace and peace are both from God.

III. That love, which is the spring of grace and peace, is from God as a Father.

IV. That we share not in his love, but only as he is our Father ; all is from propriety : first, our Father, then grace and peace from God our Father.

V. That God is our Father only through Christ— But before we draw any thing from the text by way of observation, we will speak to the terms by way of explication.

" Grace be to you," what is here meant by grace ? This is a sweet word, it perfumes the breath, it cherishes the conscience, it warms the heart, it ravishes the soul; as the spouse was ravished with the rays of Christ's glory, so Christ revives the soul with one of his gracious rays discovered to the heart; grace is the life of the soul; thou art dead till grace quickens thee, thou art lost till grace finds thee, undone till grace saves thee.   Grace is the manna of angels, the spiritual bread which those that are holy in being, are nourished with, and subsist by; angels live on grace, and stand by grace; man that shares in the grace of God, is made fellow commoner with angels, eats angels' food, and shares in angels' blessings; grace is the substance of the Scripture, the end of the law, the fulness of the gospel; Gregory calls it, " the heart and soul of God."   I am sure grace is the heart and soul of the word, it is a little word but it comprehends all good; here is more than Homer's Iliad in a nutshell, it is the epitome of all the good in heaven and earth; name any word that signifies good to the soul here or hereafter, and it is found in the index, in this little word grace.   Grace comprehends God's love to us, and our love to God, and as God's love to us is the sum of all mercy, so our love to God is the sum of all duty; grace is the new birth of the soul, whereby it takes up another nature, a new nature, a spiritual Godlike nature; as Christ was born, and thereby took on him the nature of man, and was made flesh, so man is born by grace, and thereby takes upon him the nature of God, and is made spirit; and here you have at once the great mystery of grace, in the lowest debasement of a Saviour, and the highest advancement of a sinner: for the Lord Christ could not be more debased than to be born; it was nothing so great an abasement for Christ to die as for him to be born, for being once made man, it is no wonder for to die, but being the great God, it is a wonder that ever he should be made man.   Lo, here is the debasement of Christ! yet if he had been born to a crown, to honour, it had been something, but he was born to shame, to sorrow and death. But man by grace is born to a crown, to a kingdom, he has a title to all the glory and blessedness of heaven, from the first moment of his new birth; so it is in the text, " grace be unto you and peace."

Peace in scripture is a very comprehensive term, it carries in it all happiness. It was the common greeting of the Jews. " Peace be unto you;" Thus David by his proxy salutes Nabal, "Peace be to thee and thy house;'" and the Apostle here alludes to this form of salutation; that he might mix New Testament mercy to Old Testament manners, he first stiles grace before peace, as Jacob did with his venison, he made it a savoury meat, such as Isaac loved.

Peace is the glory of heaven in the bosom of God, and brought into the world in the arms of angels; the first peace you read of in the gospel, was peace by the administration of angels, (Luke ii. 13, 14.) " And suddenly there was with the angels a multitude of the heavenly host, praising and saying, glory be to God in the highest, and on earth peace, good will towards men." And when our Lord Christ first sent out his disciples, this was the doctrine he bid them preach, (Matth. x. 12, 13.) " When you come into a house, salute it, and if it be worthy, let grace, peace, come upon it." Mark here, by the way, our Lord Jesus Christ is no enemy to good manners, he would not have christians to be clowns, which is the use of some among us, who would have their religion quarrel with good manners, no, but in whatsoever city or town you enter, salute it, and let grace, peace, come upon it, that is, wish peace to them, saying "the peace of God be upon this place, upon the head and hearts of all in it." So that peace is both a gospel salutation, when ministers and people meet, and it is also a gospel valediction, when the minister and people part. So did the Apostle, and so do I, now; "grace be with you and peace."

I observe in (Matth. x. 13, 14.) Our Lord bids his disciples, "when they enter into a house, if the house be worthy, to let their peace come upon it, but if they be not worthy, let grace, peace, return unto you;" instead of leaving peace with them, to shake off the dust of their feet against them, that is, to shew that God will shake them off as dust and tread them under feet as fuel. My brethren, your diligent attendance on the word at this place, hath comfortably prevented that part of my charge, to shake off the dust of my feet; for how beautiful have the feet of a poor worm been to you, being shod with the preparation of the gospel of Christ? And therefore, seeing our Lord Jesus Christ said, if they be worthy of their peace, abide with them; on this account I wish to you, grace and peace from God our Father, and from our Lord Jesus Christ. But what is this peace? It is the beauty of union, the harmony of the creation, the pleasure of life, the feast of a good conscience; it is that which makes life sweet, and death easy. Peace sweetens all our possessions, and all our afflictions; without this the fulness of the world is a burden, with this, poverty and emptiness are pleasant companions; without this our bread is gravelled with sourness, and our water mingled with bitterness, with this, green herbs become a feast, and our water is turned into wine; Peace, it is the most beautiful creature in the

world, and therefore it is beloved of all, courted of all;
many seek her, but few there be that enjoy her, they
do not go the right way to find her, for in the "ways of
righteousness is peace." Peace is the seminary of all
blessings temporal, as grace is of all blessings spiritual.
In grace, you have implied all holiness, in peace all
happiness; in grace all inward, in peace all outward
blessings; grace and peace are the Alpha and Omega
of all blessings, as God is of all beings; no blessing
comes before grace, and no blessing lasts longer.
Then see in this phrase of speech, the Apostle wishes
upon them, as I do upon you, all the blessings of time
and eternity, and yet he wished no more to them than
God promised to give them, (1 Tim. iv. 8.) "For
godliness hath the promise of this life, and that which
is to come;" Grace be unto you and peace, not one
without the other; though a man may have grace
without peace, as in a time of desertion or temptation,
and a man may have peace without grace, as in a
secure and unregenerate condition; grace without
peace is often found in a troubled conscience, and
peace without grace is often found in a seared conscience; as grace without peace is very uncomfortable, so
peace without grace is very unprofitable; like Rachel,
beautiful but barren. Therefore the Apostle desires, ye
should have both grace and peace. We say, the sun and
salt are the most useful creatures in the world, the one
for shining, the other for seasoning. My brethren, grace
and peace are the Christian's sun and salt; grace is the
light of their souls, and peace is the savour of their comforts; grace shines through all their faculties, and peace
seasons all their mercies. The blessings of God are become as twins, as Christ said of the spouse, (Cant. iv. 2.)

"She is like a flock of sheep that are even shorn, which came up from the washing, whereof every one bears twins, and none is barren among them." Grace and peace here are knit together by the Spirit of God in a sacred knot, not to be untied. As Castor and Pollux, when seen together, portend happiness to the mariner, so when grace and peace are found in a soul together, they portend the highest security and blessing to the believer; they are said in scripture, to be bound together, where God gives the one he never denies the other. If he gives you the upper spring of grace, he will give you the nether spring of peace, for they go both together: If he gives you the dew of heaven, you need not question the fatness of the earth; If his right hand be full of mercy, his left hand shall not be empty. Therefore grace and peace be with us from God the Father, and from our Lord Jesus Christ. Grace has a double sense, either for the grace of God to us, that justifies us, or the grace of God in us that sanctifies us. Now there is a distinct peace flowing from each of these, but still it is grace and peace.

1. Justifying grace has a peace attending that, (Rom. v. 1.) "Being justified by faith, we have peace with God"—so far as we have confidence in justifying grace, there remains no conscience of condemning sin. As there can be no bitterer war, than between conscience and the cure, so there can be no sweeter peace, than when mercy and peace meet together, and when conscience and peace kiss each other. The former is the taste of heaven, the latter is the peram-bulation of heaven, both which the believer shares in, upon his justification by faith. If Christ had peace who was made our sin, needs must the believer have

peace, who is made the righteousness of God in him.

2. Sanctifying grace has a peace attending it, and this peace differs from the former, as the root from the fruit. The peace of justification is a radical peace, the root of peace, but the peace of sanctification is the bud, the blossom of the tree; the former flows from the blood of Christ sprinkled on the conscience, the latter from the conformity that is between the word and the will, between the commands and the conscience. " As many as walk according to this rule, peace be on them and mercy," (Gal. vi. 16.) So that peace is the fruit of sanctifying grace. Now as the blood of the Paschal Lamb (which was a token of peace,) was not to be struck on the posts of the Egyptians, but upon the posts of the Israelites, so neither is the blood of sprinkling, which brings perfect peace, to be struck on the posts of the carnal sinner, but on the posts of the true believer, an Israelite indeed in whom there is no guile: no grace no peace : that is God's law. How can a sinner have peace in a state of sin, when God and conscience, when word and conscience, when law and conscience and all the attributes of God are against the sinner? "No peace, saith my God, to the wicked." Pray mark that chapter, it begins with peace, and ends in no peace. In verse 2 it is said, " he shall enter into peace," that is the righteous. In the last verse, " there is no peace to the wicked." It is the state of grace that is the only state of peace. And thus I pass from the double blessing desired, " grace and peace," to the double fountain discovered, " God our Father and our Lord Jesus Christ." But here is a question to be answered. If grace and peace be from

God the Father, then how is it said to be from Christ, and if from Christ how then from God the Father?

Answer. It is a known rule that the transient external works of God, are attributed to all the three persons in the Trinity; the same works that are attributed to the Father, are also attributed to the Son, and the works attributed to the Son, the same also to the Father, so grace and peace are here ascribed both to God the Father and to our Lord Jesus Christ; that is, they are both from mercy, and from merit; from mercy on God's part to us, from merit on Christ's part for us. They are from God the Father because he wills them to us, from God the Son because he works them in us; they are from God to Christ, from Christ to us; they are from God the Father originally, and from Christ derivatively, and to us actually; God the Father is the fountain of all grace and peace, Christ as mediator is the conduit of all grace and peace, man in union to Christ is the cistern, into which these streams of grace and peace run; God wills grace and peace to us, and Christ works them in us. God gives grace and peace to be applied to the creature, this is from the love of the Father; but the application of this peace to the soul, is from the merit of Christ the Redeemer. Thus you see there is a double spring of this double blessing. Time will not serve me further, the only observation is,

That all the grace and peace which believers share in, is derived from God the Father, through our Lord Jesus Christ; these three things opened will clear this.

I. That grace and peace are the believer's privilege.

II. That the fountain of this grace and peace is from God the Father.

III. That it is not given out from God the Father but through Christ.

1. That grace and peace are the saint's privilege. If grace is, then peace is; but grace is the privilege of every believer, and that whether you look upon it, as taken from the love and favour of God to us, this is the believer's privilege. God can as well forget Christ at his right hand, as cease his love and favour to the soul of a believer; the believers' title to all their blessings arises out of this never failing love of God: or if you take grace for the fruit of God's love to the soul, still it falls to the believers' privilege. Vocation, justification, adoption, pardon of sins, purging from sins, strength against sin, holiness, love, faith, obedience, perseverance, all these are the privileges of every believer, nay, a man cannot be a believer, without any one of them; they are as essential to the being of a Christian as reason to the being of a man.

2. As grace, so peace is the believer's privilege; there is peace eternal, peace supernal, peace internal, and peace external; there is peace external, this is peace with men; there is peace supernal, that is peace with God; there is peace internal that is, peace with conscience; all these three are to be had upon earth; and then there is peace eternal, and that is only to be had in heaven: the Apostle here doth not exclude the former, but chiefly intends the latter, peace with man is a good thing to be desired, but peace with God and conscience is much more to be desired, peace with God is the spring of all things, both within

and without, both below and above, both in time and eternity; so saith Job, "if he gives peace, who then can make trouble." Now this peace is the saints privilege, it is a legacy left to every believer, by the last will and testament of a dying Redeemer. Will you see a copy of his will? then look in (John xiv. 27.) "Peace I leave with you, my peace I give unto you, not as the world giveth, give I unto you." There is, it seems, a peace in the world's power to give, and there is a peace of Christ's bestowing. Now Christ would have us here, not to mistake the world's peace for his, for the difference is very great; for

(1.) The world's peace is a false peace, it is a counterfeit coin, it has not the current stamp of heaven upon it; but the peace that Christ gives to a believer is true peace, and perfect peace. "Thou wilt keep him in perfect peace, whose mind is stayed on Thee."

(2.) The world's peace is an outward peace; it is but skin deep, it wets the mouth, cannot wash the heart. (Prov. xiv. 13.) "In laughter the heart is sorrowful, and the end of that mirth is heaviness." The world's peace is but the shell of peace, their conscience lowers when their countenance laughs; but the peace that Christ gives is an inward and spiritual peace. (Psal. iv. 7.) "Thou hast put gladness in my heart more than in the time, that their corn and their wine increased." Thou hast put gladness in my heart; Peace is that gladness: that peace smooths the brow, but this fills the breast; as the sinner has trouble within, in the midst of all his peace without, so a believer has peace within, in the midst of all his troubles without; "In the world you shall have trouble, but in me you shall have peace."

(3.) The world's peace has only a nether spring arising out of the creature, out of worldly comforts, therefore it must needs be unclean, for an unclean fountain cannot bring forth clean water. But the peace of Christians has an upper spring, it flows from the manifestation of the love of God in Christ, it is from the sprinkling of Christ's blood on the conscience, it flows from the workings of Christ's spirit upon the soul, which is first a counsellor, then a comforter. Oh! how pure must this peace be in a believer's soul, that flows from so pure a spring.

(4.) The world's peace is a peace given to sinners, it is a peace in sin, and it is a peace with sin; as the Prophet Isaiah tells us, it is " a covenant with hell and an agreement with death;" God deliver us from that peace! Again Christ's peace is given to none but believers, it is their privilege only, a stranger does not intermeddle with this joy. (Prov. xiv. 10.) " The heart knoweth his own bitterness, but a stranger doth not intermeddle with his joy."

(5.) The world's peace is a fading dying transitory thing, it withers in the sand. " The triumphing of the wicked is but short, and the joy of the hypocrite is but for a moment." (Job. xx. 5.) Solomon does elegantly liken it to " the crackling of thorns under a pot, which is but a blaze and is gone." (Eccle. vii. 6.) So is the sinner's peace, it is for a spurt and is soon gone, but the peace that Christ gives to believers, is durable and abiding peace, "your joy no man shall take from you:" it appears in life, in death, and after death.

1st. It is our peace in life, grace brings forth present peace; it is said of the primitive Christians, " They walked in the fear of the Lord, and in the comforts of

Holy Ghost." (Acts ix. 31.) It is a remarkable expression, (Psa. xix. 11.) " In keeping thy commands there is great reward;" he does not say for keeping them, which respects the end of the work, but in keeping of them which looks at the work itself. My brethren, every duty done in sincerity, reflects a peace in conscience, as every flower carries its own sweetness: it is possible I grant a believer may not always find and feel this peace, few do; some seldom find it, few find it so always, the remains of corruption breaking forth to interrupt, or temptations to hinder, and God's desertion may darken and hide it, and a believer may seem to be totally lost, yet in this condition, which is the worst a child of God can be in, he hath a double peace.

(1) A peace in the promises, in this very condition, and what you have in bonds and bills, you account as good as money in your pockets.

(2) He has it in the seed, "light is sown for the righteous, and gladness for the upright in heart." (Psa. xcvii. 11.) Grace is the seed of peace, which Christ has sown in the furrows of the soul; and therefore peace shall spring out of the furrows of the soul: indeed this seed springs up sooner in some than in others, yet every saint shall have a reaping time sooner or later. (Psa. cxxvi. 6.) " He that goeth forth and weepeth, bearing precious seed, shall doubtless come again with rejoicing, bringing his sheaves with him?" If he stays long for the fruit, he shall have a greater crop at last; if he reaps not now he shall be sure to reap hereafter. (Psa. xxxvii. 37.) " Mark the perfect man, and behold the upright, for the end of that man is peace."

2d. This peace which is the peace of a child of God,

is a peace in death ; grace will be ministered to us
then, and that ministration shall be peace ; the sinner's peace leaves him when he comes to the grave,
though in life it fills him, yet in death it leaves him.
A believer has a twofold spring of peace, the first is
from above him, the other is from within him; that
spring that runs with peace above him, is from the
blood of Christ, sprinkled on his conscience, the
other that is from within him is from the sincerity of
his heart, in the ways of obedience. My brethren,
when we lie on our death-beds, and can reflect on our
sincerity in all God's ways, this will be peace at last ;
so it was in Hezekiah, (Isaiah xxxviii. 3.) " Remember now, O Lord I beseech thee, how I have walked
before thee in truth, and with a perfect heart, and
have done that which was good in thy sight." There
is nothing makes a death-bed so hard and so uneasy,
as a life spent in the service of sin and lust, and
nothing makes a death bed so pleasant as a life spent
in the service of Christ.

3d. Grace will bring forth peace, if not in this life,
yet certainly it will be sure after death ; if time brings
not this fruit to ripeness, yet eternity shall; grace in
time, will be glory in eternity, holiness now, will be
happiness then; whatever it is a man sows in this
world, that he reaps in the next world. " Be not deceived, God is not mocked, for whatsoever a man
soweth, that shall he also reap; he that soweth to the
flesh shall of the flesh reap corruption, but he that
soweth to the spirit, shall of the spirit reap life everlasting." (Gal. vi. 7, 8.) When sin shall end in sorrow
and misery, grace shall end in peace, in joy, in glory;
" Well done thou good and faithful servant, enter

into the joy of thy Lord." (Matt xxv. 21.) Whosoever shares in the grace of Christ in this world, shall be sure to share in the joy of Christ in the next world, and that joy is "joy unspeakable, and full of glory." I will wind up all in a threefold application by way of exhortation to three sorts of persons.

I. To such as have this grace and peace.

II. To such as have neither grace nor peace.

III. To such as have this grace and no peace.

I. To such as have both grace and peace, I will speak to them in two or three things.

1. Admire thankfully the Father, and Son: the Father's grace and the Son's love, for both had a hand in this, therefore bless both the Father for willing it to us, and the Son for working it in us. Grace and peace are the fruits of God's eternal election, for this blessing the Father gives, but the application of it to us is the fruit of Christ's redemption and intercession. How can you think of hell and damnation, and see yourself freed from it, and how can you think of the dreadful fury and vengeance of God, yourself not under it; how can you look on your state changed, your hearts renewed, grace ratified and reconciled, and your conscience quieted; how can you think of these things, but must admire the love of the Father in giving this to you, and the love of the Son in purchasing this for you? All the grace and mercy that is given to us, is by Christ purchased for us; Grace and Peace are fruits of the redeeming blood of Christ's purchase.

2. Do not envy the conditions or possessions of the men of the world; they have riches and honours, profits and pleasures, but they neither have grace nor

peace. Therefore do not envy their happiness. There is a story of a Roman that was condemned by a court martial to die, for breaking his rank to steal a bunch of grapes, and as he was going to his execution some of his fellow soldiers laughed at him, and others envied at him, that he should have grapes and they none; "now (says he) do not envy me for my bunch of grapes, for you would be loth to have them at the rate I must pay for them." My brethren, you that are the children of grace and peace do not envy the men of the world, their riches, their comforts, their pleasures, for I am sure you would be loth to have them at the price they pay for them, "for the end of these things is death."

3. Do not complain of the worst condition that the providence of God shall cast you into, in this world; it may be, you shall suffer hard things, but remember so long as thy soul is secure, never complain of hard things. My brethren, as God your Father brought you into a state of grace and peace, and thereby secured his love to your souls in Christ, can you complain of hard things? So, let the joy of the Lord be your strength, " Rejoice in the Lord always, and again I say rejoice. (Phil. iv. 4.)

II. To such as have neither grace nor peace. may I not say, I speak to many such? I would, I might not ! Are there not many that are without grace, and therefore must needs be without peace. They may have the world's peace, but they have none of this peace ; let me beg of you to get out of this graceless condition; if you love your souls do not live one day, nor one hour, nor one moment longer in a graceless state. Oh, that you would believe the words of a

dying man, for so I am to you, and such words use to
be remembered.   Oh, remember this as a testimony, I
leave with you, that the love of sin and lack of grace
will ruin and destroy every soul at last; but you will
say, how shall I get a share in this grace and peace?

1. I answer first, break off all your false peace;
we can never have true peace with God, when we
content ourselves with false peace; you will never
seek that peace which Christ hath purchased for you,
while you content yourselves with that cursed peace
which the old man has wrought in you; Oh therefore,
break off all false peace, which is not the fruit of grace.

2. Labour to see and be convinced of the miserable and naked condition your souls are in, for want of
the righteousness of Christ for a covering; without
this, oh soul, thou art miserable, wretched, poor and
naked.   Be convinced also what a miserable thing it is,
to have God our enemy!   God is the sinner's enemy,
" It is a fearful thing to fall into the hands of the living
God;" O be convinced of thy nakedness without
Christ's righteousness, and thy emptiness without his
fullness.

3. Labour to go out of yourselves to Christ for
grace and peace : " surely in the Lord, shall one say, I
have righteousness and strength ;" aye, there it is to
be found.   Labour for a thirsty frame of soul, for the
promises run far to such, "that he will fill the hungry
with good things."   Go to Christ, O soul; beg, pray,
never leave God, till he hath given thee an interest in
Christ; "for none can come to me except the Father
draw him ;" there is no pardon for the least sin out of
Christ, but there is pardon for the greatest sin in
Christ; one sin will damn the soul out of Christ, but

no sin can hurt the soul in Christ. Oh, go to Christ, soul, never give rest to thy eyes, nor slumber to thy eyelids, till thou hast made peace with God in the blood of Christ; one sting of the fiery serpent was mortal, without looking upon the brazen serpent; so one sin will damn a soul out of Christ, but no sin can damn a soul in Christ.

III. To such as have grace, but no sense of peace. This is the counsel I would leave with all such; Be much in the exercise of grace; pray much, believe much, use grace much, for the exercise and improving of grace will produce peace. There are ten duties which are to be the sphere of grace in activity, and in performing of them we shall have peace.

1. Make religion your business, the main design of your lives, be Christians to purpose; be not only Christians by the bye, " but let your conversation be as becometh the Gospel of Christ." (Phil. i. 27.)

2. Put forth renewed acts of faith on Christ every day, and remember it is as much your duty to believe in Christ to day, as if you had never believed before. Oh live by faith every day, and this will bring peace to you.

3. Maintain a constant communion with God daily; this communion with God is man's chief good; the happiness of a child is in communion with his father, and the happiness of a wife is in communion with her husband, and this is the happiness of a believer's soul, communion with God the Father, through Christ our head and husband. The seed of peace, it is true, is sown in the soul in union; but then it takes root

downward, and brings forth fruit upward. Spiritual peace will never be obtained, if communion with God be not maintained; that gives comfort in the midst of all sorrows, and satisfies all doubts, and recompenses all wants. Lo, this is the fruit of communion with God.

4. Be good at all times, but of all best in bad times; many Christians lose their peace, by remitting of their grace, and let loose their reins of religion to avoid the censures of a crooked generation. A Christian's zeal should be like the winter fire, that burns the hottest when the air is coolest, or like the lily that looketh beautiful though among thorns; so should a child of God though among sinners.

5. In all conditions, choose sufferings rather than sinning. If ever you would have peace, choose suffering rather than sinning; he that values peace with God, or peace with conscience, he must make this his choice; thus Daniel rather chose to be cast to lions, than to lose the peace of his conscience; the three children chose rather to burn in the furnace, than bow to the image. One said, He would rather go to hell free from sin, than to live in heaven with guilt on his conscience. My brethren, let me a little enlarge, because suffering may overtake us, for persecution is the genius of the Gospel, therefore let me leave four short rules with you concerning sufferings.

See that your cause be good, your call be clear, your spirit meek, and your end right. Sufferings, cannot bring out peace without either of them, but with them our sufferings shall be peace.

(1.) Let your cause be good; it is not the blood, but the cause that makes a martyr; it is not for every cause a Christian should engage to suffer; every cause will no more bear suffering than every little stream will bear a ship; nor will Christ let go sweetness to every suffering. (1 Pet. iv. 15.) " Let none of you suffer as a murderer or as a thief, or as an evil doer, or as a busybody in other men's matters." To suffer thus is neither Christian-like nor comfortable. Some suffer rather as malefactors, than as Christ's martyrs.

(2.) Let your call be clear; it is amiss to have a good cause without a call; some may suffer for the cause of God, and yet sin in suffering for want of a call. Christ calls not all to suffer; to some it is given, to others it is not. If thy call be clear, thy peace will be sweet, though thy sufferings be never so great. But you will say, How shall I know when I am called to suffer?

1st. I answer first, When truth suffers by our silence, then are we called to suffer.

2nd. When our lives will be the denial of Christ, then are we called to deny our lives for Christ.

3rd. When sin and suffering surround us, that we cannot get out, but we must either run through sin or sufferings, then I may safely conclude that Christ called me to suffer, and in this cause we may expect the peace and sweetness of his presence.

(3.) The third direction for suffering is this : Our spirit must be meek, so was Christ's ; he went as a lamb to the slaughter.

It is possible, a man may be right in his cause, and yet sinful in his carriage ; and if so, no wonder if Christ be not sweet to us. To be fierce, and raging, and reviling in suffering, it is not becoming humanity, and therefore much less like Christianity. A Christian should be like Christ. (Acts v. 41.) " And they departed from the presence of the council, rejoicing that they were counted worthy to suffer shame for his name." It becomes those that are found in the Spirit, to give blessing for cursing; the more of Christ's Spirit is in us in our sufferings, the more comfort and joy we shall receive from our sufferings.

(4.) See that your end in suffering be right; if it be self, or singularity, or schism, then Christ cannot be sweet to thee. Some have died that their names might live. Socrates died in the defence of the truth, and to prove that there is but one God ; but whether he died for honour, applause, or for God's sake, I think it is no hard thing to determine. But let thy cause be good, thy call clear, thy spirit meek, and thy end right, and then you shall have peace in all your sufferings. That is the fifth thing ; choose suffering rather than sinning.

6. If you would have peace be much in studying the Scriptures; for as God is the God of peace, and Christ the Prince of Peace, so the Gospel is the gospel of peace, which God hath given thee to lead thee in the ways of peace : " Great peace have they that love thy laws."

7. Take heed of apostacy, either in doctrine or principles. Though a believer is freed from apostacy in the state of grace, yet he is not freed from apostacy in the degrees of grace. He may fall sinfully though he cannot fall finally. Demas fell by one ; St. Peter by the other. Pray with David, (Psal. xvii. 5.) " Hold up my goings in thy path, that my footsteps slip not."

8. Make the Word of God your rule in all things ; be sure you have a Scripture warrant for all your practices. But especially keep close to Scripture, in matters of God's worship.

There are endless discourses about the mode of God's worship; I have no disputing time; it is good in difficult cases always to take the surest side. For instance, if I follow the traditions of man for the worship of God, I may sin, but if I keep close to the directions of God in the Scripture, I am sure I cannot sin; for this is the sure word of prophecy, to which you do well to take heed; therefore, in such a doubtful case, God's will is, that we take the surest side; go to the law and to the testimony; labour to be fruitful and grounded Christians.

9. Keep up the power of godliness; do not let religion down into a lifeless formality. " The righteous shall flourish like a palm tree; he shall grow like a cedar in Lebanon; those that be planted in the house of the Lord, shall flourish in the courts of our God." (Psa. xcii. 12, 13.) My brethren, it is as much a duty in them that have grace, to improve it, as for them that have no grace to get it. If you sit under the daily means, the daily waterings of God, and do not grow, do you think this will be peace in the latter end ? surely no, my brethren, your fruitfulness under the Gospel is of very great concernment. It is unfruitfulness that makes God lay his vineyard waste : it is fruitfulness that procures the forwarding your account in the day of grace.

10. Observe that excellent rule of the Apostle in Phil. iv. 8. " Finally, brethren, whatsoever things are true, whatsoever things are honest, whatsoever things

are just, whatsoever things are pure, whatsoever things are lovely, whatsoever things are of good report, if there be any virtue, and if there be any praise, think on these things." And now, my brethren, I recommend you to God, and to the word of his grace, that is infinitely able to ˚make you wise to salvation, with this benediction, which I shall make my valediction, " Grace be unto you, and peace from God our Father, and from our Lord Jesus Christ."

THE END.

T. C. Johns.
Red lion-ct. Fleet-st.

JAMES NISBET AND CO.

Have much pleasure in submitting to their Christian Friends the following unexceptionable miniature Books, neatly printed by T. C. Johns, and charged at very reasonable Prices, and well adapted for Presents.

THE

NEW TESTAMENT,

Small 32mo. a Handsome Pocket Size,

*Price in Cloth, 4s.   in Roan, 5s. 6d.   in Calf, 6s.
in Morocco, 8s.*

This beautiful edition of the NEW TESTAMENT is enriched with numerous REFERENCES, various READINGS, explanatory NOTES, &c., all illustrative of the Sacred Text, *in a Centre Column.*

There are also highly finished *Maps,* engraved on Steel, annexed to it, which will be found very valuable as well as ornamental to this little Volume.

HANDSOMELY PRINTED IN 64mo.

The BOOK of GENESIS	2s.
—————SAMUEL, 1st & 2nd . . .	2s.
—————PSALMS	2s.
—————PROVERBS	1s.
—————PROVERBS & ECCLESIASTES .	1s. 4d.
—————ISAIAH	2s.
—————DANIEL	1s.
—————JEREMIAH	2s.
—————EZEKIEL	2s.

The GOSPEL of ST. MATTHEW . . . . 1s. 6d.
——————— ST. MARK . . . . . . 1s. 6d.
——————— ST. LUKE . . . . . 1s. 6d.
——————— ST. JOHN . . . . . . 1s. 6d.
The ACTS of the APOSTLES . . . . . . 1s. 6d.
The EPISTLE to the ROMANS . . . . . 1s.
——————————— TIMOTHY, 1st & 2nd . 1s.
——————————— HEBREWS . . . . . 1s.
————— of JAMES, PETER, and JOHN . 1s.
ROWE'S DEVOUT EXERCISES . . . . . 2s.
BEAUFOY'S GUIDE to TRUE PILGRIMS . . 2s.
The BIBLE CHRISTIAN . . . . 1s.
THE CONTRAST between the Righteous and
    Wicked . . . . 1s.
DOMESTIC CALENDAR, for Reading the Bible
    in Family Worship during the year . . 6d.
CLARKE'S SCRIPTURE PROMISES . . . . 2s.
MASON'S POCKET COMPANION 1s. 6d
MARSHALL on SANCTIFICATION, 32mo. cloth . 2s.
WILBERFORCE on CHRISTIANITY, 32mo. cloth 2s.
THE SUNBEAM'S A Diary of Promises. 128mo. 1s.